Two Weekly Services
That Can Help You Trade Better:

Looking for a newsletter that shares your trading philosophy? Commodity Closeup recommends trades only if they show a high risk to reward ratio. This conservative stance has helped thousands of traders to improved profits. Why? Because discipline outperforms greed.

Commodity Closeup provides specific trading recommendations on 23 key markets. Recommended stop-loss, type of order to use, and a telephone hotline updated daily are included. Commodity Closeup is mailed first class each Thursday (50 times per year).

COMMODITY PRICE CHARTS

A complete 40-page chart service putting all types of chart information into one handy package… plus technical analysis for each commodity. This comprehensive service provides you with bar charts for all the major contracts on all the major commodities. Point-and-figure charts. Relative Strength Indexes. Covers 37 commodities including currencies, financials, stock indexes and energy futures. Jumbo 11-3/8″ × 14-1/2″ page size makes charts easy to read and update. Mailed first class after Friday's close so you have them for the next week's trading.

To start your subscription or to get more information on either weekly service described above, check the appropriate boxes on the other side of the postage-paid card.

NO POSTAGE
NECESSARY
IF MAILED
IN THE
UNITED STATES

BUSINESS REPLY CARD
FIRST CLASS   PERMIT NO. 509   CEDAR FALLS, IOWA

POSTAGE WILL BE PAID BY ADDRESSEE

Futures
The magazine of commodities & options

219 Parkade
Cedar Falls, IA 50613

Getting Started in Commodity Futures Trading

by
Mark J. Powers

Investor Publications, Inc.
P.O. Box 6
Cedar Falls, Iowa 50613

Published by Investor Publications, Inc.
P.O. Box 6
Cedar Falls, Iowa 50613

First edition 1973
Second edition 1977
Third Edition 1981
FOURTH EDITION 1983

Library of Congress Cataloging in Publication Data
    Powers, Mark J.
    Getting Started In Commodity Futures Trading
    Bibliography: p.
    Includes Index.
    1. Commodity exchanges. 2. Speculation
I. Title
    HG 6046. P68 1977   332.6'328   78-16939
ISBN 0-914230-01-8

Preface

So many people are indirectly involved in creating a book, it's hard to know where to start in expressing my gratitude. So a collective thank you goes to all those people over the years who have stimulated my thinking and encouraged my efforts.

A special thank you should go to the Chicago Mercantile Exchange, which allowed me to use material that had been developed by the CME staff.

If it's hard to know where to start, it's not hard to know where to stop. Any faults you may find should be attributed to the only one left — me.

Mark Powers

Dedicated to
Jo, Jim and Sheila

CONTENTS

Stocks vs. Commodities

The late Vince Lombardi once said, "Luck is what happens when preparation meets opportunity."

What Lombardi was saying is that, in the long run, people who are successful make their own luck by being prepared to take advantage of favorable circumstances... and that those who rely on "chance luck" have very little hope of continued success.

The purpose of this book is to introduce the beginner to the world of commodity futures trading and to aid in preparing one to take advantage of favorable circumstances that arise in the trading of commodity futures. This book will offer no sure-fire methods for making money, nor will it predict the prices of any commodity. It makes no promises to turn you into a successful trader, because a successful trader needs more than knowledge about the market. It will, however, provide you with an understanding of many of the basic aspects of futures trading — knowledge without which only "chance luck" can work in your favor.

A Word About Your Suitability for Trading

Commodity futures trading is not for everybody. As you read this book, the fact should become abundantly clear.

For example, you should not trade unless you have money you and your dependents can afford to lose. If you are in the proverbial "orphan or widow" class, do not trade. Some studies have shown that the probabilities are quite high that after a customer pays his commissions and calculates the interest income lost on margin money deposited with his broker, he will not make money.

You should not trade unless you are psychologically suited to taking large risks. Most commodity futures transactions involve a great deal of risk. Unless you are certain that you can accept that risk and still sleep at night without worry, do not trade.

You should not trade unless you are sure you can control your ego and your greed. High risk and high profit potential go together. If you cannot discipline yourself well enough to admit a mistake on a trade and close it out at a small loss or to be satisfied with a moderate gain on a winning trade, do not trade.

If you tend to live on hopes and dreams instead of on the realities of hard facts, do not trade.

If you think you can make money trading futures without doing some hard work, do not trade. Making money consistently is not easy in any line of work. And it is especially hard in futures trading.

As you read the rest of this book, keep these points in mind and try to determine your suitability to trading.

Trading Stocks vs. Trading Commodity Futures

Most of you have probably invested in stocks so you understand something about exchange markets and how exchanges operate. Stock exchanges and commodity exchanges are similar in many ways. For example, they are both membership organizations established as a means of facilitating the investment decisions of large and diverse groups of people.

The stock exchanges act to bring people with extra capital together with those who need capital to develop a business. They facilitate the transfer of ownership of corporations which are engaged in various productive activities such as steel making, auto manufacturing, banking, etc. Property rights change hands.

The commodity futures markets act to bring people together to transfer the price risk associated with the ownership of some commodity, like wheat, or some service like an interest rate. No property rights to a physical commodity change hands at the time the futures contract is entered into. The transaction is a legally binding promise that at a later date a transaction will occur involving the property rights to the actual commodity.

One can "invest" in commodities in the same way he can in stocks — in the sense that, according to the dictionary, investment is the "committing of resources with the expectation of making a profit." On the basis of that definition, it seems apparent that one also "invests" in oil wells, real estate and a whole array of other things.

It would not be accurate to leave the impression that investing in blue chip stocks and "investing" in commodity futures contracts are exactly the same thing. The two activities reside on different levels of the risk spectrum.

Commodity futures contracts fall in the high risk area of the spectrum near speculative stocks, rights, puts and calls, new issues and "penny" stocks.

Just as there is a risk spectrum for all investments, one could set up the same sort of spectrum for commodity futures contracts. That is, you can select commodities for trading that have less risk associated with them because of higher margins (less leverage) or more stable prices. For example, trading futures in a commodity like pork bellies is more risky than an equally leveraged position in lumber. Lumber prices are usually less volatile.

Further, the method of trading you select can affect the risk you assume. For example, you could use a "spreading" technique, which refers to the simultaneous purchase and sale of contracts in two different markets or for two different months. This usually has less risk associated with it than an outright long or short position. We will discuss spreads in depth in a later chapter.

Relative Size

A very basic difference between the stock market and the commodity futures market, however, is the relative size of the two markets. The stock markets are overwhelmingly larger than the commodity futures markets, and the number of people who own and trade stocks far outnumber those who trade commodity futures contracts. Although newspaper stories frequently portray the commodity markets as being "vast" with "millions of people playing the markets" where the dollar value of trading frequently "exceeds the value of stocks traded on the New York Stock Exchange," such statements are misleading.

In the case of the value of securities traded on the New York Stock Exchange, most of those securities were paid for in full and delivered to their new owners; thus, something approaching the $500 billion in value of stock traded was actually exchanged in cash through the exchange. On the other hand, futures contracts are traded on margin and less than 10% of the value of the contract is deposited with the broker in cash. Hence, only a fraction of the trillions of dollar value of futures contracts traded annually in recent years actually changed hands.

A study completed by the Commodity Futures Trading Commission in Washington, D.C., indicated that there were, as of midyear 1976, approximately 116,000 accounts in the entire commodity futures industry. Since many traders carry more than one account (one trader is known to have 17 different accounts), it was estimated that there were about 100,000 individuals and business firms who trade commodity futures contracts. These estimates include members of exchanges and brokers. On the other hand, there are about 28 million people who own securities and about 6 million who have individual accounts.

Margin and Leverage

Why do commodity futures end up so far out on the risk spectrum? Is it because the prices of beef cattle or pork bellies fluctuate so much more than the price of blue chip stocks? Not at all. In fact, the prices of many commodities fluctuate less than many stock prices. The difference is in the leverage — the amount of money needed to control a given amount of resources.

When an investor buys a stock on margin, the margin represents an equity interest in the security and the investor owes the unpaid balance as debt. In futures contract trading, the trader is not buying or selling the commodity but only agreeing to buy or sell it at a later date. In one sense, you could look at the purchase or sale of a futures contract as the purchase or sale of the right to participate in the price change. The margin payment is considered a "sign of good faith" or earnest money such as might be used in acquiring a piece of property. In other words, the purchaser promises to fulfill his contract during the delivery month.

Use of the term "margin" to describe the security deposit posted when trading commodity contracts is somewhat unfortunate, since it suggests that "margin" in the securities market and "margin" for commodity futures contracts are identical. In fact, they are quite different in concept and in practice.

The purpose of margin in commodity trading is to act as a security deposit, thus providing the broker and the exchange clearinghouse with protection from default by the customer or the brokerage firm. The level of these security deposits is set by the exchange on which the commodity is traded.

Margins on securities are set by the Federal Reserve Board and their purpose, as stated in the Securities Exchange Act, is to prevent the excessive use of credit for the purchase or carrying of securities. New purchases of stock on margin generate credit in a way that adds to the national money supply. When stock is bought, the entire purchase price is paid to the seller a few days after the transaction. If the purchaser is buying the stock on margin, the balance of the purchase price must be borrowed in order to make his full payment. Ordinarily, this balance is borrowed from the broker or from a bank and, in either case, the effect is to expand the national total of bank credit, leading to an expansion of the national money supply by the amount borrowed. This points up a major distinction between margin in commodities and margin in the stock market. Margin in commodities does not, in and of itself, involve the borrowing of money nor does it affect the money supply.

Leverage is high in commodity futures trading because margins are low. In the stock market, margins are currently at 50%. In commodities markets, margins are usually less than 10% and in some instances less than 1% of market value. Because of the low margins in commodities, one can control large amounts of resources with small amounts of capital. Hence, a slight change in the value of the total contract results in a substantial change in the amount of money in your account. For example, a 1%

change in $10,000 invested in the stock market via a non-margined account will equal a 1% change in equity — or $100. A 1% change in a futures contract valued at $10,000 is equal to a $100 change in account equity also. But in order to control that

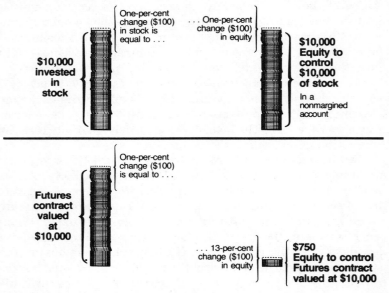

$10,000 futures contract, you probably needed to put down $750 as your initial margin. And a $100 change in $750 is equal to a 13% change in your equity. It is this leverage factor that causes commodity futures to be considered a high-risk investment. Of course, there is nothing that says you must use all of that leverage. You could arbitrarily set your personal margin higher, say at 30% and trade more conservatively.

The Time Factor

Besides the difference in leverage, another difference between trading stocks and commodities is that time is more important in commodities. You can buy a stock and put it away for years. Not so with commodities. Generally, you have to get out of a commodity position within a matter of months after you first make the commitment, or you are legally bound to accept or give delivery. However, at the time a futures contract is born, you know the exact date on which it will mature, so there is little excuse for being "caught" inadvertently.

Daily Price Limits

Unlike stock, commodity futures contracts usually have daily price limits which prohibit prices from changing by more than a certain amount on any given day. These daily price limits are instituted first, and most importantly, to limit the financial risk to the clearinghouse. Clearinghouse members must settle with each other each day, paying in or receiving the amount by which the value of each contract they owned changed that day. Second, limits act to constrain hysteria in the marketplace and let all parties have a breather when prices are changing by substantial amounts.

Market Analysis

Market and price analysis of commodity futures is similar to and yet simpler than for stocks. For those who are chartists, the techniques of charting and chart interpretation are nearly the same for commodities as for stocks. On the other hand, fundamental analysis of many commodities is much simpler, because there are far fewer commodity contracts than there are stocks, and the best fundamental research organization in the world is available free in agricultural commodity futures — the U.S. Department of Agriculture.

Selling Short

You can sell short as easily in commodities as you can buy long. A short sale in commodities can be a speculation or a hedge. It is not necessary to borrow the commodity in order to go short in the futures market, since it is not a sale of the actual commodity, but only a promise to sell and deliver the commodity at some future time. If you close out your position prior to the close of trading in that contract, no delivery is required. In the case of a short sale in securities, you must borrow the securities sold. Ultimately, you would have to obtain a similar amount of securities and return them to the party from whom they were borrowed.

Another difference: Contrary to the securities market, going short in futures does not require an uptick before initiating the position. Nor does it involve dividend payments.

Method of Trading

The "specialist" system used to maintain markets on the floors of the New York Stock Exchange and American Stock Exchange is not used by any U.S. commodity exchange. Commodity trading is conducted as an open auction, where settlement prices are arrived at by open outcry of "bid" and "asked" prices. No single person is granted the right by the exchange to "make a market" and keep a book on all the open bids and offers. The commodity markets have a number of members, each contributing to the making of the market through open competition.

In commodity trading there is no receipt or delivery of certificates with which you have to be concerned each time you trade. That happens only if you decide to make or take delivery at the consummation of the contract, in which case you will receive the physical commodity — not on your front lawn but rather in an exchange-approved warehouse or depository.

Size of Account

Most commodity accounts are small. A July 1976 survey by the Commodity Futures Trading Commission of brokers' month-end statements showed that 61.7% of all accounts contained less than $5,000 in equity.

Nearly 90% of them have less than $20,000 in equity and only a few (3.7%) have equity in excess of $50,000. Table 1 summarizes these statistics by type of account and size class. Note that approximately 76% of all of the accounts are categorized as speculative and only about one-fifth of the accounts are categorized as hedge. The remaining are omnibus accounts or proprietary accounts owned by the brokers themselves.[1]

[1]An omnibus account is one which is owned by more than one person, such as would be the case with a limited partnership, a pool arrangement or a commodity mutual fund.

TABLE 1

DISTRIBUTION OF FCM COMMODITY ACCOUNTS

(All figures are per cent in each size class)

Account Size Class	(1) Speculative	(2) Hedge	(3) Both Spec. & Hedge	(4) Cumulative % 1+2	(5) Omnibus	(6) Proprietary	(7) All Accounts 1+2+5+6	(8) Cumulative % 1+2+5+6
$1-$5,000	62.5	53.3	60.4	60.4	21.9	46.3	61.7	61.7
5,001-10,000	18.0	18.3	18.1	78.5	11.4	29.3	16.8	78.5
10,001-15,000	6.8	8.2	7.1	85.6	9.5	4.9	7.0	85.5
15,001-20,000	3.4	3.9	3.5	89.1	5.7	2.4	3.7	89.2
20,001-25,000	2.4	3.4	2.6	91.7	5.7	2.4	2.4	91.6
25,001-30,000	1.5	2.0	1.6	93.3	3.8	0	1.5	93.1
30,001-35,000	1.0	1.6	1.1	94.4	2.9	0	1.1	94.2
35,001-40,000	.7	1.2	.8	95.2	1.9	4.9	.8	95.0
40,001-45,000	.5	.9	.6	95.8	1.9	0	.7	95.7
45,001-50,000	.6	.8	.6	96.4	0	2.4	.6	96.3
Greater than $50,000	2.6	6.3	3.4	100.0%	35.2	7.3	3.7	100.0%
TOTAL	100.0%	100.0%	100.0%		100.0%	100.0%	100.0%	
%Of All Accounts	76.2	22.8	98.9		.6	.4	100.0%	

From the data in Table 1, it seems apparent that most people risk very small amounts in trading commodities. Less than one in four accounts is a hedge account and even the very large accounts, those in excess of $50,000, are small compared to accounts in the securities industry where an account of $50,000 or less is considered a small account.

Who Trades Commodities and Why?

Some people trade commodity futures as a normal adjunct to their business of producing and marketing a product. For example, if a meat packer wishes to establish the prices he will pay for cattle to slaughter in his plant during the next six months, he may buy futures. Traders who fall in this category are called hedgers. They buy and sell contracts as substitutes for merchandising transactions they will make at a later time. We will deal with this topic at length in subsequent chapters.

Other people trade commodities not as a normal part of producing or marketing a product but only in the hopes of making a profit on their transactions by correctly anticipating price movements. These people are generally categorized as speculators.

There are different types of speculators. Among them are the "scalpers" at the exchanges. They buy and sell contracts continuously, minute by minute, in large and small amounts, hoping to make a small amount on each transaction. They seldom carry a position for more than a few hours.

Another type of trader is the "position trader." He takes a position in the market and holds it for at least a day and frequently longer. He tries to take advantage of short and long term trends.[2]

One of the questions frequently asked is, "What sort of person is this speculator?"

In a Chicago Mercantile Exchange study, some 4,000 customers trading during September, October and November of 1970

---

[2]The terms "speculator" and "hedger" are unfortunate choices as they have strong emotional connotations to many people and do not always convey an accurate sense of an individual's activities in the market. A more accurate and useful classificaiton of participants would be on the basis of "commercial" and "non-commercial" users of the market.

were surveyed. These customers were trading in all types of commodity futures listed on any exchange in the United States. It was found that the typical trader looked something like this:

— male.

— about 45 years old (56% of the sample were males between 35 and 55 years of age).

— earnings in excess of $10,000 a year (47% earned between $10,00 and $25,000; 39% earned more than $25,000).

— has a good job (54% were professionals such as doctors, lawyers, dentists; top management people, or white collar workers).

— tends to be well-educated (68% of these 4,000 traders had

gone to college; 60% of them had graduated with a bachelors degree; 18% had graduate degrees).

— tends to be a short-term trader (85% were holding their positions for less than one month and 55% of them for less than 10 days). This could be interpreted in any number of different ways. It might indicate that many of them are trading without a plan.

— tends to be a small trader (55% of these 4,000 customers were trading one or two contracts each time they traded; 75%

were trading less than five contracts each time they traded).

— and last, the individual trading commodities generally has a securities account also (70 percent of the 4,000 had securities accounts).

This does not mean that these characteristics are required in order to be a successful commodity trader, because it takes a special emotional and psychological makeup to trade commodities. But it does help to remove some of the mystery about the type of individual who trades commodity futures. He is probably your next door neighbor.

Social and Economic Benefits of Futures Trading

Although economists have not yet found a way to accurately quantify all the social and economic benefits that flow from futures markets, a number of them can be identified.

The basic economic functions performed by futures markets relate to competitive price discovery, hedging (offsetting) of commercial price risks, facilitating financing and allocating resources.

Prices on an organized futures market reflect the combined views of a large number of buyers and sellers, not only of current supply and demand but also of the relationship up to 12 or 18 months in advance. This does not mean that a futures price is a prediction that will hold true. Instead, it is an expression of opinions concerning future supply and demand at a single point in time. As conditions change, opinions change — and, of course, so will price. These changes do not make the market's pricing function less useful. On the contrary, keeping the supply/demand equation current makes the system more useful than a one-time prediction.

Information generated by futures trading through the price discovery process is invaluable for planning at every stage of commodity production, distribution and processing. Planning is a normal part of every commercial business. It is necessary to achieve maximum efficiency and to minimize operating costs. To the extent that futures markets improve planning and efficiency and reduce operating costs, the benefits should accrue to the consumer and the economy.

The second major function of the futures exchange is risk shifting. A futures market is a market in risk. It is risk of price change, not the physical commodity, that is being traded on futures contracts. The futures market allows the separation of risk of price change from risk arising from other normal business functions similar to the separation of theft or fire risk from other business risks. A separation of these risks allows them to be "packaged" in special ways and transferred from those who have them but may not want them (commercial businesses) to those who do want them (speculators).

The risk of price change is ever present. This risk represents a cost which must be borne by someone. If the merchant or middleman has to assume the risk, he will pay the producer less or charge the processor more or a combination of the two. If the risk is assumed directly by the producer or processor, they will need to be compensated for bearing the risk and they will pass the cost of that along. In any event, the cost of risk assumption will become a charge on the economy.

Numerous general economic benefits flow from the hedging function. These include reduced finance charges in carrying inventory. The larger banks that finance producers, distributors and processors give their best terms for the value of the inventory that is fully protected by an adequate hedge. Most merchants, for instance, finance their operations on borrowed money. A fully hedged merchant with a good credit rating may obtain a loan of 90% of the market value of his inventory at an interest rate of say 10%. Such a merchant has a great advantage over a competitor who obtains a loan of only 75% to 80% on unhedged inventory at a cost of 12% interest. If this latter merchant is to survive in the business, this added cost has to become a charge to someone in the economy.

Market participants who do not reduce the risks through hedging are speculating. In assuming these extra risks, they may be increasing the costs to the consumer.

A futures market acts as a focal point where buyers and sellers can meet readily. This improves overall market efficiency by reducing "search" costs. Buyers automatically know where the sellers are and vice versa. They do not need to search each other out.

13

A futures market in a commodity should lead to less segmentation in the market or, to put it another way, it should foster competition by unifying diverse and scattered local markets. Local monopolists will have a difficult time maintaining their position when national markets easily accessible to all people offer their customers other alternatives.

Futures markets help to tie all local markets together into a national or international market. An integrated national market means that prices in all local markets will tend to move more closely in unison with the national market. Price relationships (basis patterns) for a larger number of locations and a larger number of related products will become more stable. This makes for more effective and efficient hedging of a wider number of risks. We will talk more about this in a later chapter.

How much is the service of the futures market worth to the consumer? That is hard to say precisely. Some studies of the use of futures markets have shown that those who use futures for hedging purposes over several seasons have a more stable income pattern from the marketings than those who do not. They do not get the peak prices but they do not get the bottom either. The futures market provides them with the opportunity to stabilize their incomes and allows them to lower their marketing margins in order to obtain a competive advantage.

Of course, a futures market can't do all things. Some people have the mistaken notion that futures markets establish prices. This is incorrect. A futures market does not cause either high prices or low prices. In an open market, prices are established by supply and demand. The futures market simply reflects the supply and demand factors and their interaction.

If a consumer boycott of a product becomes operative, if a foreign nation raises its export tax, if the foreign policy of a nation is intended in some way to affect world commodity prices, the futures market should reflect those influences, if it is working right. A futures market cannot guarantee a businessman a profit. If the businessman cannot control costs or is inefficient, the futures market will not magically make his operation profitable.

In short, a properly functioning futures market should foster and improve competition throughout the marketplace, thus encouraging efficient use of all resources.

2

Speculation Is Not A Four-Letter Word

Commodities . . . ? that's Russian Roulette!
Commodity trading is only for "high rollers."
Anybody who trades commodities loses.

Mention commodity futures trading to a group of strangers at a cocktail party, and the comments above are the most likely kinds of statements you'll hear.

So let's consider some of the reasons why people trade — and the more common reasons why some of them lose.

To review for a moment, in the first chapter we outlined two basic categories of people who take positions in commodity futures. Some trade as a normal adjunct to their businesses of producing and marketing a product. Traders who fall in this category are called hedgers. They buy and sell futures contracts as substitutes for merchandising transactions they will make at a later time. Other people take positions in commodities only in the hopes of making a speculative profit by correctly anticipating price movements. These people are generally categorized as speculators.

Why Do Speculators Speculate?

Many speculators trade simply because they want money, and the high leverage in futures trading affords the opportunity to turn small amounts of money into big amounts.

But it goes deeper than that. Some people trade because they seek a sense of excitement and risk not available to them in their daily work. The derring-do that had survival value in frontier days is still extolled in our society; yet it is often unavailable in everyday life. In an industrialized nation where most jobs are routine, a person cannot win status through on-the-job valor.

The commodity markets, though, give him the risk, the feeling of a man-alone-against-the-odds, that is not available in his everyday world. There is a certain mystique and romance associated with commodity trading. To be able to pickup the phone and call his broker makes a person a participant in an exciting, international game. It pits his skill and judgement against that of all others in the world of futures trading. To win is more than the making of money. It is a reaffirmation of his own ability and acumen; it is food for his ego — and therein lies the danger. When the ego takes over, rational decision making is impaired. A man whose ego won't admit a mistake tends to stick with a losing position too long. Consequently, people who fall in love with their positions become big losers.

A successful trader knows and understands the importance of his ego in trading, and he learns to control it. In fact, self-discipline is an important key to successful trading.

Some of the basic psychological motivations for trading can be explained by the greed/fear complex. People trade because they want money. Yet, by trading, they fear losing what they want the most. Sometimes the greed motivation becomes so strong that they overtrade. In other instances, fear becomes so overpowering that the ability of an individual to make rational decisions is impaired. A good trading plan will help control this greed/fear complex.

Another motivating factor is sheer gambling instinct. Some people trade commodities because the market is like a "Las Vegas East" for them. They enjoy the excitement of the unknown, the taking of risks, and money doesn't mean that much to them. Usually these people are losers.

There also seems to be a basic need-to-own drive in every individual. This drive manifests itself in the decision to trade futures contracts and, undoubtedly, helps explain why the general run-of-the-mill trader prefers to be "long" in the market and hesitates to go short. He would rather have no position than a short position. Before you trade, ask yourself whether any of the reasons above describe you. If so, think carefully about your suitability for trading.

Speculation or Gambling?

Even relatively sophisticated investors and investment counselors have been heard to refer to commodity futures trading as "a close relative of a Nevada casino." Gambling and speculation are distinctly different economic activities, however.

Gambling involves the creation of a risk for the sole purpose of its being taken. The dice game or horse race creates risks which would not otherwise be present. If the police raid the dice game or the race track burns down, the risks they offer no longer exists. Gambling involves sterile transfers of money between individuals. In the strict economic sense, it absorbs time and resources, yet creates no new value.

Speculation, on the contrary, deals in risks that are already necessarily present in the process of producing and marketing goods in a free capitalistic system. As livestock and crops are grown and marketed, there are obviously risks of price change which must be taken by someone. It can be those who own the actual commodity — or someone else.

For example, let's suppose you own a small ranch and decide to raise beef cattle. You know how much young feeder cattle cost, and you estimate how much it will cost you to feed them up to market weight by next fall. Based on these calculations, you decide that if you can sell your cattle next fall at 60¢ a pound or more, you can make a fair profit and the enterprise would be worthwhile to you.

The day you buy your feeder cattle you are assuming the risk that by market time next fall cattle prices will be below 60¢ per pound, which could mean no profit, or — worse yet — a loss to you.

The futures market enables you, by selling a futures contract, to shift at least a part of this risk to a speculator who is willing to assume it in hopes of profiting from a change in that future price. The point is, the risk was there. It had to be borne by someone whether the futures market existed or not. The futures market served an economic function by facilitating the transfer of the risk from someone who didn't want it to someone who did.

(This is, of course a highly simplified example of a hedge. A much closer look at this operation is the subject of later chapters.)

This does not mean that no one treats commodity trading as gambling. Anyone who approaches futures trading without a knowledge and understanding of commodities and their markets is doing just that — gambling. And it shouldn't surprise you that these people tend to be losers in the long run.

Do Most Speculators Lose?

Until recently there was little evidence to support or refute such quotes as those at the beginning of this chapter. However, Dr. Thomas A. Hieronymous of the University of Illinois has reported the findings of a study he conducted of trading results realized by 462 accounts of a major brokerage house during 1969.[1]

He concluded that, overall, about twice as many people lost money as made money. Or, to look at it another way, roughly one-third were winners and two-thirds were losers. On the average, each loser lost more than each winner made. A more re-

[1]T.A. Hieronymous, "Economics of Futures Trading," Commodity Research Bureau, One Liberty Plaza, 165 Broadway, New York, N.Y. 10006, 1972.

cent study conducted by Raymond Ross as a doctoral dissertation at the University of Illinois reported similar results. Both studies found that commission costs represented a large part of the losses.

Dr. Hieronymous also broke his findings down into the results achieved by "one-time" traders and "regular" traders.

A one-time trader he defined as a trader with an account that showed only profits or losses, suggesting that its owner had made a single trade — or a few trades in a single commodity — and withdrew. Of this group, less than 30% were in the "plus" column.

Regular traders were defined as those who had traded at least 10 contracts and who, at one time or another, had lost at least $500 and made at least $500. This group was almost equally divided between winners and losers, and their total net gains and losses, after commissions, were about equal.

Even the most experienced, most successful traders make losing trades. In fact, many have more losing trades than winning trades but still make money because the losing trades represent small losses and winning trades represent large gains. For example, if you had 10 losing trades averaging $100 each and 2 winning trades averaging $600 each, you would be a net winner of $200, even though you had more losing than winning trades.

No Winning Formula

Since there is obviously no magic formula for winning, it is important that the beginning trader understand some of the more common reasons why inexperienced traders may lose money.

1. Undercapitalization — Experience has proven that to begin trading with too little risk capital (and risk capital it must be; a trader should trade only with capital he can afford to lose) is almost a guarantee of failure. A position not adequately backed by trading capital may be forced into liquidation by a temporary adverse market move, which results in a call for additional margin that cannot be met.

2. Lack of Knowledge — Some traders, of course, lose simply because lack of know-how. It is easy for experienced traders to misinterpret or miss altogether important pieces of information that affect prices. The result can be frequent mistakes in market analysis and errors in trading decisions. Before getting involved in trading, one should know the methods of fundamental and technical price analysis, learn the different types of buy and sell orders and how they can be used, and study the production and marketing system for the commodities you want to trade.

3. Trading Too Many Different Commodities — Many new traders try to follow too many different commodities. It is difficult for even an experienced trader to keep a close watch on more than three commodities at one time. It is good advice when starting out to stick to one or two commodities and learn them thoroughly.

4. Lack of Discipline — A lack of discipline is another frequent downfall for a new trader. As was pointed out earlier, human ego is an important part of trading. When you take a position in the markets, you become emotionally involved. You defend your decision. Unless you are exceptionally objective, you can trap yourself in an unprofitable position by refusing to admit, even to yourself, that you have made a mistake.

5. Lack of a Trading Plan — Probably the single most important mistake new traders made, however, is to embark without a trading plan. A plan is like a road map. Just as you would not set out on a cross-country drive without a map, so you should not embark in commodity futures without a clear-cut trading plan.

An adequate plan forces you to set objectives and develop discipline in meeting those objectives. An adequate plan removes speculation from the personal realm of gambling.

Practice Trading

Before you open an account and lay your money on the line, it is a good idea to test yourself and your abilities by making some hypothetical trades. Appendix II contains The Commodity Trader's Scorecard, work sheets and a set of instructions for doing such practice trading. Results of your practice trading may help you decide whether or not futures trading is for you.

A word of caution is in order, however: Success in paper trading is no guarantee of success in real-life trading. You may react quite differently when faced with a real trading decision than with a paper trade.

3

The Trading Plan

People who trade commodities without a plan are like Christopher Columbus. When they start, they don't know where they're going. When they arrive, they don't know where they've been. They differ from Columbus in one important respect, however. They usually aren't as lucky in their discoveries.

As was pointed out in the last chapter, many speculators lose money because they trade without a plan. Your success as a trader will depend, to a great extent, on your ability to minimize the common mistakes made by losers.

A good sub-title for this chapter might be "Money Management," because a plan forces you to think about how you will manage your money. It is also an excellent way to control the emotional involvement that clouds the judgment of so many traders. A plan should help to reduce the frequency with which one takes profits too early or lets losses run too long. It should also help determine your suitability for commodity futures trading.

A well-prepared plan considers all aspects of your participation as a commodity futures speculator, including emotional as well as financial suitability and the strategy you will follow in achieving a goal. Plans range from the simple — which include only general considerations — to elaborate systems with completely mechanized or computerized rules of trading. Some plan is better than none at all. Even a poor plan is better than none, because no plan would provide for losing all of one's capital.

Certainly no investor or commodity trader wants to lose money, but when one takes risks, one obviously has a chance to lose money. On the other hand, there are few opportunities to make money without taking some risks. Considerations of the nature and the amount of risk that one takes are the real key to determining customer suitability and to designing an appropriate money managing plan for a commodity trader.

Exactly how much risk should a trader take at any point in time? How does he protect himself from the risks he has taken? In answering these questions, keep in mind that *your need or desire to take risks seldom is equal to your capacity to take risks.* You need to evaluate whether you are in a position to take risks separately from whether you should take risks. One should always distinguish between chances of loss on any one transaction and the consequences of the loss to the trader. Look at a transaction always in terms of the appropriateness of the risk in view of your need and capacity to assume risk. In making that evaluation you want to take a cold and objective look at your family responsibilities, your financial circumstances and your overall emotional suitability for trading. Weighing the consequences of gain against the consequence of loss is ultimately a subjective calculation, but it is absolutely essential in determining how much risk to take.

The Plan and Financial Suitability

The ideas and procedures for developing a plan, expressed in this chapter, are illustrated in a sample plan in Appendix I. Use it for your own plan or as a guide to developing one of your own.

Like a building, a plan needs a good foundation. The place to begin is with a complete review of your financial suitability for trading by determining your net worth and liquid assets. Net worth provides a guide to how much you can afford to risk in trading, and liquid assets are the only ones you can use in trading. Appendix I contains sample forms for determining your net worth, liquid assets and income available for futures trading.

You should ascertain the amount of money you will need to

meet your fixed living expenses — food, clothing, shelter, education, life insurance, savings, retirement account and investment portfolio (and alimony in case you lose!!). Only the extra money left after meeting yor regular needs should be considered as eligible for use in commodity trading.

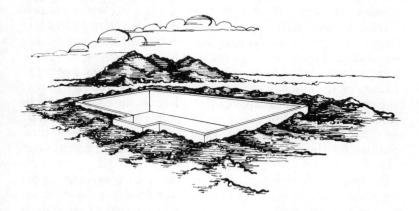

To put it bluntly, prudence dictates that you segregate from everything else you own the money you deem available for use in trading in the futures market. This makes it easier to control the urge to overtrade, and helps you to manage your money intelligently.

How much of this extra money that you allocate to trading commodities depends upon many considerations. Among them are your age, the size of your family, the type and security of the job you hold, the attitude of your family toward trading, your emotional suitability and your own personal desire for risk-taking. All of these factors should also be considered in determining your own personal trading philosophy.

If you have a net worth of less than $50,000, you probably should not be trading. But if you insist, a good guideline to follow is to commit no more than 10% of your liquid assets. If you are experienced and have large amounts of capital, you may want to go as high as 25% of your liquid assets. It would seldom be recommended to commit more than 25% of your liquid assets, no matter how great your assets are.

The Trading Strategy

Once you have determined the amount of money available for trading, you should think seriously about your philosophy of trading. By the mere fact that you have decided to trade futures, you have also decided to accept relatively high-risk investments. Nevertheless, as pointed out earlier, there are varying degrees of risk in trading commodity futures. You can trade conservatively by reducing your leverage, by judicious selection of the commodities you trade and by your method of trading. For example, trading a storage commodity is frequently less risky than trading a perishable commodity; following a "spreading" method of trading in storable commodities is normally less risky than taking a net position in a commodity. Spreading refers to the assumption of long and short position on the same business day in the same or related commodities for the same account. See Chapter 14 for more about spreads.

The first step in developing the trading strategy is selecting the commodity and contract of interest. This choice depends very much on your interests, background and knowledge. Pick the one which is most familiar and the easiest for you to follow.

Once you have picked the commodity, the real work of market analysis just begins. Before you are ready to enter a trade, you should dig deeply into the market information. Get "inside" the market. This means you must know the types and sources of information which are important in making judgments.

Some traders base their trading decisions primarily on the "fundamentals" of the market. That is, they evaluate possible future price movements on the basis of such things as a commodity's estimated production, carryover from previous years and estimated future demand, utilizing the wealth of information and data available from the USDA and many other sources. (See Chapters 6 and 7 on "Forecasting Prices" and Chapter 23, "What to Look for and Where to Find It.")

Some traders take the "technical" approach, using price charts to predict future price movements on the theory that familiar price patterns tend to repeat again and again. (See Chapters 8 and 9.)

Some blend the two approaches and take a position only when their interpretation of both the fundamental and technical factors

26

are in agreement with respect to market direction.

Still others depend heavily on the advice of a broker or advisory service in whom they have confidence.

Regardless of the approach taken, to make the decision-making process more objective and to add discipline to the approach, develop a checklist of key technical and fundamental factors and evaluate each set of factors in light of their probable impact on price. For example, are the general supply/demand statistics basically bullish, bearish or neutral? What do the technical market factors indicate? How does the current price level compare with historical price levels? You can then assign weights to each assessment and ultimately end up with a basic indicator of whether your analysis supports a long position, a short position or a neutral stand-aside position (see Part II of the trading plan, Appendix II).

Once you have a good general understanding of the expected direction of price movement, it is wise to assess the extent of the price movement and the possibility that it will occur. This is a very subjective process and has to be discerned from past price action as well as the expected interaction of the fundamental/technical factors affecting the market. Although this is a difficult step, it is a most important one. It forces the trader to think hard about how confident he is that his expectations of price movements will be met, and it provides a more definitive way of determining whether this is a worthwhile trade.

By combining all of the information about technical/fundamental factors and the expectations about price movements, you should get a clear indication of whether the weight of the analysis suggests a long, short or neutral market position.

That completes the first part of the plan — getting into the market.

Liquidation Strategy

No plan is complete unless it considers also a way out of the market or a plan for determining when and under what conditions you will liquidate the position (see Part III, Appendix II).

This means you have to consider how long you intend to hold your position. Some traders feel that if they do not reach their objective within a few weeks, they should liquidate and stand

27

aside until they get a more definite feel for the market trend. Most speculative traders avoid carrying a position into the delivery month. This stems partly from a fear of getting delivery if they are long in the market and partly from a desire to avoid the increase of margin and increased volatility frequently experienced during delivery months. A plan must include target prices reflecting the points at which you will be satisfied with the profit or will cut the losses and liquidate the position. It is important that you be realistic in setting these prices. Don't get greedy and don't rely on hopes and dreams.

To add discipline and for protection, it is a good idea, at the same time the original order is entered, to mark your target price objectives with a "stop order."

A stop order is simply a standing order to buy or sell that commodity "at the market" when a certain price is reached. As a market order, it is executed at the best possible price after the specified price is reached. For example, if you bought 5,000 bushels of March corn at $2.30 and you wanted to protect yourself against an undue loss — should prices decline instead of rising as you expect — you could give your broker an order to "sell March corn at $2.28 STOP." If the price of March corn futures did decline to $2.28, your order would automatically be executed at the best possible price, which, in a very active and moving market, might be slightly higher or lower than $2.28. Then, your position is closed.

For most commodities, the stop order is given to your broker like any other order. He transmits it to the floor of the exchange where that commodity is traded, and it is held on the books of the floor trader representing your broker's firm. When the market price reaches the price you specified in your stop order, it becomes a market order and is handled as such.

Stop orders can be used to close out your position when you have reached your profit objective, to initiate a new position, or to close out a position that has gone against you. Stop orders add discipline to your trading. They help you stick to your original objectives. The proper use of stop orders and the points at which they should ᵖlaced is a subject to which all traders should give careful ᵇᵉfore they enter the market.

Calculating the Expected Value of the Trade

One of the most valuable things you can do in planning is to assign probabilities that your target prices and either gains or loses will be achieved. As noted earlier, the mere process of assigning such probabilities causes you, the decision-maker, to consider the strength of your faith in prognostications. It forces you to think about whether your chances of achieving a gain or suffering a loss are 90%? 60%? 40%? etc.

Once that is accomplished and a probability is assigned, you have a rather simple measure of determining whether or not the trade is worthwhile. Without explaining the mathematical theory, if you multiply the potential gain to be expected from a trade by the probability of realizing that gain, you will obtain the gain or loss to be expected from that trade over the long run. Therefore, in your plan assign probabilities to your price expectations and calculate the expected values of your trade as an integral part of the planning strategy (see Part III, Appendix II).

It is important to consider commissions in the calculations. A potential profit or loss of $100 before commissions on pork bellies, for example, is really a potential profit of $55 ($100 − $45 commission) and potential loss of $145 ($100 + $45 commission).

The expected potential profit must be compared to the expected potential loss on each trade, and each trader should decide on a general rule of thumb which he can use as a guideline for decision-making. Some traders prefer to have a ratio of potential profit to potential loss of at least 3 to 1, after commissions, before they enter a trade. Others prefer a higher ratio. No matter what ratio you select as a guide to your decision to enter the market, you should have a profit objective and a loss limit in mind when you take a position.

Now you should be ready to implement your plan. The above procedure should have yielded sufficient information to provide a sound basis for your decision. It is important to remember that the objective of the plan is sound decision-making. A good decision may indeed be a decision not to trade — to stand aside until the market trend becomes clearer or until the probabilities of a successful trade improve.

An important factor here is patience. Pick your trades carefully. Do not rush in out of fear of losing an opportunity. Another one will be along shortly. Be prepared to recognize it.

The number of different commodities to be traded, the size of the initial position and the conditions under which one should add a position are also important elements of any plan. For the inexperienced, it is better to trade conservatively in only one or two different commodities with an ample cushion of cash in your account and to add to positions on strength rather than weakness. A good general policy for the beginner is to add to a position only when he has a profit on the original units, and never carry more than three open units in any one commodity. The financial graveyards are full of inexperienced people who took a plunge and wound up overtrading.

Review of Results

After you liquidate the position, review and analyze the results. find out what you did right and what you did wrong. This may be the most important thing you do. You won't progress to become a skillful trader unless you analyze why the results turned out the way they did. Learn from your mistakes as well as from the things you did right.

It should also be noted that all aspects of a plan are intertwined. Making a small change in one part of the plan may affect the rest of it in a major way. Plans should be internally consistent.

To aid you in developing a plan, some sample forms for (a) determining your financial suitability for trading, (b) determining the amount of money you have available for trading and (c) planning your strategy are included in Appendix I. After you finish the rest of the book, develop a plan using those forms and then, in conjunction with the practice trading exercise noted at the end of the previous chapter, try it out.

4

Choosing A Broker

"My advice to a prospective trader is to get the facts, make sure he has emergency funds and an understanding wife — and then get a good broker."

Not long ago, a speaker at an afternoon seminar wound up his speech with the above advice. The first question that came from the audience was, "I've already got the wife, the savings and the experience. How do I find a good broker?"

The questioner raised two important points. First, he pointed up the variation that exists among brokers in the commodity futures trading industry. Secondly, he placed his finger on one of the decisions that puzzles most new traders — i.e., what do you look for when selecting a broker?

Several years ago, psychologist William G. Baker III of the University of San Francisco conducted a study of stock brokers in an attempt to identify the personality traits of successful brokers. He ascertained that brokers who are mature, stable, sociable, self-controlled, enterprising, aggressive, ambitious, competitive and outgoing are much more likely to have customers who make money; customers whose brokers have the opposite traits or possess only a minority of these traits are more likely to be losers. Although Dr. Baker's research is directly applicable to the stock market, it has strong implications for selecting a commodity futures broker as well.

Look for someone who fits the description above but who also fits your personality, can give you guidance and is willing to provide you service. Look for a professional.

Where To Begin

Many people are reluctant to enter a broker's office, even out of curiosity. Studies show that this attitude stems largely from an unfounded belief that the public is not particularly welcome. The

typical descriptions given by many new customers upon visiting a broker's office for the first time are: "active," "confusing," "unfriendly," "noisy" and "no privacy." Nevertheless, most brokers will welcome your visit; after that initial visit you will probably deal mostly with your broker via phone.

If you already have a stock account with a brokerage firm, your present broker can introduce you to one of the men in his office who specializes in commodities. If his firm doesn't trade in commodities, your broker might be able to recommend a commodity specialist in another firm.

If you don't know any brokers to contact, there are several other ways to approach this decision. You might ask a friend who al-

ready trades commodities about his broker. You could contact
exchange and ask for a list of firms which handle commodity
trades for customers, then give one or several of them a call. You
could simply select the names of firms from the Yellow Pages of
the telephone book under "Commodity Brokers." Or you might
attend a seminar or lecture program sponsored by various
brokerage houses. These are usually advertised well in advance in
local newspapers and are generally free. Most brokers are selected
with someone else's help. A study done at the Chicago Mercantile
Exchange in 1970 revealed that four out of ten customers were
obtained by referral.

What To Look For

The best way to evaluate a broker is to visit him in his office.
Think twice before you open an account with a broker you've never
seen. There's no substitute for a face-to-face meeting.

One of the most important things about a broker are his
credentials. Is he registered with the Commodity Futures Trading
Commission in Washington, D.C.? How much experience does he
have as a commodity representative? Has he taken and passed the
National Commodity Futures Representatives Examination? Has
he been qualified to handle accounts by a training program? Is he
familiar with the literature on commodity futures trading?

You should also find out how much time your prospective broker
devotes to commodities. The picture changes rapidly in the futures
markets. He should be willing and able to devote the time necessary to follow the fast moving markets.

If you consider it necessary, a quick check on the broker's
background can be made by writing to the Commodity Futures
Trading Commission to determine if he's currently a registered
representative in good standing. Registration is required by law.

A broker should know about the materials available from the
exchanges, USDA and other sources. Some excellent work on
commodity futures trading and analyses of individual markets
has been done by the U.S. government and at such universities as
Stanford, University of Illinois, University of Wisconsin and Cornell. He should be able to guide you to those materials, as well as
some of the excellent books that have been written in recent years

about commodity futures trading.

A good broker will answer your questions directly and honestly — including telling you "I don't know, but I'll find out" when he doesn't know.

It has often been said that brokers who also trade for their own accounts are less desirable, because they suffer a loss of objectivity. Raymond Ross, in his doctoral dissertation completed at the University of Illinois, found otherwise. He found a high positive correlation between the net trading results of broker/solicitors and the results of their customers' trading. Brokers who made money trading for their own accounts tended to have customers who made money, and vice versa. Further, his research showed that the overall net trading results of customers of non-trading broker/solicitors tended to be much worse than those of brokers who also traded for their own accounts.

Consider The Firm

In selecting a broker, one must also look beyond the man to the firm. Does his office have good comunication facilities for keeping posted up-to-the-minute on prices? What sort of research facilities does the firm have, and how good are they? Surprisingly little has been done to appraise the real value of commodity futures research. Thus, you'll have to make your own judgments. You can probably judge this best by comparison with other firms. It's a good idea to ask to be placed on the mailing list for research reports and "market letters" from more than one firm, and then make a comparison over time. Obviously it's unfair to evaluate this research and advice solely on the basis of whether the firm was right or wrong in the market during some short time period. No one bats 1,000. But you can compare them on the basis of the depth and quality of the research and ask yourself if the conclusions reached are based on sound reasoning. Good research facilities are important. Ross' study also found that speculators who followed "house" research advice made money on two-thirds of their trades.

It could be that you will not want to rely solely on your broker or his firm for research. Perhaps you intend to do your own, or you may want to utilize one of the many independent commodity futures research firms that issue daily or weekly advisory letters to clients. The fees for these advisory services range from a few dollars a month to hundreds of dollars a year. The quality of the research and advice varies almost as much.

If the brokerage firm you choose is some distance away, inquire about being able to call them collect. This is a courtesy most firms offer their customers.

One of the most disappointing things that can happen to a new trader is to find that after he's opened an account and made a few small trades, his broker loses interest in him. One man recently complained, "My broker never calls me. As a customer, I don't like that. I like to think he cares about me and my money."

Your broker should keep an up-to-date log on your account and should have that log at his fingertips whenever you call. When you ask him a question about your account, he should be able to discuss with you without hesitation your position in the market, your trading objectives, stops you have placed, and other aspects of

your account. He should know what commodities you are interested in, and keep you up to date on the latest news of importance in those commodities.

Another very important service a broker can provide is to help you develop a trading plan. In fact, to test the kind of service you will receive from a broker, ask him to help you develop such a trading plan. He should know how to do it, he should have some simplified forms for planning, and he should be able to discuss with you all of the major points we touched in Chapter 3.

It almost goes without saying that you should expect fast and reliable execution of your orders. If you know people who have accounts with a broker, as them about the order execution they've received from him and his firm. Failure to execute orders quickly and accurately is inexcusable, and a sure sign that you should look elsewhere for your broker.

What Not To Look For

To this point, it sounds as though the broker should be all things to you. But there are certain things a broker cannot do and which you should not expect from him. He cannot, without legal power of attorney from you, make trading decisions without your prior approval. This means that when giving him an order for execution, you must make sure he understands exactly what you want done.

He cannot promise you profits. In fact, he's guilty of violating certain exchange rules and a Commodity Futures Trading Commission guideline on advertising if he does not, when discussing profit possibilities, mention the equal opportunity for losses.

He does have other customers to think about and can't spend all of his time pondering your account or discussing it with you on the phone.

He is also human, and no matter how experienced and diligent, can from time to time err in his estimate of the situation.

Problems

The world is made up of many different kinds of people — some good, some bad and some in between. So it is with commodity brokers. Unfortunately, there are some bad ones.

Some brokers take a very short run view of things and are more interested in getting the immediate order without giving proper thought to whether or not that particular transacton is appropriate for their customers. Some brokers care less about long-run service and more about immediate commissions.

The encouraging aspect of this situation, however, is that those people are being gradually eliminated by natural market forces (their customers leave them) and by the stringent new requirements imposed by the Commodity Futures Trading Commission.

If misunderstandings should arise or mistakes be made by one party or another, the first place to go with a complaint about a broker is to his immediate superior. Most complaints are settled there. If you're right, a settlement of the dispute will be made to compensate you. If further action is necessary, both the exchange on which the transaction was made and the Commodity Futures Trading Commission have departments to receive and investigate complaints about broker activities. Both are impartial in these investigations and are deeply committed to fairness and action when and if guilt is established. However, they need evidence, and the burden of proof is on the customer to show that the broker acted improperly.

The Commodity Futures Trading Commission Act of 1974 required the Commission to establish a reparations procedure for customers who felt they had been defrauded of their funds or in some other way injured financially by persons registered under the act. Such a procedure was established in early 1976.

Finding a good broker is not difficult, if you know what you're looking for. A true professional, interested in providing quality service and who has a strong brokerage organization behind him, can strongly enhance the profitability of your futures trading.

Opening The Account

Once a broker has been selected, it's relatively simple to open an account. Generally, it's a case of filling out some forms and depositing some money.

The first form a customer will usually be asked to complete is a New Account Information form. This asks for the usual personal information, including references (personal and credit), type of account (whether regular commodity account or managed account), instructions on sending notices and statements and your signature.

The second is a Customer Agreement Form. This gives the broker authority to liquidate any positions outstanding if the proper margin requirements are not met.

The amount of money that needs to be deposited depends on the individual brokerage house. Some will open an account for as little as $5,000, while others may insist on an initial deposit of several thousand dollars.

Types of Accounts

The type of accounts opened may vary — e.g., there are joint accounts, sole proprietorships, partnerships, corporate accounts and managed accounts. A managed or discretionary account is an account in which the customer signs a power of attorney to the broker, giving the broker the right to make trades for the account without first obtaining from the customer the approval on each trade. Don't open such an account unless you know the broker and his organization and have confidence in his integrity and ability. Most exchanges discourage the use of managed accounts and have set up special rules covering such accounts. Some commission houses forbid their brokers to accept the responsibility for managed accounts under any conditions.

Many firms also offer guided account programs. A guided account program is one that is essentially managed by a brokerage firm employee, but the customer is required to approve each transaction in advance of execution. Normally, the customer is called and consulted before each trade.

Guided accounts and managed accounts have appeal to some people who feel they don't have the time or expertise to manage the accounts themselves and would prefer to have someone else do it for them or at least help them do it. A person seeking such services may also want to consider some of the commodity mutual funds, limited partnership arrangements or even computerized advisory services.

Several large brokerage houses have established and are marketing commodity mutual funds. Just as the name suggests, an individual can buy an interest in the fund and participate in the profits or losses of the fund activity in proportion to his ownership in it.

Limited partnerships generally operate in the same manner. They are composed of an established number of limited partners

38

and a general partner. Each of the limited partners assumes limited liability for any losses incurred by the partnership. That liability is limited to the investment made. The general partner, however, has unlimited liability.

The attractive thing about limited partnerships and commodity funds is that the individuals investing in them, except for the general partner in the case of limited partnerships, have limited liability; they can lose only the amount they have invested. And when a group of people pool their funds, it provides some efficiencies in the management of the money and assures a sufficiently large sum of money so that the account has greater "staying power" than any one of the individuals might have if they were trading separately.

You should be very wary of participating in any venture of this kind, however. Before making any initial investment, you should thoroughly examine the background of the individuals managing the account and the rules and procedures under which the fund's assets will be invested.

It's hard to pick up a financial newspaper today without encountering an ad for someone selling a computerized commodity futures trading advisory service. Some people are attracted to the mystique that is associated with computer technology. The advent of the computer as a trading tool was inevitable. The computer is a very efficient means of analyzing large amounts of data and of testing a large number of trading strategies to identify those which seem profitable. Nevertheless, the computer is no better than the person programming it and establishing the criteria for analyzing the data input into the computer and output from it. Garbage in and garbage out is an old saying in the computer industry.

Before you lay out very much money for computerized advisory services, check carefully into their past record of achievement. Many such programs are very simplistic and rely heavily on technical analysis largely because the rules of thumb generated by technical analysis are easily programmable on the computer. The more sophisticated and better programs rely on a combination of technical analysis and fundamental analysis. In addition, the good models are sophisticated enough that they contain internal feedback procedures whereby the computer learns from its experience. Thus, as the economic environment changes, the model in the computer conducts trial and error procedures to identify those parts of the model which must be updated to reflect things learned from past experience. These types of models, which have been used successfully to teach a computer to play chess with such skill that even expert players lose to it, are now finding their way into the futures trading field.

If you're looking for outside advice and management help, check carefully into what you're getting before you sign a contract. And most importantly, watch the size of the management fee.

5

The Order

One of the most important and perhaps the least understood aspects of commodity futures trading is the order that a customer gives to his broker to assume or close out a position in the market.

An order is, by definition, an instruction given by a customer to his broker directing the broker to buy or sell a particular futures contract or contracts during a certain time interval. Within these two broad categories of buy and sell orders, however, is a wide variety of order types, each with a specific purpose. So let's examine the above definition one phrase at a time, to see how each works.

Time Element

Time is an aspect of all orders, and there are several ways in which timing may be specified when placing an order.

"Day" orders are good only for the day they are placed. If not executed, they expire at the close of trading on the day on which they are entered.

"Open" orders remain in effect until either executed or cancelled or until the contract expires.

"Good 'til cancelled" orders are the same as open orders.

"Good through (date)" orders remain in effect until the close of business on the date specified. Variations include orders that are "Good for this week" or "Good for this month."

"Time-of-day" orders call for execution at a specific time or specific intervals during the trading session. For example, "Sell 2 July pork bellies at the market at 11:30 a.m."

41

"Off-at-specific-time" orders are similar to "Day" orders but have an added time contingency in that they remain in effect only until a specified time during the trading session. If the order is not executed by that time, it is automatically cancelled. For example, "Sell 2 May pork bellies at 55.00. Good 'til 12:00 PM, Chicago time."

"Fill-or-kill" orders are those to be executed at a specific price or better immediately upon receipt in the pit on the exchange floor. If the order cannot be executed immediately, it is cancelled, and the customer is notified of the latest quote. These are also sometimes referred to as "immediate or cancelled" orders or "quick" orders. Such orders must be filled in total or in part immediately upon receipt. Any part of the order not filled immediately is cancelled automatically.

"On-the-opening" orders must be executed during the opening of trading, which is a short period of time — usually counted in minutes — at the beginning of the day's trading during which an opening price range is determined in the trading pit. If not filled then, the orders are cancelled.

"On-the-close" orders must be executed during the closing of trading, which is a short period of time — again measured in minutes or fractions — at the end of the day's trading activity. If not executed before the closing bell, the orders are cancelled.

Price

In addition to the time element, all orders must include instructions as to the price at which the transaction is to be made. The order may designate a specific price at which it must be executed, or it may leave the price to be determined by the market. A number of alternative types of price instructions may be used.

The one with which most traders are familiar is an order to buy or sell "at the market." "Market" orders are to be executed at the best possible price obtainable at the time the order reaches the pit. Example: "Buy 2 pork bellies at the market."

"Limit" orders are those to purchase or sell futures at a designated price or better. If it is a limit order to buy, the price designated must be below the current market price. If it is a limit order to sell, the price designated must be above the current market price. A limit order enables the customer to execute a transaction at a better price than that prevailing at the time the order is entered, if the market price reaches (actually trades or is bid or offered at) the level specified. Of course, the customer takes the chance that his order will not be executed because the price level he has designated for execution is not reached.

A limit order never becomes a market order. For example, consider the limit order, "Buy 2 May pork bellies at 54.50 limit." This transaction will be made only at a price of 54.50 or *less*. If it had been, "Sell 2 May pork bellies at 54.50 limit," the transaction would be made only at 54.50 or *higher*.

A "market-if-touched" order is one to buy or sell futures "at the market," when the price reaches the specified level. This order is similar to a limit order in that the designated price to buy must be below the current market price and that to sell must be above the current market price. Unlike limit orders, however, market-if-touched orders are always executed if the price moves to the designated level because they become market orders at that time. An example of such an order is, "Buy 2 May pork bellies at 54.50, market-if-touched."

Stop Orders

A "stop" order is one to buy or sell at the market when the market reaches a designated price. They are referred to as "stop-loss" orders when placed to close out a position in the event prices move against the trader. A stop order to buy must be entered above the prevailing market price. A stop order to sell must be entered below the prevailing market price. It is these two characteristics that distinguish a stop order from a market-if-touched order.

A stop order to buy or sell at a specified price does not guarantee, however, that the order will be filled at the price specified, even though the market sells or is bid at the stop price. If the market is moving quickly and passes through the stop before the broker has a chance to execute the order, the execution price may be higher or lower than the stop price.

43

Stop orders are used for three purposes: To protect the profit on an existing long or short position; to initiate a new long or short position, or to stop losses by closing out an unprofitable long or short position. An example of a stop order is, "Buy 2 May pork bellies at 54.50, stop."

A "stop-limit" order is one that has a designated limit above which the customer will not buy and below which he will not sell. A stop-limit order enables a trader to take advantage of the stop order, yet also to be sure of getting a price within a definite range. Stop-limit orders may be executed when the price is bid at or above the stop price, buy they cannot be executed outside the limit specified. In effect, once a stop order is elected, it becomes a limit order. For example, "Buy 2 May pork bellies at 54.50 stop, limit 54.80" means that if the market sells or is bid or offered at 54.50, buy 2 May pork belly contracts. If you can't get them done at 54.50 or better, keep trying to buy them up to a price of 54.80, but in no event buy them at a price above 54.80.

"Scale" orders are orders to buy or sell two or more lots of the same commodity at designated intervals. For example, "Buy 2 May pork bellies at 52.50 and one each ½-cent down for 5" is an order to buy two May pork bellies at 52.50 and then one more each as the price declines by ½-cent intervals until the total of five additional contracts have been purchased.

Combination Orders

Combination orders are two orders that are entered at the same time, with the cancellation of one contingent upon the execution of the other. A combination order may also be an order to buy or sell one commodity at a specified price in one month when prices reach a specified level in another month — or in another commodity. Commodity brokers who accept combination orders assume no responsibility for simultaneous or exact price execution, however, as it is physically impossible for a broker to be in two places executing two orders at the same time.

Combination orders may be classified as "alternate" orders and "contingent" orders. Alternate orders are a group of orders entered at the same time with instructions that, upon execution of

44

any one of the orders, all remaining orders are cancelled. Example, "Buy 2 May pork bellies at 54.50 or 2 July pork bellies at 55.00."

Contingent orders are entered with the understanding that the execution of one order is dependent upon the execution of the other. They are also referred to as "when-done" orders. These orders may instruct the simultaneous purchase and sale at a stipulated price, or they may instruct the execution of one part of the order before the other part of the order is considered entered. Example: "Buy 2 May pork bellies at the market when August pork bellies sell above 55.00."

"Spread" orders are used to establish or close out spread or straddle positions and can be used in a variety of ways.

An "inter-market spread" is the purchase of a particular commodity future on one market and the sale of a contract for the same commodity on another market. Example: "Buy 2 May wheat, Chicago, at the market and sell 2 May wheat, Minneapolis, at the market."

An "intra-commodity" spread is the purchase of a futures contract for a given month and the simultaneous sale of a futures contract for the same commodity in a different month on the same exchange. Example: "Buy 2 May pork bellies and sell 2 July pork bellies when July is 3 cents over May."

An "inter-commodity spread" is the purchase of a futures contract for a given commodity and the simultaneous sale of a futures contract for a different but related commodity. Example: "Buy 3 July grain sorghum at the market, sell 10 July corn at the market."

When entering a spread order, the buy part of the order is always given first.

Placing the Order

It is important when placing orders to give your broker complete and clear instructions — whether you want to BUY or SELL; the QUANTITY (quantity in some commodities is given in number contracts, while in others it is given in number of units of the commodity. For example, "2 pork bellies" refers to two contracts; "5 wheat" refers to 5,000 bushels or one contract of wheat); the EXCHANGE on which you wish to trade (some commodities are traded on more than one exchange); the MONTH you wish to trade; the length of TIME you want the order to stand; the PRICE; and, of course, the COMMODITY. This may sound like extremely rudimentary advice, but it is surprising how many misunderstandings result from failure to ensure that the broker knows exactly what his customer wants done.

6

Forecasting Prices

One of the most popular myths in commodity price forecasting is that there is a magic formula for accurately predicting prices and that someone, somewhere, holds the secret to that formula.

A few years ago a member of a major commodity exchange told me excitedly that, after eight years of trading and searching, he had discovered the method for forecasting pork belly prices. A few months later he had to sell his membership on the exchange to pay his debts. Currently, he is working as a brokerage house clerk. Apparently he had staked all he had on his newly discovered secret, only to learn — as countless others before him — that his magic formula was really a witch's potion.

The price of a commodity at any given instant does not pop from a bubbling cauldron but is the result of decisions on the part of both a buyer and a seller. Presumably, both traders, after careful analysis of all the factors, have concluded that that price was the best for them under the circumstances.

How did they arrive at their decisions? Most likely through a combination of fundamental analysis and technical analysis. Fundamental analysis refers to the study of those elements that affect the physical supply of and demand for a particular commodity. Technical analysis refers to the study of market activity itself: Prices, trading volume, open interest and other numerical data.

This chapter contains a cursory look at fundamental analysis. Those who would like to delve deeper into the subject can find it in any good basic economics text. This does not mean to imply that fundamental analysis is more important or better than technical analysis in price forecasting. As a matter of fact, most successful traders utilize both approaches — the fundamental approach for identifying long-term trends, technical analysis for timing of trades and identifying short-term trends.

Fundamental Analysis

A contractor starting out to build a house has a definite objective in mind — namely, the completed house. Likewise, the price analyst must have a definite objective. It can be narrow and specific, such as an explanation of the movement in beef prices during the last six months, or more general, such as the probable effects on prices of a new government agricultural program.

The building contractor needs certain things to accomplish his objective; i.e., a detailed blueprint or plan, tools, materials to work with and a technique. The price analyst also needs a plan. He needs a knowledge of basic economic concepts in order to avoid costly errors and to assure that he remains on target. He must have material to work with in the form of data and information, and he needs techniques for utilizing the data to build, step-by-step, toward his objective of accurately forecasting commodity prices.

A good place to start is with the meaning of a couple of pretty important words — "supply" and "demand."

Demand

The term "demand" is used by different people to mean different things. It is often — and not quite correctly — considered synonymous with "consumption" or with "quantity" of a commodity moving into market channels. To an economist, demand refers to the quantity of a product or service which buyers are willing and able to buy at a given place, time and price. Normally, the quantity that people will buy varies inversely with the price. That is, as the price goes up, the amount bought goes down, and vice versa.

In general, consumer demand for a product or a service depends on four main factors and may change when any of the factors change: (1) Real income or purchasing power of consumers — as people have more money to spend, they will usually spend it; (2) the number of consumers — as the number of people grows, so does the total demand for products; (3) the price and availability of substitutes — chicken as a substitute for pork; hence, if the price of chicken goes up relative to the price of pork, people will tend to eat more pork and less chicken; and (4) consumers' personal tastes and preferences — if people suddenly decide they like pork better than beef, their preferences will be reflected in increased demand for pork.

As noted, the price of the product and the quantity bought are closely related. However, this relationship varies, depending upon the commodity. If sirloin steak goes up 50% in price, housewives might start pushing their shopping carts right past the steak cooler. However, if the price of table salt were to rise by 50%, sales of salt are not likely to fall very much. In one instance, there are substitutes; in the other instance (salt), there are none and it's a necessity. By the same token, a 10% change in the price of pork may cause a 12% change in the amount of pork purchased.

The degree to which the quantity bought changes in response to a change in price is described by the frightening term, "price elasticity of demand." This is nothing more than an index number devised by economists to describe how far purchases will go in one direction when price goes in the other. For example, the price elasticity for all beef has been estimated at — .95.

49

This means that a 10% *increase* in the price of beef is associated with a 9.5% *decrease* in the amount of beef bought. Expressed another way, it means that people tend to tolerate moderate beef price increases and go on broiling hamburgers.

A full understanding of elasticity and what it means will enable you to estimate the amount of price change necessary to clear a market of a given amount of product. For a complete discussion of this subject, a good reference is *The Marketing of Agricultural Products* by Shepherd & Futrell, Iowa State University, Ames, Iowa.

Supply

Just as you can't cut a piece of cloth with one blade of scissors, you can't determine price by considering demand only. The other blade of the price-determining scissors is supply. Recent experience has shown that the demand for commodities remains relatively constant over short periods of time. This is particularly true in developed economies such as the United States, where consumer habits change slowly and incomes do not fluctuate sharply. Therefore, supply must be given careful consideration in price analysis and forecasting.

Generally speaking, the short-term supply of a commodity is made up of the carryover from previous growing seasons, the current year's production and imports. There is no carryover, of course, for unstorable commodities like live cattle or hogs, but in commodities such as grains carryover is an important part of supply.

Most data published on commodities by USDA and other sources deals with supply, because it is more readily measured than demand. Periodic reports based on growers' stated intentions as well as measurement of actual yields at the end of the season provide a relatively accurate indication of the forthcoming supply of a commodity. Ask your broker for such reports or get on the mailing lists at U.S. Department of Agriculture, Commerce and Treasury to receive their reports directly.

As used by economists, the term "supply" means the quantity of a product or service that would be made available by sellers at a specified place, time and price. Just as buyers will take different amounts of a commodity depending upon the price, so sellers are usually willing to sell different amounts at different prices. Normally, the quantity of a commodity offered for sale varies directly with the price; that is, when the price goes up, the amount offered for sale goes up, and when the price goes down, the amount offered for sales goes down. As in the case of demand, the concept of elasticity also applies.

The quantity of a commodity offered by sellers at a given price is also influenced by whether or not the commodity is storable. The willingness to sell from stocks on hand depends upon the owner's comparison of current prices with what he thinks he might get if he held on to his commodity a while longer. On the other hand, the supply obtained directly from current production is affected more by such things as weather, yields, acres planted or number of animals bred, quantities and prices of feed, and other costs of production.

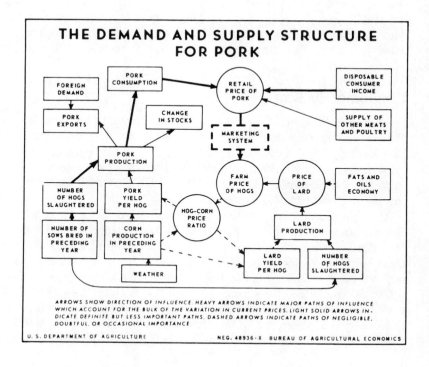

THE DEMAND AND SUPPLY STRUCTURE FOR PORK

ARROWS SHOW DIRECTION OF INFLUENCE. HEAVY ARROWS INDICATE MAJOR PATHS OF INFLUENCE WHICH ACCOUNT FOR THE BULK OF THE VARIATION IN CURRENT PRICES. LIGHT SOLID ARROWS INDICATE DEFINITE BUT LESS IMPORTANT PATHS. DASHED ARROWS INDICATE PATHS OF NEGLIGIBLE, DOUBTFUL, OR OCCASIONAL IMPORTANCE

U. S. DEPARTMENT OF AGRICULTURE   NEG. 48936-X BUREAU OF AGRICULTURAL ECONOMICS

The longer-term supply of a product is determined by the total number of potential producers; the capacity of the facilities they operate; their proficiency as producers; the physical characteristics of production of the commodity — such as the length of life of fruit trees; their own personal expectations; the relative costs of production for alternative products; and certain social and institutional influences, such as the historical tendency of corn farmers to continue to plant corn.

Armed with an understanding of what it is that makes up supply and demand for a commodity, the analyst is then ready to organize these elements in such a way that he can judge their collective effect on price. In other words, to develop a "model" — a diagram of what affects prices and how it affects them. It should be noted that models are simplifications of reality. No model can include all of the relationships that affect price, and, indeed, it would be a waste of time to attempt to do so. The important thing is that the model include the major factors and show the real interrelationships between them. The diagram on the preceding page is a model of how supply and demand interact to affect the prices of pork. The lines connecting the elements show the interrelationships.

Consumer is King

All demand begins, of course, with the consumer. In the absence of a demand by consumers for a product, there would be no demand by retailers, wholesalers or processors. This demonstrates the importance of beginning a price forecast with an analysis of consumers' demand for the end product or at least working from the point closest to the consumer.

An experienced analyst learns to study those factors that affect demand and supply at each level of the system. He learns, for example, that when the packers are operating plants at less than optimum capacity because of a lack of hogs for slaughtering, they bid up the price of hogs. And that during periods of inflation, the price of beef usually rises more than the price of pork. He also learns that these factors do not operate instantaneously, that there are time lags built in. It takes weeks for a rise in the demand of pork at retail to be fully transmitted back

52

to the farmers in the form of higher prices for hogs. Likewise, an increase in the supply of hogs at the farm level is not transmitted into lower retail prices right away.

When analyzing the effects of changes in supply and demand, the analyst must be careful not to confuse causal relationships with movements that are simply associated. Some years ago a researcher reported that annual changes in the price of pork seemed to be related to changes in the price of beef. Some jumped to the conclusion that changes in prices of beef caused changes in pork prices. Later, analysts discovered that changes in pork prices were almost completely accounted for by changes in market supplies and consumer incomes. The reason for this apparent cause-and-effect relationship was that beef and pork prices are affected by the same domestic demand conditions. Naturally, therefore, they tended to fluctuate together.

Prices are not generated automatically by the factors of supply and demand. Prices are actually "discovered" through a process of give and take on the part of the buyers and sellers. Market traders collect, analyze and interpret all the information and facts they can about supply and demand. Then on the basis of their analyses, they make bids and offers, back and forth, until finally two people agree that a particular price is satisfactory to both. When the transaction is made, the price is generated. It's like a giant computer.

Where to Get Data

Where does the analyst go to obtain his data about supply and demand and the many factors affecting each? As mentioned before, most of the data is available directly from reports of the U.S. Department of Agriculture and several private market reporting agencies. These reports tell in great detail the daily, weekly and monthly price movements, market receipts and other associated factors and are useful in following current situations as well as in long-term forecasting. Most of the government reports are available free. Anyone working regularly in the field of price forecasting and analysis should ask to have his name placed on the mailing list of the government agencies issuing reports. For a list of the available reports, write to: Superintendent of Documents, Government Printing Office, Washington, D.C. 20250. Chapter 23 lists a great many USDA reports available on specific commodity groups as well as a number of private sources.

Private market-reporting services are available for many commodities. In addition, many trade organizations collect and publish information about their industry on a regular basis. Magazines, newspapers and wire services report information about USDA statistics and the markets on a daily basis. Many of the articles contained in *Futures* Magazine deal in depth with analysis of individual reports and commodities. Your broker should be able to keep you posted on the timing of the reports, and he should also be able to give you a quick summary of the contents of reports after they are released.

In addition, most exchanges provide relatively complete statistical summaries and pamphlets explaining, in a simplified way, the fundamental supply and demand factors affecting prices for individual commodities. For example, the Chicago Mercantile Exchange publishes a daily bulletin containing summaries of the previous day's futures trading and the important cash market statistics. They also publish a yearbook containing the same information for a whole year, special periodic summaries of important USDA reports and an excellent series of pamphlets explaining how to analyze the fundamental factors affecting each of the major commodities traded.

Knowing the release date of a report is crucial for the trader. Markets anticipate reports, and prices will adjust prior to release of the report in anticipation of what the report will contain. Sometimes, of course, the market is wrong in its anticipation, and prices that went up expecting a bullish report will immediately go down when the report is found to be bearish. Most smart traders try to be out of the market or at least in a protected position at the time major reports are released. This is just good common sense. Do not try to outguess the market. Take time to study and analyze new information before committing yourself to a position.

Government Policies

As in most aspects of life, the government plays a major role in the pricing of products, and all fundamental analysts learn to watch closely the activities of the federal and state governments — in encouraging or discouraging production, controlling imports and exports through embargoes and quotas, storage programs, and in establishing price ceilings and floors. There are a myriad of such government programs in existence, and virtually all affect prices in some way.

7

More About Forecasting Prices

Remember the old comedy record of a Frenchman describing the first American football game he had ever seen? Looking at commodity price movements on a day-to-day basis without an understanding of the underlying patterns can make about the same amount of sense.

These underlying patterns take several forms. Some movements reflect seasonal influences, some are cyclical. There are also trends to be considered. All of these price movements may be further divided into those of short-term and those of long-term duration.

Short-term price fluctuations are due mainly to sudden shifts in the demand for, or supply of, a commodity as the result of reactions to weather conditions, political moves, international developments, rumors, technical "signals" or chance occurrences. Long-term price fluctuations are the result of fundamental or gradual shifts in demand and supply resulting from more enduring factors such as changes in production technology, consumer preferences or population growth.

Seasonal Movements

All agricultural commodities have some seasonality in crop production and marketing. Perishable and semi-perishable commodities which are not stored by dealers have to be moved into consumption as soon as possible after production. As the available supply of these products increases, consumers will buy the added quantities only at lower prices. When the supply falls off, consumers are willing to pay higher prices. That's why prices are usually more volatile for perishable commodities than for the non-perishables.

Non-perishable commodities (those which can be stored) are usually lowest in price at harvest time but tend to rise during the rest of the year only by an amount sufficient to cover the accumulated cost of storing. Consequently, the season's supply is fed into consumption in relatively uniform amounts from month to month. As a result, prices are more uniform throughout the year than for perishable commodities.

Seasonal variation in commodity prices is frequently misinterpreted. The true seasonal movement in prices can be observed only by taking average prices over a long period. And keep in mind that this represents history — it does not necessarily predict the future. The average or so-called "typical" seasonal price movement does not occur regularly each year. In fact, month-to-month changes in price are quite different in different years. The seasonal price variation merely represents a general tendency.

Wheat provides an excellent example, as it is one of the commodities that tends to follow a distinct seasonal price pattern. Generally, low prices in wheat occur during the summer harvest season, with higher prices in winter and spring.

Cyclical Movements

Almost any regularly recurring movement can be called a cycle. But in commodities, this term is usually applied to the more-or-less regular rise and fall of production and price over an extended period of time. Cycles are self-energizing, which means that one part of the movement follows or is caused by another part. This makes cycles, to a certain extent, predictable.

There are several well-known cycles in the production and price of a commodity. High prices not only encourage new producers to enter into production but influence existing producers to produce more. As market receipts increase, prices decline until they reach a point where some producers become discouraged and drop out while others simply reduce their operations. As the contraction continues, prices rise until they again reach a level that encourages expansion, marking the beginning of a new cycle. The graph

58

on this page, showing changes in hog prices and pork production, demonstrates this action.

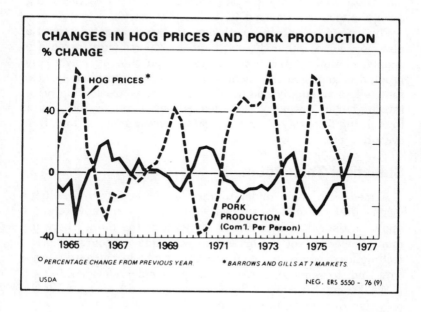

CHANGES IN HOG PRICES AND PORK PRODUCTION

Often there are time lags associated with cyclical movements. For example, livestock marketings tend to lag behind production on the upswing of the production cycle because, as production increases, a larger proportion of available animals must be retained for breeding purposes. On the downswing, a smaller than average number of animals are retained for breeding and farmer marketings are therefore larger than the total number of animals on farms would indicate. In anticipating the effects of the production cycle on price, you have to take into account this shifting lag of production and receipts. Further, the length of time it takes production to change will vary according to the time it takes to bring the commodity to market. For example, in hogs, it takes three to four years for a cycle to be completed; in cattle, it takes six to eight years.

Trends

Long-term changes in supply or demand, whatever the causes, may result in gradual increases or decreases in prices. Such long-term changes are referred to as "secular trends."

The steady growth in population, the gradual development of new uses for a commodity without a proportionate increase in supply, changing customs, changes in purchasing power, and gradual changes in the technology of production all may have some effect on supply and demand over the years, forcing prices into higher or lower ranges. Meanwhile, of course, the price is fluctuating from day-to-day, season-to-season and, possibly, from cycle-to-cycle.

Statistical Techniques

Armed with some understanding of the supply and demand factors that can affect commodity prices, you are now ready to apply statistical techniques to analysis of the data. There are many. Selection of a particular technique or combination of techniques depends on the nature of the problem, the nature of the data and, to some extent, on your personal preference.

We'll treat only a few of the more popular methods here. We can only familiarize you with the basics. It would take a separate book to explain any one of them — and many have been written.

Ratios

For long-run forecasting, a great many experienced traders consider certain ratios — such as the hog/corn ratio and the egg/feed ratio — as reliable indicators.

The hog/corn ratio is used in forecasting hog prices. It is calculated by dividing the price of hogs per hundred-weight by the price of a bushel of corn. (If the price of hogs is $20 per hundredweight and the price of corn is $1.50 per bushel, the hog/corn ratio would be $20 \div 1.50 = 13.33$.)

Changes in this ratio give you an indication of the profitability of hog feeding and help you forecast an increase or decrease in

the number of hogs fed. Low ratios (below 12) suggest n̶ₐ̶
profit margins and low future production, while high ratios
indicate higher profits and greater future production.

Similarly, the egg/feed price ratio is an indicator of the
profitability of producing eggs. An egg/feed price ratio of 10
indicates that 10 pounds of feed is equal in value to one dozen eggs.
A ratio below 9 is considered low, in that it has a depressing effect
upon egg production.

Monthly Hog/Corn Ratio

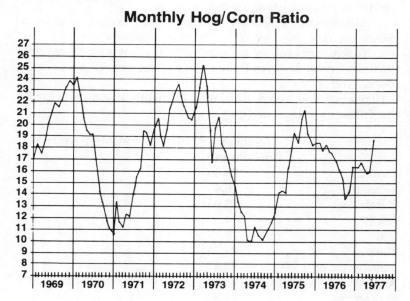

Moving Averages

A moving average is a flexible trend line that has been
"smoothed out." If annual or monthly data are used, the moving
average will reduce the effects of cycles, seasonal variations and
irregular movements, giving you a better idea of underlying
supply and demand strength. But the longer the period chosen, the
greater the likely time-lag between a change in the trend of prices
and the indication of this change by the moving average.

Active traders prefer to plot moving averages over short time
periods. Five-day, 10-day or 20-day moving averages are com-

monly used although some methods use 4-, 9- and 18-day moving averages. The example in this chapter is based on a 12-month period. The method, however, applies to any time period.

To build a moving average:

1. Select a time period or number of weeks that seems to best represent the cycle or seasonal element that you are most interested in smoothing out. As an example, if you want to eliminate the seasonality in pork prices to identify the long-term trend, you should use a 12-month period.

2. Average the prices for that 12-month period in order to obtain the first number of the moving average.

3. To figure out the second number in the moving average, drop the price for the first month and average the next 12 prices in the series. And so on.

Here's how you would calculate a 12-month moving average for the following retail pork prices:

	Average Price/Pound	Moving Average
January	76.68	
February	76.40	
March	76.03	
April	74.63	
May	74.72	
June	74.72	
July	75.37	
August	74.44	
September	71.64	
October	69.49	
November	66.13	
December	63.98	874.23 ÷ 12 = 72.85
January	63.89	861.44 ÷ 12 = 71.88
February	64.82	849.86 ÷ 12 = 70.82
March	65.29	829.12 ÷ 12 = 69.09

Index Numbers

High on the list of statistical measures most useful are those telling you how much change has occurred from one period to another or how change in one element compares with change in another element. For example, you may want to use an index to compare the production of corn in one year with the production of corn in another.

The usefulness of index numbers is by no means limited to changes in the price or production of single commodities. They are widely used to express changes in such complex economic areas as the cost of living and business cycles. These, of course, involve combining many prices or quantities in such a way that a single number can be used to indicate overall changes. The "cost-of-living index" is perhaps the most well-known of these; the Dow-Jones index of leading stocks is almost a household word. We are more concerned here, however, with a simple index that pertains to one commodity.

Suppose, for example, that we wanted to develop an unweighted index to measure the change in average farm prices of fat steers from 1964 through 1971. We would divide each year's price by the 1964 price and multiply by 100.

Year	Price	Index
1964	22.66 ÷ 22.66 × 100 =	100.0
1965	25.39 ÷ 22.66 × 100 =	112.0
1966	25.86 ÷ 22.66 × 100 =	114.1
1967	25.58 ÷ 22.66 × 100 =	112.8
1968	27.13 ÷ 22.66 × 100 =	119.7
1969	29.95 ÷ 22.66 × 100 =	132.1
1970	29.64 ÷ 22.66 × 100 =	130.8
1971	32.35 ÷ 22.66 × 100 =	142.7

This would give us a rough but handy single number to indicate these relative price changes.

Indexes are particularly useful in analyzing seasonal patterns. For example, in grain prices seasonal indexes can aid in estimating the profitability of storing a crop as opposed to immediate sale.

Seasonal indexes can also be used to estimate specific price levels during the year but only when reliable annual price forecasts are available. For example, if the average price of fed steers at Omaha for a particular year is reliably estimated to be $30 per hundredweight and the seasonal price index for June is 97.80, the estimated June price would be $30 × .9780 or $29.80 per hundredweight. Through additional simple statistical techniques, you could also estimate the probability of achieving that price.

The main point of all this is simply that indexes properly constructed and used can be very powerful forecasting tools.

Correlation

In Chapter 6 it was pointed out that an analyst must fit together supply and demand to determine how they relate to market prices. Correlation analysis is used to identify these important factors for inclusion in a supply and demand model.

Correlation is nothing more than a measure of the degree of association (not necessarily cause and effect) between two or more factors. Most fathers, for example, would find a high correlation between a teenage son's request to use the car and Saturday nights.

Correlation may be determined and expressed either mathematically or graphically. Correlation studies are classified as "simple," meaning the study of relationships between only two factors, and "multiple" or the study of the relationship of one factor to a group of other factors. We'll deal here only with "simple" correlation as shown on a graph.

Suppose we want to measure the relationship between the price of lumber and the number of housing starts in the U.S., assuming the preceding data.

The first step is to put the data on a "scatter" diagram, as shown in the accompanying graph. The vertical scale represents lumber prices and the horizontal scale represents housing starts. Dots are inserted in he diagram representing price and housing starts for each month. That is, the dot for any one month is opposite the point on the horizontal scale corresponding to the houses started and opposite the lumber price on the vertical scale. After all the data have been plotted, a line is drawn through the field of dots representing the average relationship between the two factors.

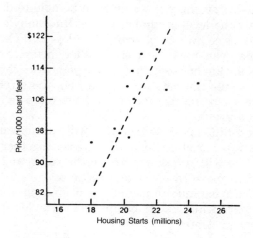

	Average Monthly Price/1000 Bd. Ft. 2 × 4's	U.S. Housing Starts (thousands)
January	$ 82	1,810
February	95	1,794
March	98	1,938
April	97	1,951
May	96	2,046
June	109	2,008
July	118	2,091
August	119	2,219
September	119	2,029
October	106	2,038
November	108	2,228
December	110	2,433

If the level of lumber prices depended only on the number of housing starts, all of the dots would lie on the line, and you would have a very powerful forecasting tool. If you know the number of housing starts, you would then be able to determine fairly accurately the level of lumber prices. But many other factors affect the price, which is why the dots are "scattered" around the line. You have to look at other factors, therefore, like other uses for lumber to help improve your price forecasting accuracy. The closer the dots are to the line, the stronger the relationship between the two factors and the more reliable the forecasts on the graph.

If the relationship is positive, the line will run upward to the right and the two variables tend to increase together. If it is negative, the line will run downward to the right, and the two variables tend to move in opposite directions.

This is a good technique to use at the beginning of analysis, because it suggests which relationships and variables are worthwhile exploring in depth.

Analyzing the Data

One last word of warning. Don't confuse the fundamental analysis with statistical analysis. And don't use one without the other. The mechanics of statistical analysis alone would be quite insufficient for effective price analysis. In fact, many successful commodity traders do not use formal statistical techniques. Qualitative or deductive reasoning plays an important role in price analysis, since many relationships or causes and effects cannot be statistically measured. Fundamentals are essential in filling the gaps. Using both, you won't fall into the common trap of arriving at erroneous conclusions drawn from purely statistical manipulations.

8

Technical Analysis

Technical analysts approach commodity price charts in much the same manner as cryptographers attempting to decipher a code. They have no less expectation that "written" in those squiggly lines is a message containing the ultimate secret to forecasting commodity prices — if only the code could be broken.

Their reasoning? That even if you knew where to find all the fundamental information about the supply and production of a commodity . . . even if you had the time to add it all up and also allow for such fleeting factors as weather, strikes and crop disease . . . you still wouldn't have the clue to market response. Because it is not these things that affect futures prices, but how traders react to them. And, according to the theory of technical analysis, the only place where all the factual supply and demand data plus the mass moods, hopes, fears, estimates and "guesstimates" of everyone in the market are crystallized is in a commodity's price, volume and open interest. Technical analysts thus believe that by studying HOW prices have acted, you can obtain more insight about future price movements than you can by studying WHY prices have acted a certain way. They believe one can learn more by studying the price movements than by studying the factors that affect prices.

There are two basic types of price charts used in technical analysis: Bar charts, which are also sometimes called line charts, and point-and-figure charts. Both kinds of charts are easily con-

67

structed. All you need are the price information, some graph paper and a pencil.

If you don't want to be bothered or don't have the time to build and maintain your own charts, there are numerous chart services available that provide ready-made charts for a fee. Some of these provide only one type of chart, while others such as Commodity Price Charts provide a combination of all types of charts and also offer interpretation of the charts. Ask your broker or check *Futures* Magazine's annual reference guide.

The first step in constructing any chart is to decide on the frequency of the prices to be plotted — that is, daily, weekly or monthly, Normally, if you are interested in short-term trading, you would keep your charts on a daily basis. If you're interested in intermediate or longer-term analysis, weekly price charts may be more suited to your purpose.

The Bar Chart

If you've ever seen a commodity price chart, chances are it was a bar chart. They are by far the most popular, because they're easier to keep than point-and-figure charts and because all the informa-

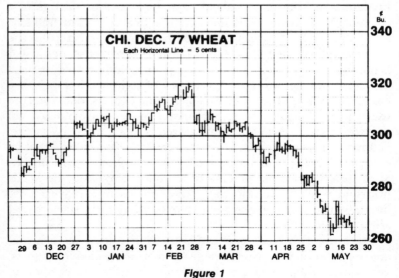

Figure 1

68

tion needed to update them can be found in most local newspapers.

Figure 1 is a typical bar chart. The numbers running up the right side of the chart are the prices in cents per pound. Similar charts for other commodities would use price scales in keeping with those commodities. For example, a wheat chart would show prices in cents per bushel with minimum variations of ¼ cent per bushel, a hog chart in cents per pound with minimum variations of 1/40 of a cent (2½ "points") per pound.

Across the bottom of the chart is a daily calendar with the weekends left out. That is, each square contains only the five weekly trading days. This prevents a two-day "gap" in the chart between each two sets of weekly data, making the chart easier to read.

At the end of each trading day, a vertical line is drawn on the chart directly above that date on the calendar. The top of this line marks the point of the day's highest price. The bottom of the line marks the lowest price at which that commodity traded that day. The closing price is shown by a short horizontal "tick" extending to the right.

The Point-and-Figure Chart

"All well and good," say the point-and-figure chartists, "but look at what you've missed. That one little line stands for thousands of trades and price fluctuations. It doesn't tell you nearly enough."

And they have a case. In a sense, a point-and-figure chart is to a bar chart what a moving picture is to a still photographer. Depending on the scale to which it is built, a point-and-figure chart can show you every single price fluctuation in a commodity throughout the entire trading period.

As with bar charts, the vertical axis of the point-and-figure chart shows prices (see Figure 2). This time, however, the spaces — not the lines — represent the prices. The reason for this is that prices are marked on the chart by filling in the boxes with an "X" or an "O." Because point-and-figure charts display price changes without regard to time, the bottom scale has no calendar.

Entries are made on a point-and-figure chart whenever a pre-determined price change occurs. The best way to understand this is with an example, so let's build a point-and-figure chart for December 1977 New York silver.

471.00					
.90	X				
.80	X	O			
.70	X	O			
.60	X	O			
.50	X	O			
.40		O			
.30		O			
.20					
.10					
470.00					

Figure 2

The minimum price fluctuation for silver is 1/10 of a cent per ounce, or 10 points, so we'll mark off the point scale in 10-point increments. To record every one of the 10-point jiggles in silver prices, however, would make our chart extremely sensitive . . . so, let's agree not to take any action until the price moves at least 20 points in the same direction.

To begin charting, let's say that right now — right at this very moment — December silver is quoted at 470.50 cents. To show this, we'll put an "X" in the 470.50 box in the first column as our starting point. Then, after jumping around between 470.60 and 470.40 for a few minutes, the price of December silver touches 470.70. This is a 20-point move, so we add another "X" to the first column at 470.70 and then — only then — fill in the 470.60 box to show the travel of the price. If the price continues up and reaches 470.90, another "X" is added at that price and at 470.80. And so forth.

Now, for reversal. Even though we decided that a 20-point change in the price of silver in one direction was worth recording, we now have to decide how far it must go against the trend to be significant. Let's say that it has to reverse at least 40 points to be meaningful. In charting jargon that's called a "4-box reversal." This means that if December silver drops from 470.90 (our last "X") to 470.50, we must make a new mark on the chart. We used

"X" to show up-moves, so let's use "O" for down-moves. We place an "O" opposite 470.80, 470.70 and 470.60 for continuity. We have to move to the next adjacent column to do this, because those boxes in the first column are already filled.

Then, if December silver continues down to 470.30 (remember, we're charting 20-point moves in one direction) we mark an "O" in the boxes for 470.30 and 470.40. And so on.

You can readily see that a point-and-figure chart this sensitive would almost require your presence on the trading floor or a ticker in your office for you to keep it accurate and up-to-date. Of course, most people cannot be on the floor of the exchange and, besides, one does not need such a sensitive chart to trade successfully. These types of charts can be made less sensitive to the little wiggles in price and more useful in identifying major turning points in price trends by the size of the price change recorded and the size of reversal needed before the change is recorded. Realistically, for example, a point-and-figure silver chart in recent markets probably would have boxes measured in 10 cents or perhaps even 50 cents per box, not tenths of a cent, and it might take a price change of $1 per oz. to mark a reversal, not .4 of a cent as our example indicates.

But there are some guidelines which apply to all point-and-figure charts, regardless of values assigned to boxes or reversals. For example, suppose you want to build a 3-box reversal chart which notes only large significant moves and can be developed from the daily high-low price data carried in your local newspaper. The general rules for developing such a chart are:

(A)　X's represent price increases; O's represent price decreases.

(B)　The spread (difference) between the high and the low for the day is the important data to get from the newspaper.

(C)　To start the chart, begin with a day in which the spread between the high and the low represents at least three boxes on the chart[1]. If the close is above the mid-point for the day, the first column is X's. If below, the first column is O's.

---

[1]You will need to decide how sensitive you want the chart to be and select the size of box and number of boxes for reversal accordingly. The procedures for charting are the same, irrespective of what box you select.

(D)   If the most recent entry is an X (O), review the daily high (low) first. If the high (low) is at least one box higher (lower) than the last entry, add the appropriate number of X's (O's).

(E)   If the daily high does not require drawing more X's, then consider the low. If today's low is lower than the highest X by 3 boxes or more, begin a column of O's beginning one box below and one box to the right of the highest X.

(F)   If the daily low does not require drawing more O's, then consider the high. If today's high is higher than the lowest

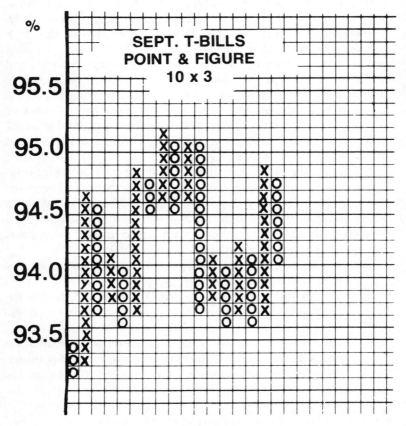

Figure 3

72

O by 3 boxes or more, begin a column of X's beginning one box above and one box to the right of the highest O.

(G) A simple buy signal occurs when the current column of X's rises one box higher than the top X in the prior column of X's.

(H) A simple sell signal occurs when the current column of O's fall one box lower than the lowest O in the prior column of O's.

To demonstrate this charting method, consider several actual contracts over a period of time (Figures 3 and 4). There are a number of buy and sell signals, several of them false. Can you find them?

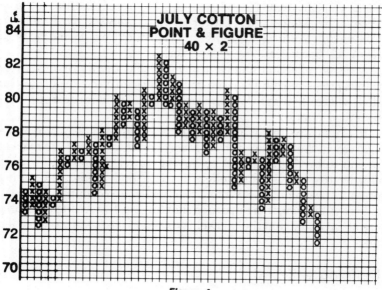

Figure 4

Although the point-and-figure technique can be applied in any market, among the most useful are those in which good fundamental analysis is difficult to accomplish and where the price moves are subject to a broad spectrum of political and economic factors, e.g., currency, Treasury Bills, GNMA's, etc. Point-and-figure charts become especially powerful tools when combined with good fundamental analysis.

73

Interpreting Bar Charts

By recording price movements as they develop, charts provide a continuous picture of how prices are reacting to market forces. The objective of chart analysis is to discern from this picture the trend of prices, and to ascertain when that trend changes. Although it is not the intent here to provide a comprehensive discussion of chart formations and their interpretation, a few of the basic formations will be reviewed in order to give you an idea of how many chart analysts think and how they interpret pictures of price moves.

If you'd like to dig deeper into the subject, there are several good books you can read. Two of them are *Technical Analysis of Stock Trends* by Magee and Edwards and *Concepts on Profits in Commodity Futures Trading* by Houston Cox, formerly with Reynolds Securities, Inc., New York.

A bit of reflection makes it obvious that there are only three things prices can do: They can go up, they can go down or they can stay where they are. Whichever happens, it is meaningful to a technical analyst.

If prices are in an uptrend, it is because buyers are more aggressive than sellers at that general price level, and the market is said to be characterized by buying power. When prices trend downwards, it is because sellers have the upper hand, and selling pressure predominates. When prices move in a seemingly random, sideways fashion, it is construed that buying and selling pressures are about equal and the market is considered to be in a congestion area.

Defining a Trend

An uptrend in the price of a commodity is characterized by a series of higher and higher lows — i.e., attaining levels above previous highs and lows. A market is in a downtrend when the highs and lows get progressively lower — when each price decline reaches lower than the immediately previous low price and each increase falls short of the previous high price.

To mark an uptrend in prices, a chartist draws a straight line connecting two or more low points in the price move. As long as prices remain above this trend line, the uptrend is considered to be intact as buying power is stronger than selling power and one should be long (Figure 5).

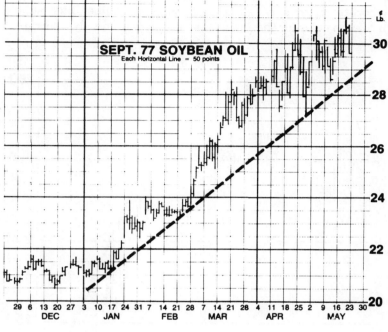

Figure 5

To identify a downtrend, a line is drawn connecting two or more high points in the price move, as shown on the chart on the next page (Figure 6). So long as prices stay below this downtrend line, the trend remains down; selling pressure is deemed to hold the day, and one should be short.

The end of an uptrend is signalled when a new high "wave" fails to reach or exceed the previous high recorded in the formation of that trend. The end of a downtrend is indicated when a new low wave fails to penetrate a previous low mark. The ending of a trend, however, does not necessarily imply the start of a new trend in the opposite direction. It could mark the beginning of a sideways movement or congestion area.

75

No market ever starts in one direction and keeps going in that direction without some backing and filling along the way. There are price swings within price swings. There are REACTIONS (short-term price declines) within bull markets, and RALLIES (short-term price rises) in bear markets. These intermediate moves do not alter the trend of the market but merely interrupt it for a time.

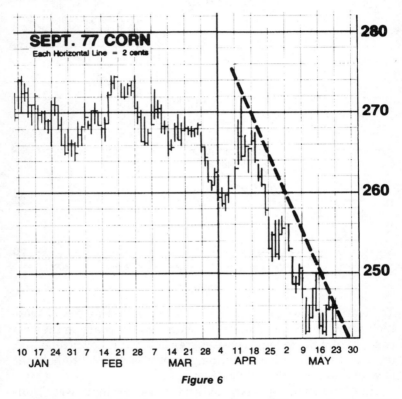

SEPT. 77 CORN
Each Horizontal Line = 2 cents

Figure 6

When a trend is broken and prices move sideways for a while, the congestion area so formed can have an effect on price movements at a later time. A congestion area made during an uptrend can tend to act as a "support" for prices during a later downtrend. A congestion area formed during a downtrend may offer "resistance" to the upward movement of prices when they turn up again.

76

Generally speaking, a support area is a price range where buying pressure increases rather abruptly, and a resistance area one where selling pressure suddenly appears in force.

Chart Formations

As we have stated, one of the major objectives of all technical market analysis is to identify the end of an old trend or the start of a new one. A number of chart formations have come to be accepted by chartists as important indicators of trend changes, as they have in the past marked the top of an uptrend or the bottom in a downtrend.

A price "bottom" is a level where buying power begins to absorb all offerings, the demand for futures contracts begins to exceed the supply, and prices rise. Conversely, a price "top" is an area where selling pressure intensifies, buying power is not sufficient to ab-

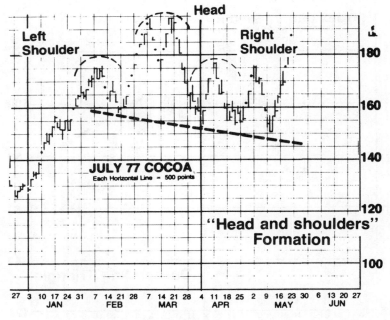

Figure 7

77

sorb all offerings, and prices turn downward.

Various chart formations have over time become associated with these important turning points in the market. Perhaps one of the most reliable and easily identified of these is the so-called "head-and-shoulders" formation. When you find this formation it usually means a major market move is beginning.

The head-and-shoulders top formation looks like a "W" with an extended middle leg. As shown on the accompanying chart, it begins with a sharp rally and a following sharp reaction to form the left shoulder. The head is formed by another, more extended rally and decline. Then a third, smaller rally and decline form the right shoulder. The formation is considered to be completed — and considerably lower prices in store — when prices decline out of the right shoulder and penetrate the "neckline."

The head-and-shoulders bottom formation is simply the inverse.

Other important chart formations include the ascending

Figure 8

78

triangle, the descending triangle and "gaps."

A *descending triangle* formation results when the market is unable to make consecutive highs at higher levels. As prices approach previous highs, increased selling pressure appears ... while at the same time prices encounter strong support at a particular price level each time they descend to that level. Thus, buying power is limiting the decline; but because offerings get progressively weaker on each rally, each rally falls short of the one before it.

Descending triangles often develop at the end of extended advances. When prices finally break through the bottom of the triangle, it is frequently an indication that a further decline is imminent.

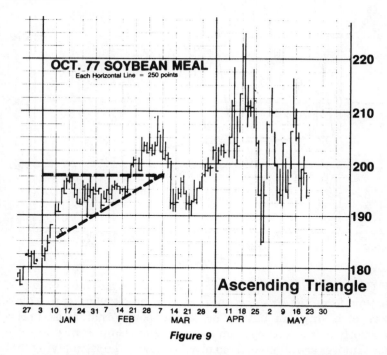

Figure 9

An *ascending triangle* is indicative of a market bottoming out, and suggests an advance in prices. This formation results when consecutive market lows strike progressively higher, while highs run into repeated resistance at about the same price level. Although selling pressure limits the advance at a certain price level each time, buying power gets stronger and stronger with each reaction ... and each price dip is therefore shallower than the one before. If prices finally break out on the upside, it is often an indication of higher prices to come.

A *gap* is simply a price area where no trading takes place. In an uptrend, a gap occurs when the day's lowest price is higher than the previous day's highest prices. In a downtrend, the case is the reverse.

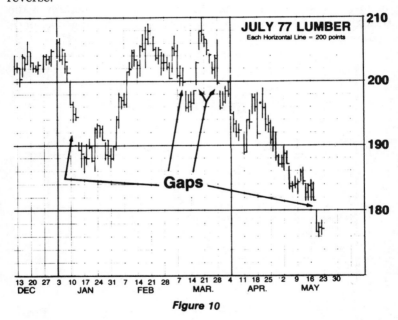

Figure 10

Gaps can be "read" in a variety of ways. A gap out of a top or bottom formation is sometimes called a "breakaway" gap, indicative of a surge in buying or selling power that causes price abruptly to break away from the formation. Gaps formed in steep price moves are often referred to as "runaway" gaps, implying that prices have run off and left all opposing factors far behind. A gap at the end of a long move may be an "exhaustion" gap — the last lunge of an expiring price move.

To a beginning analyst, the subject of charts may seem almost incomprehensible, and you may wonder if the whole thing is nothing more than the figment of a hyperactive imagination. As a matter of fact, a good imagination is an asset in identifying price formations. The patterns are seldom as symmetrical as those chosen for our examples, and it does take some imagination to see them. But with experience, you will find it easier to identify not only the basic formations noted here but also many variations of them.

Of course, interpretation of chart formations is only part of the technical analyst's job. You must use your knowledge of past price action, along with considerations of such other important factors as trading volume and open interest to fully evaluate the relative strength of buying and selling pressure in the market. Volume and open interest will be the subject for our next chapter.

9

Volume And Open Interest

Two important elements of technical analysis are the daily trading volume and open interest.

A technical analyst would no more think about ignoring the statistics on volume and open interest than he would consider eating his morning eggs without salt and pepper. These statistics are, in a sense, seasonings. When mixed with the other information available, they heighten the sense of what's happening in the market.

When we speak of volume of trading, we are referring to the total of purchases or of sales, not of purchases and sales combined. That is, each time a transaction is completed — whether it involves the establishment of a new position or an offset of an old position — the volume is increased by one.

"Open interest" refers to futures contracts that have been entered into and not yet liquidated by an offsetting transaction or fulfilled by delivery. As with volume, the open interest figure is for one side of the market only, not for the long and short sides combined. However, unlike volume, the effect of a transaction upon open interest does depend on whether new positions are being established or old ones closed out.

When trading in a new delivery month begins, there are no contracts in existence, so the open interest is zero. This is in contrast to the stock market, where a new issue may begin trading with many shares available for trading prior to its opening. In the futures market, a new contract comes into extistence only when a new buyer and a new seller complete a transaction. If the buyer is offsetting by buying back a previously sold contract or the seller is offsetting by selling a previously purchased contract, there is no change in the open interest.

Thus, the rules for determining changes in open interest are as follows:

1. Open interest increases only when a new contract is made; i.e., a new purchase is matched with a new sale.
2. Open interest decreases when an old purchase is liquidated by a sale and the opposite side of the transaction is an old seller buying back his previous short position.
3. Open interest decreases when a short makes a delivery on a contract and a long accepts delivery.

4. There is no change in open interest when a new purchase is matched with an offsetting transaction (sale of a previous purchase) or if a new sale is matched with an offsetting transaction (purchase of a previous sale).

All open contracts must ultimately be closed out in one of two ways — by offsetting transaction or by making or taking delivery of the physical commodity.

And if all this has started the fog horns blowing, maybe an example will help. Let's assume that you now have no position in the market but decide today to buy one futures contract of plywood. If the seller on the other end of your transaction was closing out a previous long position in plywood, the open interest would not change. You would have, in effect, "replaced" him in the market. He was long. Now he isn't, and you are.

On the other hand, if your seller was initiating a new short position, there would be a new long (you) and a new short (him) in the market, and open interest in plywood would go up by one.

Now let's assume it's some time later and you have a nice $800 profit in your plywood position and decide to sell and take those profits. When you do, you close out your long position. If the buyer on the other end was closing out a short position to stop his losses, your transaction would reduce the open interest by one, as the plywood positions outstanding would be reduced by one long (you) and one short (him).

On the other hand, if his was a new long position he would "replace" you and the open interest in plywood would remain unchanged.

Finding the Information

Statistics on open interest and volume of trading are easily available from the exchanges, from your local broker and in many major metropolitan newspapers. In addition, the Commodity Futures Trading Commission (CFTC) publishes monthly statistics on open interest and volume of trading for all of the regulated commodities. The CFTC also provides information about the nature and size of traders who hold the open contracts. Any trader who holds a position in any one future of a regulated commodity in excess of a particular amount — which amount is set by the CFTC — must report daily his trades and the number of contracts he holds in his position. In making this report, the trader also classifies his positions as either speculative or hedging. These data are then compiled by the CFTC and reported each month. There are

85

some traders who believe this information provides good indications of the relative buying or selling strength of the people in the market.

Interpreting Changes

In analyzing open interest and volume, you should consider the total figures for all the months of a particular commodity and not the open interest or volume of the individual options (months) separately. A word of caution, however. For best results, the months to be aggregated should all be within the same "crop year." Supply and demand factors in two separate crop years are not always related. You could have an increase in total open interest for the aggregate of the two years, with price trends in each of the years moving in opposite directions. This could cause a misreading of market signals. By separating the figures for the two years, a more reliable technical interpretation can be reached.

Changes in open interest and volume of trading have forecasting value only when considered in connection with price changes. Almost any book on technical analysis provides a summary of rules of thumb for relating changes in open interest and volume to price action. Most such *rules of thumb* and their rationale go something like this:

1. If the open interest is up and prices also are up, this indicates new buying and a technically strong market. The increase in open interest means new contracts are being created, and since prices are advancing, buyers must be more aggressive than sellers.

2. Open interest going up while prices are going down indicates short selling or hedging and a technically weak market. Again, the increase in open interest means new contracts are being established. However, since prices are decreasing, sellers must be more aggressive than buyers.

3. If the open interest is going down and prices are also descending, this implies long liquidation and a technically strong market. Since open interest is declining, offsets and liquidations by old buyers and old sellers are more numerous than new commitments by new buyers and new sellers. Inasmuch as prices are declining, these old buyers (who are now selling) must be more aggressive in their market activities than the old sellers (who are now buyers) in

their covering operations.

4. If the open interest is down and prices are up, this indicates short covering and a technically weak market. Again, since open interest is decreasing, old buyers and old sellers must be closing out commitments; but increasing prices suggest that the old sellers who are covering their positions by buying back their contracts are more aggressive than new sellers. Hence, the market is considered to be technically weak.

5. If the volume of trading "follows" the price — that is, if volume expands on price strength and declines on price weakness — this indicates the market is in a technically strong position and should go higher. By the same token, if the volume of trading expands on price weakness and declines on price strength, the market is considered to be in a technically weak position, ripe to go lower.

Like all rules of thumb, however, there are many pitfalls in their rote application. One of these is the effect of seasonality.

Seasonal Patterns

As in many aspects of commodity futures trading, there are seasonal influences and patterns in open interest and, to a much lesser extent, volume of trading. This is particularly true in commodities which have a seasonal aspect to their production or consumption. For example, the seasonal change in the open interest in grains follows the same general pattern as the seasonal change in the visible supply of grains. Thus, there is a tendency for the open interest in such commodities as wheat, soybeans, corn and oats to be at its low point for the year just before the harvest of the new crop and for open interest to gradually increase and peak at about the time of the peak in storage stocks. These seasonal changes in the open interest result from changes in hedging requirements. As a commodity is put into storage, the number of hedged transactions made in the market increases. Because hedge positions are frequently longer-term positions, the open interest naturally grows as hedging increases. Then as stocks move out of storage and hedges are lifted, the open interest tends to decline.

The *gross* seasonal changes in open interest are relatively unimportant in measuring technical market strength or weakness. A more important statistic is the *net* change, after allowing for the seasonal trend. It is diffiuclt to precisely measure these net changes, but if you follow the procedures we outlined in an earlier chapter for developing a seasonal index, you can remove much of the seasonality in the data. After that it's a matter of measuring the deviations from year to year and determining whether the deviation is comparatively large or small.

Generally speaking, volume of trading has little seasonal tendency, and what little there is is relatively unimportant. There may be a slight tendency for trading volume to increase during heavy crop movements, but such increases are not consistently repeated.

Internecine Warfare

As we have pointed out, there are many different systems for forecasting prices. Practically all of these systems, however, are based upon the same general considerations. They assume that two types of forces influence prices: The fundamental conditions of supply and demand and certain technical factors which arise out of the characteristics of trading and the psychological reactions of the traders themselves. By studying either one or both of these methods, one can predict price changes, many believe. The two approaches do not always make good bedfellows, however, and the battle lines have been drawn for years as to which of these analytical methods is more useful. The fundamentalists can point to numerous instances in which they were "right" and the technicians were "wrong." Technicians can show an equal number of cases that went their way.

Most "orthodox" analysts look upon chartists with skepticism, mainly because they think that, in order to predict prices, it is necessary to understand the causes of price change. They argue that anyone — such as a chartist — who bases his predictions on evaluation of market action (prices, volume and open interest) rather than upon the causes (supply and demand forces) is suspect. Yet many of these same analysts would grant the validity of the story of the old Indian woman who could predict the appearances of Old Faithful without having the foggiest notion as to what caused the geyser. And most of them would also readily admit that if the ability to predict prices were no better than the ability to evaluate causation, many a successful stock market and commodity trader would be making a living in some other way.

Those who are accustomed to applying rigorous scientific tests to methods of analysis can find plenty of inconsistencies in the various systems of chart reading. Yet these systems seek to provide a means of evaluating short-term market moves which even the most skilled users of fundamental methods do not pretend to be able to predict. In view of this fact, the least the fundamentalist can do, in all fairness, is to give chart reading a sympathetically critical hearing.

Purist chart readers, on the other hand, might do well to pay more attention to the criticism offered by fundamental analysts. Chartists' explanations of market action often are — well, over-imaginative. Some so studiously ignore fundamental forces that even in the face of violent price-shattering events they may be found calmly making their price predictions for weeks ahead, to within a fraction of a cent.

In point of fact, *most successful traders combine fundamental and technical analysis.* Many of the arguments propounding the superiority of fundamental analysis to technical analysis, or vice versa, are therefore really moot. The two methods of analysis are complementary; they supplement each other.

Random Walk

Recently, new fuel has been added to the controversy — namely, the random walk theory. Adam Smith, in his best-selling book, *The Money Game,* included a chapter entitled, "What the hell is a random walk?" He answered the question when he wrote that prices have no memory, and yesterday has nothing to do with tomorrow.

To put it another way, the random walk theory states that today's price change is totally unrelated to tomorrow's price change and that one cannot predict future prices on the basis of past prices.

If Adam Smith's economic model is a correct description of

reality, there are several obvious implications. It can be shown, for instance, that such price series cannot contain any cyclical or seasonal variation. This implies that so-called technical methods of investment analysis may be far less useful in predicting futures price changes that is commonly believed.

Economists have probably spent more time seeking to determine the validity of the random walk theory than they have on any other single pricing model. Research on the random walk model goes back to the early 1900's. Holbrook Working, Professor Emeritus of Stanford and considered by many to be the dean of all economists working in the area of futures trading, was the first to do a definitive study of the random walk model as it is related to grain futures prices. He concluded that the random walk model did appropriately describe commodity price behavior for the wheat market. His work led to subsequent attempts to apply the model to the stock market, and the vast majority of the work on the stock market has reached the conclusion that the random walk model is a very good approximation of stock-market price action.

Most studies using commodity prices, however, have rejected the model, although not always for the same reasons. Dr. Working himself, for example, reported a tendency for corn prices to deviate from random walk. Dr. Hendrik Houthakker, formerly of the Council of Economic Advisors and currently at Harvard University, and Dr. Seymour Smidt of Cornell University have conducted studies and concluded that on the basis of their information, the random walk model is an incorrect approximation of commodity futures prices. Labys and Granger, in their book, *Speculation, Hedging and Commodity Price Forecasts,* conclude that most price series of commodity futures contracts approximate a random walk, although on some occasions seasonal patterns are found, particularly in daily price-changing series.

Economists and commodity futures traders have argued that purely speculative markets would have to approximate the random walk model, because if they produced price series with predictable patterns, these patterns would soon be "traded" out of existence. The obvious question, then, is: Why has research shown that some commodity futures series do contain predictable components?

There seem to be several possible reasons: (1) Commodity futures markets are not purely speculative markets, since in them goods are actually sold by producers and bought by consumers. (2) The production of many commodities is highly seasonal in nature. Demand is also seasonal, and since the cost of trading is so small, you would not expect all of the seasonal pattern to be "traded out" but only enough for it to be barely profitable to use this pattern in determining a buying or selling policy. (3) It might also be argued that some commodity markets are not sufficiently developed to eliminate completely every predictable component. Dr. Houthakker comments that commodity price developments are watched by relatively few traders, most of whom are quite set in their ways. Even in the most active futures markets, the volume of serious research by participants seems to be quite small. It is, therefore, possible that systematic patterns will remain largely unknown for a very long time.

In summary, the random walk model is probably not descriptive of most commodity markets, although it is probably descriptive of some markets for selected periods of time. In any event, the random walk theory does not say that price changes are unpredictable if one uses all available information. It only postulates that they are unpredictable if based solely on considerations of previous price changes.

10

Hedging, Part I

Malcolm C. Forbes, founder of *Forbes* magazine, once drew up ten commandments "for those who earnestly seek to fight successfully the battle of life." His fifth commandment was "Take out life insurance."

If we were to write a ten commandments of those who "earnestly seek to fight successfully the battle of business," our fifth commandment might be "Take out price insurance — hedge."

Most businessmen would not think of operating without insurance against fire, theft, explosion, and other natural disasters. But physical loss or damage to goods are not the only risks businessmen face. The risk of loss due to price change looms equally large.

It is a simple matter, of course, to get policies for fire or other physical risks. Yet, no matter how many insurance companies you go to, you won't find one that will write a policy to protect against losses due to price changes. The reason, obviously, is that fires are usually independent events. When fire burns down the one man's building, it does not destroy the buildings of all his competitors. This means that an insurance company can calculate the probabilities of a claim on an individual basis.

Price changes, however, are not independent in their impact. They affect all competitors at the same time and generally in the same way. That is why you cannot buy price insurance. Still, a form of "insurance" is available through a technique called hedging in the commodity futures markets.

There are many different definitions of hedging, many different circumstances under which hedging can be accomplished, and many different types of hedges. A simple "short form" definition of hedging we prefer is: Transactions or positions in any futures contract which (a) represent a temporary substitute for a transaction or position to be made or taken at a later time in a physical marketing channel; (b) are economically appropriate to the reduction of risk in the conduct and management of a commercial enterprise, and (c) arise from potential changes in the price of assets, liabilities and services (existing or anticipated) associated with the operation of a business enterprise.

This definition fits all commodities traded on futures contracts, including currencies and interest rate futures. It makes it clear that hedging is associated with risk reduction in the management of a business and that, in order for such risk reduction to occur, the prices in the futures market must be substantially related to the value of the assets, liabilities and services being hedged.

For example, a firm that knows it will need raw materials six months from now hedges (to reduce the risk the price will go up over the next six months) by entering the futures market and buying a contract of those raw materials now, thus establishing its price. Later, when the time approaches that it actually needs the commodity, the firm purchases the actual commodity from its normal suppliers and cancels its obligation in the futures market by selling the futures contract. The futures contract thus acts as the temporary substitute for the later transaction.

On the other hand, a firm carrying inventory that it knows it will be selling in the coming months hedges by entering the futures market and "selling" that inventory now, establishing its price. Later, the firm will really sell its inventory through its normal channels and cancel its obligation in the futures market by buying back the futures contract. Again, the futures acted as a temporary substitute.

So long as the actual material and the commodity futures contract are identical or closely related, hedging can be a very effective tool for reducing price risks. If they are not closely related, the "hedge" will not reduce risk and may increase it. When one hedges, he trades the risk of change in price level for the lesser risk of change in price relationship between two related prices — the cash market price and the futures market price.

The purchase or sale of the futures contract offsets the opposite position in the cash market. Ideally, the loss in one market will be offset by a gain in the other, and the threat of loss through price change will be considerably reduced.

The purpose of hedging, then, is to seek protection against major price changes by neutralizing the impact of price fluctuations.

Let's take a specific example and follow it through. Let's assume you are a small meat packer, and you know you are going

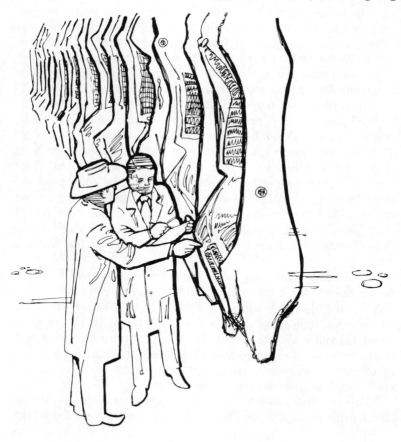

to need about 400 head of fat cattle next December to slaughter and pack. Let's further assume, for the sake of discussion, that December cattle on the Chicago Mercantile Exchange are quoted today at $43 per hundred pounds (or 43 cents per pound). At this price, you know you can conduct a profitable beef packing business — but you can't be sure what actual, live, on-the-hoof cattle will be selling for come next December.

So you decide to hedge. You do so by buying 10 futures contracts of December cattle (400,000 lbs. or about 400 head). And let's say you did pay 43 cents per pound for them.

Disregarding a few other factors, which we will get deeper into later, let's assume that by the time December rolls around and you are ready to buy the actual cattle, the cash price for fat steers has risen to 47 cents per pound. Ordinarily, your profit margin on your beef business would be so slim with cattle at this price that you might even consider cutting back on your beef packing. But your hedge has done its job and you can, in effect, buy cattle now for 43 cents per pound — not 47 cents.

How? Because the increase in the cash price will have been reflected in the December future price, particularly as the delivery month approaches. The extra 4 cents per pound you have to pay for live cattle — your "loss," so to speak, while you waited until December to actually buy — will be approximately offset by your 4-cent profit in the futures market. So, you can buy your cattle through your normal supply channels for 47 cents per pound, and offset your futures position by selling 10 December cattle contracts for about a 4-cent-per-pound profit to you.

As we said before, this is somewhat oversimplified, but it demonstrates the basic concept of the "buying" hedge.

A "selling" hedge is conceptually the same but would be used, for example, by a silver processor who holds a large inventory of the metal and wishes to reduce the risk of its value declining over time as a result of a drop in cash silver prices. In this case, any loss in his inventory worth would be approximately offset by the profits on his short sale of silver futures.

Whatever the reason, hedging provides protection against major price swings when the price of the product traded in the cash market (the market of immediate payment and delivery, e.g., wholesale market) is closely related to the price of the product described and priced in the futures market.

Businessmen hedge because they want to establish a price which they can be quite certain of realizing within a small range of error. When they hedge, they give up the opportunity for obtaining a better price of course; but at the same time they protect themselves against obtaining a dramatically worse price.

Who Hedges and Why?

A review of the companies that do, can or should use the futures market as a tool in corporate strategy reads like a veritable "Who's Who" of U.S. industry. Among readily recognizable names are Swift & Co., Armour, Oscar Mayer, Kroger, A & P, General Foods, General Mills, Kellogg, Kraft, Coca Cola, Nestle, Hershey Foods, National Biscuit, Weyerhauser, Georgia Pacific and Boise Cascade. The list goes on and on. A review of Commodity Futures Trading Commission Records as of July 30, 1976, revealed that 745 corporations were listed as carrying hedge positions of 25 contracts or more in various futures contracts. Although this figure involves some double counting, the significant point is that a large number of corporations do use the futures market for hedging.

Firms such as these use the futures market as a business management tool in a diverse number of ways, depending on the special circumstances of their line of business. Dr. Holbrook Working, noted agricultural economist, after careful and extensive observation of the business use of the futures market by handlers of commodities, defined and identified a number of types of hedges. Briefly, as identified by Dr. Working, the uses of hedging are:

The Carrying Charge Hedge. This is undertaken for purposes of obtaining at least partial payment for the cost of storing products, as in the case of a grain elevator operator who buys corn in November with the intent of storing it until the following summer. He hedges by attempting to sell the July futures at a price difference sufficient to cover the cost of the product plus all storage costs from November to July.

The Operational Hedge. This involves the placing and lifting of hedges over short time periods as temporary substitutes for merchandising transactions. It is widely used in the milling industry. There is no intent of earning storage charges in the use of this hedge.

Anticipatory Hedge or Forward Pricing Hedge. This involves the purchase or sale of futures in anticipation of a formal commitment to be made later, as in the foregoing example of the meat packer. The operator carries an open position in the futures market for a time without an offsetting cash commitment.

The Selective Hedge. This comprises hedging on the basis of price expectations. The motivation is not so much to avoid risk, as such, but to preclude major losses. Thus, a firm would hedge incompletely; they would not carry short hedges at all when a price increase is expected.

The Risk-Avoidance or "Insurance" Hedge. This is the kind of hedge the silver processor used in the example above to protect his inventory. It involves the carrying of equal and opposite positions in the same commodity in a futures market and the cash market. It is the typical textbook example.

Several Benefits

Dr. Working's description of the use of futures markets as a management tool makes clear that, properly employed, hedging can be one of the most important elements employed by a manager in his overall mix of strategies for achieving company goals.

There are at least six important benefits to properly used hedges:

First, hedging provides protection from adverse price fluctuations, thus permitting a business manager to escape, in large part — rather than having to overcome — the uncertain impact of price changes on his operations. By reducing exposure to price change uncertainty, hedging can help protect profit margins and stabilize income.

Second, and perhaps equally as important, is the flexibility it provides a firm in its corporate strategy of buying, selling and pricing. Most particularly, it provides flexibility and control in the timing of purchases and sales. Being able to buy earlier or sell later than your competitors — or even vice versa — may be the key ingredient in obtaining better prices.

Third, where the product is stored or inventoried, hedging can free working capital that would otherwise be tied up in inventory. Buying a contract for the future delivery of a product requires only a fraction of the value of the product paid out in margins. This allows a businessman to control the same amount of resources with much less capital. This, in turn, has some added benefits in the form of reduced fixed capital investment and interest charges, since the businessman may be able to reduce the size of his storage facilities.

Fourth, for products that are inventoried or stored, hedging can substantially reduce the costs of storage, since futures prices for different months will tend to reflect such costs. "Carrying charge" hedges are designed for just such purposes. See Chapter 13, "Hedging in Action," for example.

Fifth, fixing of costs and prices in advance facilitates business planning.

Sixth, the benefits which can be reaped from an effective hedging program should increase the borrowing capacity and credit-worthiness of a business. A banker will be more willing to offer his best terms against an inventory intelligently and effectively hedged than he will with one not hedged.

All of this means that to the extent hedging reduces the cost of marketing, society and the national economy benefit.

Commodity Characteristics and Hedging

In considering the applicability of the different types of hedges to a particular commodity and in trying to understand the price relationships between cash and futures markets (the essence of hedging), you should study the production and marketing characteristics of the commodity involved. Some commodities are perishable, some storable, some semi-storable, some continuously produced, and some seasonally produced.

A little reflection on the types of hedges and the commodity characteristics mentioned above should make it obvious that only certain types of hedges are applicable to particular commodities. For example, a carrying charge hedge, the traditional hedge used by grain elevators for hedging the seasonally produced and storable grains, is not applicable to non-storable commodities like cattle or hogs. The forward pricing hedge is most applicable here.

It follows that the key to hedging in any of the categories mentioned above is the playing off of price relationships in two different markets so that losses from your position in one market (cash or futures) are offset by gains from the position in the other market (cash or futures). The essence of these two price relationships is called the basis.

The CFTC and Hedging

The Commodity Exchange Act authorizes the Commodity Futures Trading Commission to establish limits on the number of transactions and the size of positions that any speculator can maintain or control in any futures. The Act requires that hedgers be exempt from such regulations. Because of this exemption, the CFTC must define who is a hedger and institute a procedure for granting the appropriate exemption from trading and position limits.

The CFTC has established such speculative limits for nine commodities (cotton, potatoes, eggs, soybeans, corn, wheat, oats, barley and flaxseed) and for purposes of granting exemptions has defined hedging for those commodities. Generally, the level at which limits are set is sufficiently high so that only very large traders are constrained by them.

The definition established by the CFTC for hedging is conceptually similar (but more complete) to the definition given earlier in this chapter. Specific transactions for which exemptions from the limits are automatically granted by the CFTC generally fall in the following categories:

a. Sales of any futures which offset the ownership or fixed price purchase of the same commodity.

b. Purchases of any futures which offset the fixed price sale of the same commodity or its equivalent byproducts.

c. Certain types of cross-hedges and anticipatory hedges. A cross-hedge is one where the commodity being hedged is not the same as the commodity represented in the futures contract, e.g., sweet corn being hedged in the Chicago corn contract. An anticipatory hedge is a purchase or sale of a futures contract to protect the price of a cash commodity you do not yet own or have not yet sold but anticipate that you will own or have available for sale, e.g., a farmer who has wheat planted but not yet harvested or a processor who will need corn for his milling plant. The CFTC has special filing requirements and may impose special restrictions on such positions.

The CFTC also recognizes a wide variety of other transactions as hedges. For those transactions to qualify for exemption from the speculative limits, however, the trader must obtain permission in advance from the CFTC.

Generally speaking, the procedure for obtaining the exemption is quite simple. Contact the CFTC office nearest you, and they will provide you with all the information for filing.

Hedging is Not an Automatic Reflex

More and more businessmen are coming to recognize that the decisions on hedging are not and should not be made in isolation from their tax strategies, their accounting methods and their financing strategies.

A hedge transaction that, viewed alone, seems like a good idea may indeed be unnecessary or even unwise when its full implications are considered in light of its effect on taxes or in light of the hedger's ability to bear the risk without hedging.

The steps in making the decision of whether to hedge or not to hedge are quite straightforward and apply equally well to farming, merchandising, banking, etc. A manager must address the following questions:

a. How much risk exposure do I have, i.e., how much money could I lose if prices go against me?

b. What is the probability that I will suffer a loss, i.e., is there a 30%? 40%? 50%? chance that the price will move adversely by 10%? by 20%? by 40%?

c. What will it cost me to hedge, i.e., interest on margin, commissions, basis variation, spread between the bid and the ask price?

d. Can I afford not to hedge? Should I carry this risk myself?

In answering these questions, the manager has to have a good understanding of his operating costs, his market prospects, his tax strategy and the overall nature of his risks. It is very possible that in the total operation of a firm one risk will be offset by another, thus obviating the need to hedge either of them individually. (For example, under LIFO accounting methods for valuing inventories, one may find different net exposure than under FIFO.) Sometimes a careful review of market prospects and calculation of the potential adverse price move indicates that the risk of loss is quite small compared to the cost of hedging. If the firm is well capitalized and can stand that risk quite easily, it may decide not to hedge. On the other hand, even if the risk is small and the firm poorly capitalized, then it would be wise to hedge.

Further, timing of the hedge position can be important. As pointed out earlier, technical market analysis can be a useful means of identifying the proper time to hedge. Consequently, it behooves hedgers to have good charts of prices. It is very possible that, given the outlook for prices and the chart signals, a hedger could afford to carry a certain risk for a short period of time until the market has moved to a more appropriate level for hedging.

Tax rules with respect to hedgers are somewhat different than they are for speculators. The Supreme Court, in the Corn Products Refining Co. case, ruled that hedging transactions which are an integral part of manufacturing or are done for the purpose of price protection must be treated as ordinary income or loss. Therefore, business firms which keep their records on an accrual basis and value their inventories at market at year-end must take into account gains or losses on the open futures contracts that are hedges against the cash commodity or against forward sales or purchases.

If the hedger values inventories at cost or the lower of costs or market unrealized gains, losses are usually not taken into account until the futures market transactions and their corresponding cash trades are closed. Therefore, taxpayers who value their inventories at the lower of costs or market have an opportunity to defer income tax liability from one period to the next by closing out all loss futures positions and simultaneously placing their hedges into another delivery month.

All of this is quite complicated and very dependent upon the overall position and business strategy of the business firm. Accounting rules have a particular importance here. That's why it's so important that the manager of a firm involved in hedging integrate the hedging decisions into the overall strategy of the business management firm.

The important point here is that hedging should not always be an automatic reflex. The decision to hedge should be considered carefully in light of its costs and its benefits. For a further explanation of this concept and an example of this decision-making process at work, see Chapter 16, "Money, the Ultimate Commodity."

11

Hedging: The Basis

Here's a practical example from a few years ago that shows you the significance of basis in hedging.

The telephone range and Bart Jones answered it. It was Bob Thompson, his commodity broker, calling to talk to him about hedging the cattle he had on feed.

"Your cattle should be ready for market in June," Bob said, "and right now June futures are at $41.50. I think you ought to sell them now and lock in that price."

Jones thought for a minute. The 80 head he had on feed would be about the equivalent of two futures contracts. June cattle futures prices had been rising steadily, but recently had leveled off in the $41 to $42 range. He doubted they would be much higher by June, and they could be lower. At $41.50 he figured he'd have about a $4 per hundredweight profit margin.

"O.K.," he said, "Sell two June contracts at $41.50." Ten minutes later Bob called back to tell him the two contracts were sold at $41.50 and instructed Jones to send him $1,500 in margin money. Jones did so and then relaxed, figuring he had sold his cattle at $41.50 and secured his $4 per hundredweight profit.

When June rolled around, Bob called again to suggest that Jones lift his hedge by buying back the futures and delivering his cattle at his normal market — a meat packing plant located about 15 miles away. Since Jones knew that delivery on the futures contract was not the normal route followed in hedging, he did as Bob suggested. He lifted the hedge at $42.50, futures prices having gone up slightly, and he sold his steers, which graded out USDA Choice, to the nearest packer for a price of $41.

But when Jones calculated his net, he found that he had lost $1 per hundredweight on the futures transaction, not counting his commissions and interest he could have earned on the margin deposit — and, he had sold his cattle for $1.05 per hundredweight

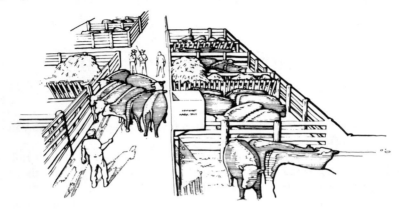

less than the futures had been on that day. His net profit was only $2.50 per hundredweight. He was puzzled by it all; he wasn't sure whether he had been sold a bill of goods by his broker about "locking in" $41.50 or whether the local packer had cheated him by giving him so much less than the futures price.

Jones had made his mistake by assuming that the futures price quoted to him equated with prices at his local market. He forgot about the most important element in hedging. Calculating the basis, or adjusting the futures price to represent his local area.

The Important Difference

A futures contract represents a specific time, quality, quantity and location of a commodity. When Jones sold the futures, he was entering into a contract for the delivery of 40,000 pounds of Choice grade fat animals delivered in Omaha, Neb., or Sioux City, Iowa (or at certain other delivery points at a premium or discount). Hence, in judging whether or not the futures price at $41.50 was the "right" price for him at that time, Jones should have first determined how the futures price related to the price where he usually markets his cattle.

106

Had Bart Jones known that the prices for his local area were usually $1.50 under the futures, he would have known he was not locking in a net price at $41.50 on his hedge and that the $41 price paid by his local packer when deliverable futures were selling at $42.50 was "about right."

The essence of profit or loss in hedging is the basis. This is true for any hedge in any commodity. The basis is the difference between two prices representing *different locations, different qualities, different markets or different times.* Hence, if one is hedging a product of different quality in the cash market than is reflected in the futures contract, he must account for that difference in the basis calculations. We will use the term "basis" in this discussion to mean the aggregate of all these, or simply the difference between a trader's local cash price and the futures price at any given time.

Before beginning a hedging operation, close attention should be paid to historic price relationships for the time period covering the proposed hedge.

With futures contracts such as those for live cattle, feeder cattle, and live hogs — which are continuously produced, non-storable commodities — the relationship of the cash price to the futures price has relatively little meaning except during the contract month. Hence, it is sometimes difficult to get a good hedge for commodities such as cattle that are ready for market in a non-delivery month. Accurate estimation of what the basis will be for a particular delivery month is, therefore, most important in effective hedging of these commodities. If the producer accurately forecasts the difference between his price and the futures price at the time of the sale of his product, he will have a virtually perfect price-protecting hedge.

For a semi-storable or storable commodity, such as corn, the basis primarily reflects two main factors — the cost of storage between two time periods and locational differences.

Because there are costs for storing actual corn and there are virtually no similar costs for holding futures contracts, cash prices usually gain in relation to futures prices during the storage period. The price of cash corn, therefore, should usually be below the price of futures by the amount of storage cost from any given point in time to the date of maturity of the futures. March futures, for

107

example, will usually be below the May futures by the cost of storage between March and May.

Futures markets are not always "normal." When immediate supplies are scarce, futures markets often become "inverted" — that is, nearby contracts are at higher prices than the more distant contracts.

The pork belly market during the late spring of 1973 is a good example of this. Late in 1972, the February 1973 pork belly contract was selling at as much as a 600-point premium to August 1973 bellies. This premium reflected short near-term supplies and high cash prices, as well as traders' expectations that the "hog cycle" was beginning to turn upward and that supplies could be considerably more plentiful by late summer.

Then, as succeeding pig crop reports in December 1972 and March 1973 indicated that, because of a variety of factors, farmers' farrowing intentions would apparently not be met as soon as had been expected, the premium gradually shrunk. By May 1973, the premium of March over August was only 200 points — still an inverted market but less so than before.

Fully storable commodities — such as wheat, for example — are also subject to these influences. In fact, futures for all commodities are affected to some degree by such factors as temporary weather conditions, import/export agreements, near-term shortage or over-supply and other factors. These should be made a part of any evaluation of your basis in a particular commodity futures contract.

In actual practice, the basis for the par delivery area represented in the futures contract tends to narrow toward zero as the delivery time for the futures contract approaches. The reason for this is simple. If on April 1 the cash price of the commodity were $1 below the April futures price, merchants would buy the actual commodity, sell the April commodity future and make a certain profit. As they did this, the two prices would rapidly converge until the basis had narrowed and the profit opportunity had disappeared. This convergence of the cash and futures prices during the delivery month means simply that the futures price tends to reflect actual values in the cash market. This convergence does not usually occur during non-delivery months. Hence, for non-storable commodites the basis

108

is likely to be unstable and difficult to predict accurately in the non-delivery months.

Calculating the Basis

There are two primary methods of determining the basis for any local market: (1) historic price relationships and (2) actual cost calculation.

To calculate the basis with the first method, you simply obtain past futures prices and compare them with prices at your local market for the same quality product. Usually, you will find that basic patterns repeat themselves year after year. Hence, you can learn to predict basis levels for particular months. If you were figuring the basis for live cattle at Kansas City, Mo., you might find that Kansas City prices have normally been 50 cents per hundredweight below the prices paid at the specified futures delivery point of Omaha. The basis would, therefore, be 50 cents, and any producer who normally markets at Kansas City would adjust the futures price by 50 cents per hundredweight when figuring his basis.

To calculate the basis with the second method, you must obtain the actual cost of transporting the cattle from the local market to the location represented by the futures contract. Hence, in this instance, to determine the basis between Kansas City and Omaha via this method, you estimate the costs for transportation (including shrink), interest charges, insurance charges and the like and use this total to adjust for your actual basis at Kansas City.

If Jones had calculated his basis correctly using costs, he would have had the figures at the top of the next page, and he would have known that a $41.50 futures price really meant $40 at his local market.

As mentioned above, there are many factors that cause the basis for any local market to vary over a period of time. These include such things as changes in local supply and demand, changes in local production costs, the predicted size of a future crop, changes in government programs and local market receipts.

The basis may not work out perfectly because the price relationships described above don't always follow their theoretical models

Allowing for Basis

Jan. 15	Sell June futures @		$41.50
	Transportation differential	$1.00	
	Interest & commission	.15	
	Other marketing expenses	.35	
	Basis		$1.50

Expected net localized price $40.00

June 10	Sell live cattle @		$41.00
June 10	Buy back futures @		$42.50
	Loss on Futures	($42.50-$41.50)	$1.00
	Net realized price for cattle ($41.00-1.00)		

Summary: Expected price from hedge   = $40.00
                Realized price   = $40.00

— that is, cash and futures don't always move up and down in unison. Nor do they always converge exactly at delivery time. And there is the difference in the strength of the relationship between the cash and futures prices for semi-storable commodities like pork bellies as opposed to non-storable commodities like live hogs.

Another bug in the theoretically perfect hedge is the fixed size of the futures contract which must be used to hedge. A cattle futures contract on the Chicago Mercantile Exchange is 40,000 pounds, which equates roughly with 40 head of fat cattle. If you are feeding 60 head, the sale of one contract leaves one-third of your cattle unhedged. The sale of two contracts would "over-hedge" your herd.

Despite all these imperfections, however, hedges do work — and even an imperfect hedge may be better than no hedge at all.

In summary, the Bart Jones example above illustrates several key ingredients in any hedging program. They are:
a. Know your costs of production so that you can determine whether the futures price is allowing you to hedge at a profit.
b. Know what the futures price represents in time, quality, quantity and location and how that corresponds to the commodity you are hedging.

c. Know your basis — the relationship between your local price and the futures price.

When you know these things, you can apply the basic principles to hedging any commodity.

It should also be emphasized that a perfect hedge is not necessarily one in which you get a better price by hedging, but rather it is one in which you achieve your target price through correct calculation of the basis.

In summary, it should be emphasized that hedging is not an operation that should be taken lightly. It takes hard work to hedge effectively. Hedging decisions should be given as much attention as any other aspect of the business. Hedging will not guarantee a profit. If a business manager can't control his costs in the cash market, hedging will not help him. Hedging will not make a good manager out of a poor manager, but it can make a good manager an even better one.

12

Your Banker and Hedging

One of the most important relationships a hedger has is with his banker. A good banker can assist a hedger in a number of ways, not only in lending money but also in providing advice. Bankers are in a unique position to teach their customers how to use futures markets, and it is in their best interest to do so since futures markets and hedging provide a lender with an opportunity to improve the quality of his loans.

A good loan can be made even better by hedging. Producers who have learned this are finding, with increasing frequency, hedging helps them secure loans.

Futures trading can aid the overall profitability of a business by providing a good deal of flexibility in the timing of purchases and sales, thus allowing a businessman to select the most favorable time of the year for making his price decisions.

As pointed out earlier, when a producer hedges, he "locks in" or assures himself of achieving a price within a fairly small price range. Thus, when he comes to his banker for a loan, he will be able to assure the banker of the exact price, within a small margin of error, that he will receive for the product he has hedged. The banker, therefore, has a greater assurance that the loan will be repaid.

The Loan Package

When a banker makes a loan secured by hedged collateral, it is usually a good idea to coordinate the management of the hedge account at the brokerage house and the management of the loan account at the bank. This coordination has to start at the very beginning, when the terms of the loan are being considered. At that point, the banker will be interested in what the loan is to be used for and from what source the funds for repayment will come.

In considering the first question, it is usual on most loans on hedged collateral that the funds loaned be used not only for the business purpose stated by the borrower but also that the banker agree to the use of the funds for meeting margin calls on the futures exchange. Just as a speculator should not speculate with too little capital, a hedger should not try to hedge without sufficient capital to meet expected margin calls. A banker who would refuse to take this second step and lend for purposes of making margin calls on hedged collateral could soon find his customer without a hedge (brokers are required to close out accounts when margin calls are not met), thus reducing the quality of his loan and removing any guarantee of the price to be obtained for the hedged collateral.

The second question, pertaining to the source of funds for repayment, goes to the heart of cash flow management. When the futures market price moves in favor of the hedger's futures position, the cash market has moved against him. For example, assume a farmer sells hog futures to hedge hogs he is fattening. If the price declines, the farmer will have a gain on his futures transaction, but his hogs will be worth less. But the gain on the futures side will be paid into the farmer's brokerage account each day, and that money is available for payment to the bank to reduce the amount of the loan.

On the other hand, if the price of the futures increases, the farmer will have lost money on his short futures position, and he will be required to pay, in cash, to his broker the amount of the loss. This loss will be offset by the increase in the value of his live hogs. The greater value of the live hogs allows the banker to lend additional sums on the same collateral without changing the percent of the loan relative to the value of the collateral.

For example, suppose a hog farmer plans to buy 600 feeder pigs weighing 40 pounds each and to use his own feed, fattening them to 200 pounds each. Suppose, further, that at the time he buys the feeder pigs, he hedges by selling four futures contracts (each contract represents 30,000 pounds or 150 hogs) for fat hogs at

$41.66 per hundredweight. If the banker requires the hogs and the farmer's feed as collateral for the loan and lends 85% of the value of the fat hogs, the farmer will have a loan of $42,500.

Now, if the cash and futures prices for the fat hogs decline to $35 per hundredweight, the banker will find that the value of the collateral (42,000 = 1,200 cwt. × $35 per cwt.) has fallen below the original amount of the loan — a dangerous situation for the banker. It is likely he will ask for a pre-payment on the loan to restore the 85% ratio of loan to collateral value.

Since the farmer has hedged, he will have no problem making the pre-payment because, as the futures price fell from $41.66 to $35.00, the farmer's brokerage account was credited in cash with the gain on his futures position. The money, except for the original margin in the brokerage account, can be withdrawn and transferred directly to the bank to reduce the loan without actually closing out the futures position.

If per chance, the futures market had risen to $45.00 per hundredweight, the farmer would have been called upon to meet a margin call because the market would be above the level at which he previously sold. This increase in price would result in the loan (42,500) being worth only about 78% of the value of the collateral ($54,000 = 1,200 cwt. × $45 per cwt). The bank should be willing to increase the loan back to the 85% level of the collateral value. This amount can then be used to meet the margin calls.

From this example, it becomes clear than the management of the hedge account and the loan account need to be coordinated. The hedge becomes important in upgrading the quality of the loan and assuring repayment. Management of the loan account becomes important in maintaining the hedge. And the key to good management in both is good management of the cash flow.

There are several important points for both hedgers and lenders to keep in mind. These include:

1. A hedge will not make a bad loan a good loan. Loans should be made on the basis of whether the underlying purpose for the loan is justified, not on the basis of whether it is hedged or not.

2. Hedging is not for everybody and should not be undertaken solely for purpose of securing a loan.

3. Whether the collateral is hedged or not will have no impact on the interest rates charged for the loan. Research has shown that

the most likely impact will be an increase in the debt-to-equity ratio or the lending of a larger amount of money on a given equity base.

4. The hedger and the lender need to have a thorough understanding of the hedger's cost of operation and his margin of profit represented in any hedge transaction.

The biggest danger confronting both the lender and the hedger is that the "hedger" will succumb to the temptation of "speculation" and thereby take positions in the futures market which jeopardize his loan as well as his whole financial structure. It is not unusual for a producer to sell a futures contract, thus hedging, and after a short time he finds that the market has moved against him, causing a loss. He reasons that if he simply "hedged" a little more at this higher level by selling even more contracts, he will recover his loss and even "make a little money" when prices ultimately fall. Alas, prices don't fall but continue rising. He finds himself strapped for cash to meet the margin calls. His banker finds out what he has done when he comes in for a bigger mortgage on the farm.

Another temptation is for the hedger to trade in and out of his position, removing the hedge when prices move slightly against him and trying to put it back on at a better price. The usual result of this activity is huge commission costs and a great danger of being whipsawed, i.e., the hedge won't be "on" when a major market move occurs.

A third temptation is that the hedger, particularly after initial successes, begins to think that since he is so intimately familiar with the market he can "out-speculate those speculators." He, therefore, begins to speculate heavily out of all proportion to his financial ability, thus jeopardizing his loan and his business.

The banker can protect against these happenings by keeping tight control of the hedge and the hedger. Any banker who makes a loan on hedged collateral should include as part of his control procedures the following: (1) Frequent consultation with the hedger for purposes of reviewing his strategy, (2) insistence that the borrower and the broker sign an agreement requiring that the banker receive a copy of all orders entered into the account, (3) that any profits accruing to the account be kept in escrow for the bank until the account is closed and the loan repaid and (4) that the broker provide a monthly statement of account activity to the banker.

The hedger should also assure the banker that other accounts will not be opened for purposes of speculation. It is also not unusual for bankers to require hedgers to sign agreements that, under special circumstances, allow the banker to "take over" management of the hedge account and even make delivery of the collateral on the futures contract.

13

Hedging in Action

Even if the only real hedging you'll ever do is in an argument with someone else, if you are going to trade futures, it is important to know basically when and how farmers, processors and others hedge their products and services in the futures markets. Their hedging can have an impact on futures prices that mean profit or loss to you. In previous chapters you learned about the importance of basis and the importance of your banker in hedging. Now let's make the process of hedging come alive with some real down-to-earth examples. We'll see how important it is to know your costs of production and to calculate accurately your breakeven point as well as your basis.

For the first part of this chapter, you are going to be short hedging cattle again. Then you will be in the meat packing business and will buy futures to protect the price you will pay for hogs you will actually buy at a later date. We could as easily make the example a grain elevator in North Dakota buying wheat from a farmer. The concepts are essentially the same, although the arithmetic would be different. Lastly, we'll demonstrate the use of the grain market to earn storage charges for grain you have harvested. Again, we could easily make the commodity gold or silver or any other storable commodity. The concepts would be the same.

To do an effective job of hedging, the first thing you need is good information. You must know your costs in the cash market . . . the relationships between your price at the local level and the futures price (the basis) . . . and you should have knowledge of what the futures price is and what it represents. The last is especially important, because the futures contract very specifically defines the quality and location of the commodity being traded. If the quality or location of the commodity a hedger is concerned with in the cash market differs from the commodity deliverable in the futures market, he should take that into account in calculating the net localized price he is trying to establish in the futures. And, last, you should have a knowledge of the fundamental economic and seasonal factors that affect the prices of your product and how these act over time.

The Short Hedge — Cattle[1]

Let's assume that you are operating a feedlot and in January you bought 189 feeder cattle averaging 703 pounds in weight. The accompanying table on pages 122-123 summarizes your hedge program. You intend to feed them to an average of 1,100 pounds each. Total cost for the purchase of the animals averages $38.09 per hundred pounds, and you estimate that it will cost you $47 per hundredweight to feed them to their finishing weight of 1,100 pounds. Your estimated breakeven point is $41.31 per hundredweight (total weight divided by total cost).

Using procedures learned in the previous chapter, you estimate your basis for cattle in your local area at $1.50 per hundredweight. That should be added to your breakeven price along with any profit you hope to make. Let's assume that you expect a $30 per head profit (equivalent to $2.73 per hundredweight). Adding the basis and expected profit to your breakeven point provides you with a target price of $45.54 per cwt. That's the price at which you must sell the future on your hedge.

The 189 head of cattle is the equivalent of five contracts of fat cattle. Since you expect that they will reach the 1,100 pound level by June, you select June futures for your hedge. Let's assume that on five successive days, starting in late January, you sell one futures contract each day for an average futures sale price of $45.40 per hundredweight. You are now hedged, i.e., you have sold the cattle you are raising on a futures contract.

Now assume that time passes, the cattle gain weight, and on

---

[1]This example represents an actual hedge experience. It is furnished by Douglas Johnson, Guarantee State Bank, Beloit, Kan.

June 11, 188 head (one died) are sold to a meat packer for $40.60 per hundredweight. On that same day, you buy back your five June futures contracts at $42.05 per hundredweight. Note that the basis ($42.05 − $40.60) is equal to $1.45 per hundredweight — not quite equal to the $1.50 you had estimated. Note also that the sale price of $40.60 per hundredweight is $.71 per hundredweight below your breakeven point. This loss on the sale of the animals is more than compensated for, however, by the $3.35 profit made on the futures side.

Overall, you end up with a net profit per head of $19.39 — a little more than $10 less than you expected when you bought the feeder cattle. Why? First of all, the cost per pound of gain was underestimated. It actually turned out to be $2.05 per hundredweight higher than had been estimated. The animals were sold at a slightly lower weight than had been anticipated — one animal died, and feedlot, marketing and interest costs had been slightly higher than expected. The result was that the breakeven price was underestimated. This demonstrates the importance of accurate estimation of the costs.

Despite the loss in the actual feeding of the cattle, there was a $6,450 net gain in the futures transactions for an overall profit of $3,646.70 or $19.39 per head. Had you not hedged, you would have had a loss of a little over $2,800 or about $14 per head. In this instance, hedging definitely paid off. (Check through the summary of the cattle hedge on the next two pages.)

Hedge Hogs

One of the hedges we talked about before is a forward-pricing hedge for a continuously produced, non-storable commodity. So let's work through an example of a live hog long hedge and see how you can protect the price you will have to pay for hogs. Although this example refers to live hogs, the concepts explained (know your basis, establish a target price, etc.) are applicable to long hedging for any commodity including industrial commodities like copper, rubber, etc. and other foods like cocoa, coffee, sugar, etc.

For purposes of illustration, we'll assume that you get interested in hedging hogs on March 7 and decide to find out about protecting the price of hogs you will be buying in June. On March 7, June hog futures were selling for $40.50 a hundredweight.

121

Summary of Short Cattle Hedge

I. Estimated Costs, Breakeven and Target Prices

Jan. 26 — bought 189 feeder cattle weighing
    703 lbs. at $38.90 $50,613.73
        Estimated gain 397 lbs. at $47 cwt.   35,265.51
                       Total costs estimated $85,879.24

1,100 lbs. × 189 head (207,099 lbs.) divided into
$85,879.24 = $41.31 estimated breakeven cost.

Estimated sale date: June 16   (Use June Futures)

Breakeven	$41.31 cwt.
Estimated basis	1.50 cwt.
	$42.81 cwt.
Profit desired	2.73 cwt. ($30 per head divided by 1,100 lbs.)
Target price	**$45.54**

II. The Hedge

You need to sell 207,900 lbs. of June live cattle futures (5 contracts of 40,000 lbs. each) to assure a $45.54 price and a possible profit of $30 per head.

Jan. 31 — sold 1 June futures at $44.00
Feb. 2 — sold 1 June futures at   44.50
Feb. 5 — sold 1 June futures at   45.00
Feb. 5 — sold 1 June futures at   45.50
Feb. 8 — sold 1 June futures at   48.00

200,00 lbs. sold at average futures price of	$45.40 cwt.	
June 11 — bought 5 June futures @	42.05 cwt.	
Difference	3.35	(× 200,000 lbs. = $6,700.00
		Less commission
		($50 per contract) 250.00
		$6,450.00

III. The Results

June 11 — sold 188 head at $40.60 cwt.
(delivered to packer June 11) averaging 1,093 lbs. $83,426.50

Actual purchase costs	$50,613.73	
Actual feedlot costs	33.040.74	
Actual marketing costs	23.83	
Actual interest	2,551.50	$86,229.80

Feeding loss	**$ – 2,803.30**
Futures gain	**+ 6,450.00**
Net	**$ 3,646.70**

Actual breakdown	**$41.96 cwt.**	**Projected breakeven**	**$41.31**
Actual cost of gain	**49.05 cwt.**	**Projected cost of gain**	**47.00**
Actual basis	**1.45 cwt.**	**Projected basis**	**1.50**
Actual profit	**$3,646.70 or**	**Projected profit**	**$5,670 or**
	$19.39/head		**$30/head**

Since you're attempting a long hedge, you will be *buying* futures. There are two costs involved — a commission cost, which you must pay your broker (in our example, that's approximately 12¢ a hundredweight), and interest on margin. (This cost is somewhat hidden. It's the amount of money your margin could have earned if it were in a bank savings account, for example, rather than on deposit with your broker.) For our example here, it's about 3¢ per hundredweight. So, the total cost of buying the futures is $40.65 per hundredweight.

As explained in the preceding chapter, if you were buying hogs somewhere other than in the Peoria area or hogs of a quality substantially different than that priced on the hog futures contract, you should take into account the location difference (location basis) and quality difference (quality basis) in estimating the net price you would have in the hogs if you received them in actual delivery on the futures contract. We'll assume here that you normally buy hogs in Peoria, and by the time you get them to your plant the price is equivalent to the Peoria top price. We'll also assume that you're buying the same quality as is represented on the futures contract — 200-220 pound USDA 1, 2, 3, or 4 quality hogs.

Futures vs. Cash Hog Prices
(Prices in dollars per hundredweight)

		Closing June Futures Price	Top St. Louis Cash Price			Closing June Futures Price	Top St. Louis Cash Price
March	7	40.50	40.75	June	2	49.27	48.00
	14	42.95	41.00		3	49.65	48.00
	21	43.85	40.75		4	49.20	48.75
	27	45.50	40.25		5	49.15	49.25
April	4	45.55	41.00		6	49.25	49.25
	11	46.80	42.25		9	50.10	49.50
	18	46.70	42.25		10	50.50	50.25
	25	47.75	42.50		11	50.77	50.00
May	2	47.70	44.75		12	50.80	49.75
	9	47.00	47.25		13	52.20	51.00
	16	48.60	49.00		16	53.55	52.50
	23	48.95	48.75		17	53.70	53.00
	30	49.20	48.75		18	54.65	53.50
					19	56.05	56.00
					20	56.85	57.50

As shown on the accompanying worksheet below, the target price you expect to pay for hogs by hedging them on the futures market is, therefore, $40.65 cwt.

Now comes the $64 question — or maybe we should call it the $40.65 question. Do you expect to be able to buy hogs in the cash market in June for less than $40.65? Or do you look for cash prices above that? If you expect them to be less and are reasonably certain your expectations will be realized, you probably won't want to hedge. If you expect them to be considerably higher than $40.65, you will. We'll say that you are looking for a price of over $45 a hundredweight in June, so you decide to hedge.

Let's determine now exactly how your hedge would have worked out. Time passes and June 20 arrives. On that date June futures are selling at $56.85. Since you bought for $40.65 and sold at $56.85, you have a net gain on the futures of $16.20 per hundredweight.

Worksheet for Live Hog Hedge

Futures price for June	$40.50
Commission	.12
Interest on margin	.03
Total cost	40.65
Location difference (transportation and shrinkage from Peoria — or, normal price (differential)	0
Quality difference	0
Target price	**40.65**
Expected cash price	**45.00**
Buy futures (including commission and margin) on March 7	40.65
Sell futures on June 20	56.85
Net gain or loss on futures	+ 16.20
Purchase live cash hogs on June 20	57.50
Minus gain on futures	− 16.20
Actual cost of live hogs	**41.30**

On June 20 you also buy the actual, walking-around live hogs and get them to your plant at the equivalent Peoria top price on that date of $57.50 per hundredweight. That $57.50 per hundredweight is a dollar more than you expected to pay, and $16.85

over what your target price was when you hedged. However, since you have a $16.20 gain on futures, you can apply that to the actual cost of the hogs. This makes the total net cost of the hogs equal to $41.30. Not quite the target price but close. The hedge did its job. It protected against major price risk.

The target price was not met exactly. Why? Because the futures price and the price you paid in the cash market for actual hogs were not exactly equal at the time you offset your futures contract. If they had been equal, you would have paid exactly a net of $40.65 for the hogs. For example, had you removed your hedge on June 6, you would have paid $49.25 per cwt. for your live hogs, but since futures were at the same price, the gains would have exactly offset the losses and the net price would have been $40.65. If you had removed the hedge on June 2, you would have paid only $39.58.

A couple of caveats. Our packer here was long; that is, he had purchased the futures. When the buyer goes into the delivery period — in this instance, any time during the month of June — he may receive delivery of hogs on the futures contract; and he could receive them in Peoria, East St. Louis or any of the other Exchange-approved delivery points. You need to keep this fact in mind whenever you carry a long position into the delivery period for any commodity.

The Storage Hedge

Now let's turn our attention to another type of hedge — the storage hedge, i.e., a use of the futures market to help pay the costs of storing a product. This type of hedge is possible because the normal relationship between cash and futures prices for storable commodities is a futures price higher than the cash price and the more distant futures higher than near-term futures, reflecting the cost of storage.

Anyone who owns the product will be induced to store it for a period of time only if he expects to be able to sell it at a sufficiently high price to pay his storage costs. Conversely, people who buy the product will have to pay storage charges if they buy it in advance of their time of need. To avoid having capital tied up in storage and other facilities, they are willing to pay a slightly higher price at a later time if someone else will store it for them. Hence, distant futures prices are normally above near-term or cash market prices. As the futures month approaches the delivery

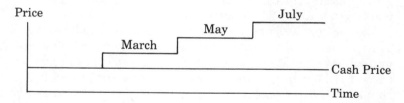

period, cash prices will converge toward futures as carrying charges are earned or become less. This phenomenon allows businessmen to put a product in store, sell it forward on a futures contract and, as the basis narrows, earn a profit which helps cover storage costs. It should be obvious that such a hedge is not practical in non-storable commodities.

A word of caution: Not all markets for storable commodities are always normal, i.e., futures prices above cash. Sometimes they become inverted, i.e., cash above futures. In that instance, the storage hedge does not work.

Let's assume that a farmer has harvested 20,000 bushels of corn. On Oct. 10 his local grain elevator offers him $3 a bushel, the going cash rate. At that same time the Chicago May futures price is

$3.60. Since the farmer owns the corn, he has these alternatives:
  (a) either selling the cash product for immediate delivery,
  (b) selling it on a cash forward contract or
  (c) selling it on a futures contract through a short hedge.
If he does none of these, he will be speculating in the cash market.

In considering his alternatives, let's assume that the farmer decides to store his corn on the farm and hedge it by selling it in the May futures, thus earning at least some of his storing costs. In evaluating May futures, he needs to consider whether a May futures price of $3.60 provides him, after the storage period, with a net local price high enough to cover storage costs, interest, insurance, etc., plus a profit to make the storage worthwhile.

Let's assume that he plans to sell the cash product sometime in April. He calculates that he will need $3.40 as a target price to cover the cost of storage, 35¢, plus 5¢ profit. His present basis (cash to May futures) is 60¢ under May. Historical basis patterns for his area show that the local basis narrows to about 10¢ under May in April. This will give him a target price of $3.50 a bushels ($3.60 − $.10 for location basis). His hedging costs are 2¢ a bushel, thus his net target price is $3.48 per bushel.

Assume he sells four contracts of May futures at $3.60 a bushel. Time passes, April 15 arrives, and the cash price of corn at his local market is $3.45. May futures have fallen to $3.53, indicating a basis of 8¢. He sells his corn on the cash market and lifts his hedge. He nets $3.50 per bushel on the hedge. The transaction can be summarized as follows:

Cash Market	Basis	Futures Market
October 10		
Harvests 20,000 bushels of corn, local price $3 per bu.	$.60	Sells 4 May futures at $3.60
April 15		
Sells 20,000 bushels of corn, local price $3.45 per bu.	$.08	Buys 4 May futures at $3.53
+ $.45	$.52	+ $.07

(Hedging costs are estimated at 2¢ per bushel. Hence net basis gain is $.50.)

128

Another quicker way of doing the above calculations is simply to look at the change from the buying basis to the selling basis. Add the basis gain to the original purchase price, subtract the costs of hedging and you will know the net price received. When using a carrying charge hedge, remember these two rules:

   a. If the basis is narrowing (selling basis is less than the buying basis), you are earning at least part of your storage charges.
   b. If the basis is widening (the selling basis is above the buying basis), your hedge is costing you more money than not hedging.

This points up the importance of knowing your basis patterns and selecting the most opportune time to lift your hedge. These storage hedge rules are equally applicable to grains, gold, silver, etc.

Trying Other Examples Yourself

So that is what a short hedge, a long hedge and a storage hedge look like. We could not cover examples in every commodity, hence we covered only two livestock and one grain hedge. However, the principles we used throughout are applicable to a wide number of other commodities. Work out some examples for yourself to determine how well the hedge works. You could also plug in some hypothetical situations in which the futures price goes up and you lose money on futures.

You will find that as long as prices eventually converge to your expected basis, your hedge will work out as you expected it would. That's what hedging is all about — knowing your basis patterns. When you hedge, you essentially trade the greater uncertainty associated with absolute price change for the lesser uncertainty associated with basis change or relative price change.

Selecting a Hedge Broker

In selecting a broker for hedging, you should look for someone who is interested and willing to service hedge accounts. Some registered reps prefer to handle hedge accounts. Others are not willing to spend the time and effort necessary to do a good job. A suitable broker should be able to explain the various aspects of hedging to you, aid you in calculating price relationships and be willing to help you give and receive delivery, if necessary. A good broker should also be able to provide fast and reliable execution of orders.

What About Delivery?

Although about 98% of all futures contracts are offset and not delivered, there are times that it would be advantageous for a hedger to accept delivery ... when, for a particular location, accepting or giving delivery is the most profitable alternative. At that same time, at another location, it may not be the most advantageous. In deciding whether you want to give or take delivery, you should calculate all of your costs involved in accomplishing the delivery and then compare that to the best price you can get in another market.

Decision-Making on Hedging

The internal organization of the decision-making machinery on hedging for a firm is quite important, because hedging should be a part of a firm's total management strategy. It's important that the top people in a firm, including the president and the board of directors, be aware of how and why the futures market is being used for hedging. If they understand that hedges do not always work out perfectly and that there will be times when the gains and losses in the futures market will not exactly offset the gains or losses in the cash market, the chances of futures trading becoming an integral and useful part of the management decisions of the firm are much greater.

For decision-making, some firms establish committees to review the basic economic data, estimate risk exposures, coordinate the decisions that need to be made between buying and selling and make the actual decisions in the futures market. Other firms have one man with the responsibility for trading, with a committee to provide basic outlook data and advice and guidelines on his use of the futures market.

In all cases, there should be a close liaison between the comptroller of the firm and the man having responsibility for the hedging because hedging is basically a financial operation and can have an important effect on the finances of the firm. It can also have implications for tax purposes.

How Much to Hedge

A major concern facing all hedgers is deciding just how much to hedge. Should you cover 100% of your exposure, or is 50% sufficient? How about 10% of it, or none?

There are no hard and fast rules. The proportion of your risk to hedge is a personal decision a manager should make. Generally, the answer to the question should be based on some, or all, of the following factors:

a. Your net capital. The greater your capital base, the more risk you can withstand. If you are well capitalized and unhedged and prices move against you, the loss may not be catastrophic. On the other hand, if you are poorly capitalized, you probably can't afford to take very much risk. A small adverse price change could mean bankruptcy. In those instances, hedging to protect small positive price margins, or to protect against further losses, may be well advised.

b. Your expectation about prices. When you put on a hedge, you have essentially accepted a price. When you decide if you want to accept a price, whether it's one available in the futures or in the cash market, you need to have a standard against which you can compare the available prices. The standard should be either a forecasted price (your forecast or someone else's), a break-even price, a budgeted price, or some acceptable price you have identified. You also need to consider the strength of your expectation; i.e., the probability that the forecasted price, or expected price, will be realized if you do not hedge.

c. Your cash flow detector. Hedges require cash deposits at your broker. If your futures position loses money, that money must be deposited in cash with your broker on a daily basis. If you do not meet variation margin calls, the broker will liquidate your position. You may then find yourself unhedged at exactly the time you need it.

Hence, in deciding how much you want to hedge, keep in mind how the variation margin calls may affect the cash flow needs of the rest of your business.

14

Fact And Fiction About Spreads

Joe Boswell first appeared on the commodity trading scene about six months ago ... the morning after a dinner party where he had listened for almost an hour while a well-dressed stranger described commodity conquests in numbers that boggled his mind.

In the succeeding months, Joe became a trader. He won some and he lost some, the latter category unfortunately predominating because — in spite of the reasonable guidance he was getting from his broker — Joe's own preparation for trading commodities did not extend much beyond that party conversation.

It was also during this time that Joe first heard of a "spread." He knew it to be a trading strategy calling for buying a contract for delivery in one month and selling a contract for delivery of the same or a different commodity in another month and that it is considered a conservative method of trading. A little further investigation revealed to him that by spreading he would be trading two contracts for only a little more commission than he'd pay to trade one, and — in the case of the cattle spread he was considering — he would need only $300 margin instead of the $700 necessary to trade one contract outright.

Joe figured that was a good deal. He would be getting two for almost the price of one ... and he would be being "conservative," which suited his Midwestern upbringing perfectly. So he bought June live cattle at $41.00 and simultaneously sold December live cattle at $44.00. Two days later, June cattle were at $39.50 and December cattle were at $45.00. By spreading, Joe had without delay lost $1,000. In retrospect, had he taken an outright position of one contract in either of those two months, the most he would have lost over that time period would have been $600.

Joe has since disappeared from the commodity trading scene and is still wondering — among other things — how a "conservative" method of trading could result in his losing more money than if he had not been so "conservative" and been simply long or short.

What Joe didn't know (and what his broker had apparently failed to impress upon him) is that spreading transactions in and of themselves are not necessarily conservative methods of trading. Sometimes the prices for different futures months of the same commodity fluctuate independently, making such spreads more risky than outright positions. This is particularly true for perishable commodities like eggs, cattle and hogs.*

Semantics

The term "spread" and "straddle" are sometimes used interchangeably but frequently confused. The term "spread" is often used to refer to the simultaneous purchase of a futures contract for delivery in one month and sale of a futures contract for the same commodity for delivery in another month; e.g., the purchase of May corn and the sale of July corn. The term "straddle" is frequently used to refer to simultaneous trades which arch across two different markets — for example, the purchase of July pork bellies and the sale of July hogs.

In order to avoid confusion, we'll use only the term "spread," calling these "intra-commodity spreads" and "inter-commodity spreads," respectively.

The objective of a spread is to make a profit by correctly anticipating variations in the relative market strength of the two positions involved. A spread trader is *not* concerned with the absolute price change in either one of the contracts but only with the relative price changes *between* the two futures contracts.

---

*Even though brokers offer special margins for spreads, be careful; not all of the things they call spreads are economic spreads.

For example, assume that February pork bellies are trading at 40 cents and May pork bellies at 45 cents. A trader who believes that a five-cent premium for the May contract is not justified — or will not be justified prior to the expiration of the February contract — may buy the February pork bellies and sell the May pork bellies at the prevailing five-cent-per-hundredweight differential. Later, if the absolute price levels change so that February is at 46 cents and May is at 49 cents, the differential will have narrowed to three cents — leaving a two-cent profit (minus commissions) on the transaction.

Obviously, if one is to favor being long one contract and short another, as he must in a spread, he must have reason to believe that forces affecting the two are related. They must be related, else the two prices will act independently and one will be in the position of having two distinct outright trades and not a spread at all. Buying cocoa and simultaneously selling corn, for example, is not considered a spread. It is merely the establishment of two unrelated trading positions. On the other hand, the purchase of milo versus the sale of corn (or vice versa) is a true spread because, while there are forces tending to make these two markets act somewhat differently, the two commodities are substitutes for each other in the livestock feed economy and, indeed, their price movements are related.

"Time" Spreads

"Time" spreads involve the purchase of a futures contract for delivery in one month and the sale of a futures contract in the same commodity for delivery in another month — for example, the purchase of a futures contract of corn for delivery in May and the sale of a futures contract of corn for delivery in July. The purpose here is to take advantage of discrepancies that arise between the two prices as a result of the difference in the time of maturity of the two contracts. In order for such a spread to have any economic logic, of course, the supply/demand elements affecting the price for one of the time periods must also have an effect on the prices in the other time period.

Time spreads can be very risky in some commodities and nearly riskless in others. Those time spreads which would be near the low end of the risk spectrum would involve the completely storable, seasonally-produced commodities — like the grains. Those at the other end of the spectrum would be in the highly perishable commodities, like fat cattle or eggs. In the middle would be spreads in continuously-produced, fully or semi-storable commodities which may have variable carrying charges — like pork bellies or silver.

For the seasonally-produced, completely storable commodities, prices between futures months are related to the cost of carrying the commodity in storage from one time period to

the next. Such costs include storage, handling, insurance, shrinkage, interest on investment and commissions. In a normal market, where the price system provides an incentive to producers who store products, the nearby months usually sell at a discount to the more distant months, the difference between the two representing the carrying costs. In a normal market, therefore, the price of May corn will usually be higher than the price of March corn.

If the price differential between these two months exceeds the total cost of carrying, smart commercial traders will buy a March contract and sell a May contract; and then in March, if the differential has not returned to reflect carrying costs, take delivery of the corn, store if for a month, and re-deliver it in May to cover the short sale. The profit on the transaction would be the difference between the sale price plus the sum of the carrying costs and the transaction costs ... and the price of the

March contract. Because traders will take advantage of such profit opportunities, the carrying costs usually limit the amount by which the price of the May corn contract will exceed that of the March corn contract.

It is important to note, however, that there are no such carrying cost constraints on the amount that March can sell over May. In fact, this sometimes happens. When it does, it is referred to as an "inverted" market. An inverted market results from a shortage of immediately available supplies. It reflects an economic disincentive to storage and encouragement for storers to sell their grain. Since the far-out months are selling at discounts, the market indicates it expects this near-term supply/demand imbalance to correct itself in the short run.

As indicated earlier, spreads in storable commodities are generally at the low end of the risk spectrum because the prices of different months are related to carrying costs, and usually these carrying costs establish a limit, albeit an imperfect one, on the forward premiums. However, in some storable commodities — such as silver — short-term interest rates constitute a major part of the carrying cost. If short-term interest rates are quite volatile, carrying costs will fluctuate accordingly.

Such time spreads also work well for continuously produced, storable or semi-storable commodities, such as pork bellies. In such commodities the normal spread relationship will change, however, between months as the in-to-storage movement changes to out-of-storage. Remember that these discounts and premiums being paid in the market reflect essentially the strength of the incentive for holders to store or not store a product. It is for this reason that "normal" carrying charges for the months when the product moves into storage will be different than those for such commodities when the product moves out of storage.

How Profitable?

Properly handled, spread trading can be very successful. This was established by Dr. Richard Meyer of the University of Florida. His object for study was pork belly spreads. The equa-

137

tion he used for determining the total carrying costs in the pork belly market was:

Total Carry Costs = $X1 + (X2 \times A) + (X3 \times .10 \times A)$
where:
X1 = commission costs in cents per pound
X2 = interest on margin money in cents per pound
X3 = insurance and storage costs per month in cents per pound
A = number of months between the contracts included in the spread.

Using that formula and various rules of thumb about the proportionate relationship between price differences and total carrying costs, Dr. Meyer analyzed the profitability of pork belly spreads between 1965 and 1971. His results show that spread trading under certain conditions could have been quite profitable. He concluded that — using almost any of the rules of thumb he devised — one could have earned between 15% and 20% annual return. Of course, you have to be careful about interpreting his results, which were derived after the fact, as being applicable in the future. Times change, markets change, and price relationships change. Dr. Meyer's study was completed under a Fellowship in Futures grant from the Chicago Mercantile Exchange, and a copy may be obtained by writing to Education Department, Chicago Mercantile Exchange, 444 W. Jackson Boulevard, Chicago, Illinois 60606.

Perishable Spreads

Time spreads in perishable commodities are high-risk transactions. Except under special circumstances, they are frequently more risky than an outright net position in the commodity. This is the problem Joe Boswell had earlier. The reason is because supply/demand elements affecting the price of the commodity in one month may have very little effect on the price for another month. Take eggs, for example. None of the eggs deliverable in May are available for delivery in July. Further, if people eat fewer eggs in May, they do not necessarily make up for it by

increasing their consumption in July ... nor do they necessarily continue reduced consumption in July. Because these supply-demand relationships are independent, the two prices are independent. Their relationships change often and sometimes substantially, making the risk great on spread transactions in eggs.

Nevertheless, from time to time a trader will find, after careful economic analysis, that some contract months in commodities such as eggs or cattle are clearly over-valued and some months are clearly under-valued. In this instance, buying the under-valued contract and selling the over-valued contract can be profitable.

An example is found in a recent preliminary report by John Hendershot, another Fellowship in Futures recipient, who studied price relationships between nearby and distant futures in cattle. His research indicates that a model including the number of cattle on feed, the average market weight of fat cattle, the steer-corn price ratio plus a seasonable variable will aid a trader in identifying such trading opportunities in cattle.

However, you should be aware that such transactions are, in effect, two outright positions and not legitimate spreads, as there is very little natural economic connection between the two positions — this is true whether or not your broker calls them spreads.

Inter-Season Spreads

The time spreads referred to above are all intra-season spreads. There are also profit opportunities in spreading between seasons or crop years — for example buying this year's soybean crop and selling next year's. These types of spreads do work and are legitimate when the commodity is storable so that one season's supply can be carried over to the next season for delivery. This is possible in the grains, but not in pork bellies, where Exchange rules prohibit it.

Inter-season or inter-crop spreads are not restricted to crops that are grown in the soil. There is a seasonality to the production cycle in broilers, plywood and other commodities, as well as periods of in-storage movement and out-of-storage movement. It is important to note, however, when effecting transactions covering two distinct seasons, that an important event always occurs during this interim — namely, a new harvest or a turn in the cycle, which means major changes in production.

Spreading Location Basis

There are instances where the same commodity is traded on two different exchanges, and the contracts call for par delivery at two different locations. In this case, if all other elements of the contracts are equal, the difference in prices on the two exchanges should be equal to the transportation cost between the two locations represented in the contracts. If, for whatever reason, the difference in prices between the two contracts should exceed transportation costs, it will be profitable for commercial traders to buy the lower-priced contract on one exchange and sell the higher-priced contract on the other exchange, thus locking in a profit equal to the amount by which the price differential exceeds transportation costs. If these profit opportunities do not disappear by the time delivery can occur on the contracts, you need only take delivery on the lower-priced market, transport the product to the par delivery point of the other market and re-deliver in fulfillment of your short position.

For example, if you were in a position to buy wheat in Kansas City, ship it to Chicago and re-sell it at a profit, you would do so. Hence, any time the contract in Kansas City sells below the contract in Chicago by more than the transportaton costs, some traders will be buying the contract in Kansas City and selling it in Chicago.

Spreading Quality Basis

Just as par locations differ between contracts for the same commodity listed under different exchanges, quality specifications also sometimes differ. A smart trader will be aware of what the normal price differential should be for the various grades and qualities of a commodity. If the two contracts don't sell at these normal differentials, he will buy one contract and sell the other. As the time for delivery approaches, the two prices should come to reflect the actual value in the spot market. To the extent those actual values reflect the normal differentials, the trader will have profited.

Inter-Commodity Spreads

As noted above, there are physical relationships between certain commodities. Sometimes the supply and demand elements for two commodities are tied together because they are substitutes for each other, as corn is a substitute for milo or grain sorghum. Sometimes one commodity is derived from the other, such as soybean meal and soybean oil are made from crushing soybeans. Sometimes one commodity is the raw material used in the production of a finished product, as with feeder cattle and fat cattle.

Because of these physical and economic relationships, the price fluctuations in the two commodities are related. As a result, a price change in one commodity directly affects the price of another. This places constraints on the extent to which prices in the two commodities can diverge. For example, as the price of corn rises relative to the price of milo, livestock feeders will start substituting milo for corn. This will reduce the demand for corn, thus slowing its price rise, and increase the demand for milo, encouraging it to rise in price.

Likewise, reduction in the demand for soybean oil and soybean meal will be reflected in the demand for raw soybeans, and thus limit that product's price moves. Normally, the price differences between soybean oil, soybean meal, and soybeans will reflect processing margins. If a trader expects the processing margins to widen, he should buy meal and oil and sell soybeans.

Spotting Spread Opportunities

Visualizing the spread between months can be done in a number of different ways. One good way is to keep a daily price table noting the closing price on each side of the spread and the difference between the two. For example:

February Pork Bellies	May Pork Bellies	Difference	Profit Buy Feb.-Sell May
48.90	50.00	+ 1.10	
49.00	49.80	+ .80	+ 30
48.00	49.50	+ 1.50	− .70

Such a table allows you to tell at a glance how the price moves alter spreads.

It is also a good idea to obtain a history of several previous years' price action. However, you don't want to become too dependent on past history. Disease effects, droughts, monetary problems, governmental programs and other factors will change price patterns from year to year.

Spreading and Taxes

The Tax and Revenue Act of 1981 dramatically changed the tax treatment of gains or losses from commodity trading. Prior to 1981, some people employed spread positions in commodity futures as a means of deferring taxes and of turning short-term gains into the lower taxed long-term gains. The tax act changed all that. Major revisions included:

a. Futures transactions have no required holding period.

b. The maximum tax rate on all speculative futures transactions is 32%.

c. Futures losses can be carried back three years against futures gains or carried forward against securities gains.

The tax act specifies that any gain or loss in futures contracts be treated as 60% long-term capital gain or loss and 40% short-term capital gain or loss. This ratio applies irrespective of the length of time the futures position is held. The following shows how a tax of 32% on profits for an individual in the highest tax bracket is derived.

Example of Tax on Profits

Day 1 Buy regulated futures contract (Treasury bill contract, gold contract, etc.)

Day 2 Close out transaction — sell regulated futures contract

Profit from transaction $100

Classification of $100 of Profit

Long term capital gains: $60
Taxed at 20%

Short term capital gains: $40

Tax on this portion amounts to $12

Tax is 50% of $40, or $20

The combined maximum tax is $32

In addition, the new tax act marks all commodity futures contracts to market at year-end and treats all of these "unrealized" gains and losses as if 60% of the capital gains and losses on them were long-term and 40% were short-term "realized" gains or losses; i.e., each futures contract is repriced daily to reflect the market's official closing price. The profit or loss resulting from this repricing is realized on that day in the equity of the investor's account.

The new tax rules, therefore, require gains and losses to be taken into account not only when futures positions are closed out, but also on all open positions on the last business day of each taxable year.

Carryback and Carryforward of Losses

If a taxpayer, other than a corporation, has a net commodity futures loss for a tax year, the amount of loss may be carried back to each of the three taxable years preceding the loss year against marked-to-market gains. Of the amount carried back, 60% will be treated as long-term capital loss and 40% will be treated as short-term capital loss. The loss is carried first to the earliest of the three prior years and no losses may be carried back to any taxable year ending on or before June 23, 1981. However, the loss may be carried back only to the extent that it does not exceed the "net commodity futures gain" for that year defined as the lesser of regulated futures gains or the net capital gain for that year, and that the carryback does not increase or produce a net operating loss for that year.

Losses which are not used up by the carryback may be carried forward indefinitely. They are considered as 60% long-term and 40% short-term capital losses and are carried forward under existing rules related to capital losses generally. Carryback of losses is not available for investors in stocks, bonds, options and other alternative investments. It is another advantage which exists for investing in commodity and financial futures.

Summary

In conclusion, then, several points are worth reiterating:

1. Certain normal price relationships exist between futures contracts for the same commodity, based on time, quality and location differences between the contracts. Because these natural economic factors tie pieces together, the premiums and discounts between futures have approximate natural limits placed on them. Spread transactions to take advantage of these natural relationships *can* be relatively low-risk, yet profitable transactions.

2. Unless the price differences between two contracts are related to natural economic bonds, the risks in spread transactions may be very high. These natural bonds are extremely weak in perishable commodities. Hence, it is wise to study commodity futures price relationships with respect to time, location and quality differences before instituting a spreading program. This necessitates reviewing past price transactions and studying marketing patterns for the physical commodity.

3. In nearly all spread transactions, commercial traders have a distinct advantage over public speculators. Commercial traders have easy access to the actual commodity and the facilities necessary for storage, processing and disposal, should they actually decide to give or receive delivery in order to realize their profit from the spread. It is generally a wise practice, therefore, for speculators to liquidate futures positions prior to delivery, unless they have made specific arrangements to accept delivery and hold the product for re-delivery later.

4. Spreading is far from riskless. The low margins required for spread transactions can result in small gains or losses in absolute terms but can have the same proportionate impact on the value of the margin investment as a larger swing in an outright position

that requires higher margins.

5. When spreading, try to spread approximately the same dollar amounts on each side of the transaction. Frequently, the contracts will not be of equal value, particularly in inter-commodity spreads. If they aren't of approximately equal value, you may end up in the unfortunate position of having a gain on the small side and a loss on the larger side, which nets out to a pretty good-sized loss. You'll be right but lose money. You'll win the battle but lose the war.

6. Do not yield to the temptation of establishing a spread in an attempt to recover from a losing outright position. Such tactics virtually always backfire. The spread transaction will not offset the loss, but will only initiate a new position which could work to compound the loss.

7. Consult first and often with your tax advisor.

Spreading can be profitable and should be considered as a possible part of every trader's strategy and trading plan. It can hold relatively low risk in certain circumstances. For the beginning trader, spreads in low-risk situations are one of the best ways to learn about the market without being subject to the possibility of sharp market losses.

15

Financial Futures — An Introduction

We are all familiar with the dollar bill. We recognize and accept it as payment for debts. These dollar bills are simply pieces of paper manufactured by our federal government and declared by it to be legal tender for the payment of taxes and other debts.

In the commodity futures world, money has always been important as a medium of exchange. Recently, however, it has taken on even more importance as a tradable "commodity."

The opening of foreign currency and interest rate futures in Chicago has made every commodity trader realize that money is also a commodity and that it, too, has a price just like everything else. Money's price is quoted in two ways: (1) A foreign exchange rate, reflecting the purchasing power of one country's money relative to another country's and (2) an interest rate price, reflecting the value of money as an income-producing asset.

Just as the value of a bushel of wheat fluctuates relative to the value of a bushel of corn, so too does the value of the U.S. dollar fluctuate relative to the value of the French franc. This price for money is called an exchange rate and represents a sort of external price other countries are willing to pay for our money.

Just as wheat may be used to produce flour, money may be used to earn income by lending it to people who, say, build houses. The price of money here is the interest rate cost of borrowing it. This interest rate price for money reflects the value sellers (lenders) and buyers (borrowers) place on the use of money for a certain period of time. In both cases — the exchange rate price and the interest rate price — supply, demand and political events determine the level of price.

Money is the ultimate commodity, and no commodity trader's education is complete without an understanding of the futures market for money. Indeed, the money futures markets are the most fascinating and potentially the largest of all. The next few chapters will provide you with a very basic introduction to these markets. The first chapter will give an introduction to the role of money in the general economy. An understanding of that role is essential to evaluate the price movements for money. Subsequent chapters will discuss foreign currency trading, GNMA futures and Treasury bill futures.

Money

If we did not have money, goods would be exchanged through barter, an inefficient and time-consuming process. If a person wanted to trade his output with someone else, he would first have to search among other willing sellers until he found an opposite party with a product he wanted. Second, the two parties would then have to agree on a price which represented equivalent values. Even if they agreed that three chickens and two hogs were equivalent to one cow in value, one party might end up with two hogs more than he wanted.

Man, in his wisdom, realized at some point in his development that an intermediate good, which everybody could readily recognize and accept in exchange for all other goods, might make for a lot fewer headaches in bargaining and doing business. Thus, money was born. Producers could sell their output in exchange for the intermediate good (money) to anyone who wanted to buy. They would not need to waste time looking for someone who had a product they actually wanted. Prices of all goods could be expressed in terms of the intermediate good and the amount of payment could be matched to the price. No longer would a fellow get more hogs than he really wanted. He could take the intermediate good and buy precisely the number of hogs and chickens he desired.

Money, as shown above, performs several functions. It serves as a medium of exchange — everybody accepts it as payment. It serves as a store of value — it can be used to buy things. It serves as a unit of measurement — $300 will buy one horse.

Through the years, many different things, ranging from cigarettes to gold, have served as money. At times, more than one intermediate good has been used as money by various countries of the world. But this reduced the efficiency of transactions because producers had to quote the price for each product in terms of each of the monies. Since it was virtually impossible to maintain a stable relationship between the various monies, most countries reverted back to the use of a single intermediate good as money. Today all countries of the world use paper money.

Although all countries use paper money, each country tends to use a different name for its money (e.g., dollar, peso, franc, etc.) and because of differences in the political stability, natural resources, levels of workers' productivity, opportunity for foreign investment, etc., some countries' money commands a higher price relative to the U.S. dollar than do other countries' money.

Money in the Economy

Money is the grease that makes an economy run smoothly. Imagine the economy of a country as one big machine. This machine represents all the mills, factories, farms, offices, and shops that turn out the goods and services consumed in the society. Everyone with a job works on this big machine. Some are repairmen, some are operators, but all of them are producing goods and services the people use.

Naturally, all of the workers are paid and these workers use their money to buy things produced by the machine. Thus, a nice smooth circle is completed of people working on the machine, being paid by the machine and buying their goods and services from the machine.

If the people buy all that is produced, then everything is in balance and the economy for this country is healthy and stable. Sometimes, however, imbalances appear and interrupt the smooth flow of labor, money, and goods and services. When this happens, prices change and we get increases or decreases in economic activity.

149

These imbalances may arise because of leakages in flows of spending by the machine or by the people. For example, people may decide not to spend all of their money on goods and services but may decide instead to *save* some of their income. Thus, they do not buy as many cars and television sets. Since the flow of money back to the machine is reduced, the machine slows down its production. Fewer people are needed to run the machine, and total income and total buying power are reduced. Economists refer to this set of affairs as a recession.

Usually, however, these savings find their way back to the machine through the hands of businessmen who borrow the funds from the people and reinject the money back into the spending flow by increasing the size of the machine, i.e., building plants, buying new equipment and inventory. Depending upon how much of the savings businessmen want from people, they raise or lower the price (interest rate) they are willing to pay people for the use of their money. These activities, which are analogous to modernizing and expanding the machine, create new jobs and increase total income, thus bringing the flows of spending back toward a balance.

A second imbalance, or drain on the flows, can be caused by taxes collected by the government. Taxes are paid to local, state and national governments and have the same slowdown effect that savings have. However, just as with savings, the tax money finds its way back into the system because the government hires people and buys goods and services.

Just as increases in savings and taxes can create imbalances in the system through withdrawals, imbalances can also be created by people refusing to save and simply demanding more goods and services from the government. The government can either refuse the demands or pay for them by raising taxes or by printing money which is then given to the machine in payment for the goods and services. Refusing the demands and raising taxes are not always popular with the people; hence, governments frequently opt to print more money. Frequently, this is more money than is necessary to keep the machine running smoothly. In order to meet this output, the machine foregoes repairs and hires untrained workers. All the income is used to produce goods to meet current demand and none is used for expanding, rebuilding and updating the machine. This results in reduced efficiency. Ultimately, costs increase and the machine reaches the limits that it can produce. To alleviate this, consumers need to be convinced to postpone their purchases. This is best done by raising prices. This is referred to as inflation. Hence, when too much money gets into the system, the result is inflation.

Money, the Machine, and the Banking System

It should be obvious from the above that if the flows of money spending match the flows of goods and services, prices will remain stable and the machine will run smoothly. If imbalances in flows of money occur, the machine slows down or works at such a furious pace it generates more momentum than it can handle. Thus, the amount of money and the smoothness with which it flows from individuals back to the machine through the land, labor and capital become most important in determining the health of the economy.

In order to make this all flow smoothly in an economy, every country has a banking system through which they facilitate the flow of funds and adjust the supply of money. Banks serve as depositories for people's savings. They act as intermediaries by making these savings available to businessmen for investment expenditures and the vital function of furnishing business and government with credit. Through their lending function, banks are able to adjust the money supply to make the flow of spending match the flows of goods and services, land, labor and capital.

Naturally, most governments do not allow banks to operate willy-nilly in this system. Instead, the governments establish a Central Bank which acts to regulate the actions of commercial banks and to manipulate the expansion and contraction of the money supply. Thus, the ultimate control of the money supply rests with the government.

In the U.S., the Federal Reserve Board, through its network of regional federal reserve banks, acts as the Central Bank. Its methods of operation differ only in degree from Central Banks of other countries. The Fed operates to control the money supply by controlling the amount of excess reserves in the banking system. Long ago banks found it prudent to maintain reserves against their deposits in order to meet the normal cash withdrawals of their customers. Current federal law requires them to maintain

151

certain minimum reserves. The amounts over and above the minimums needed are called "excess" and are funds available for lending. The Fed controls excess reserves by:

a. Adjusting the required ratio of reserves to deposits. By lowering the required reserve ratio, the Federal Reserve decreases the amount of reserves that member banks are required to maintain in their accounts and makes additional reserves available to the member banks. Thus, a reduction in the required reserve ratio from 12% to 10% would increase the amount of excess reserves and thereby increase the amount of money available for lending. By raising the required ratio, the opposite would occur.

b. The purchase or sale of government securities, T-bills, bonds, etc. When the government buys the securities, they increase member bank reserves and vice versa.

c. Through loans of reserves to member banks.

A commercial bank may be short on reserves relative to its demand for loans and may then borrow from the Federal Reserve. The bank will pay a rate of interest known as the discount rate. The Fed can set the discount rate at whatever level it wants. By raising this rate of interest, borrowing is made more expenisve and commercial banks will be less inclined to borrow reserves. They will have to raise the rate of interest to customers, and as the price of credit to customers goes up, usually the demand for such credit will go down. Conversely, by reducing the discount rate, borrowing is made less expensive and banks will be more inclined to borrow reserves and make loans to their customers.

Thus, the Central Bank of the government acts to regulate the actions of the commercial banks and thereby to regulate the supply of money to accomplish specific objectives related to levels of employment, personal income and price stability.

The extent to which the Central Bank accomplishes these objectives has a great influence on the interest rate price and the international price (foreign exchange rate) of a country's money. The alert trader will watch closely the monetary policy of a country and the action taken with each of the monetary tools. They are among the most important elements in determining long-run strength or weakness in a currency.

Inflation

Money by itself is really useless. It takes on value only when it is used as a medium of exchange. Thus, the value of money lies in what it can buy.

Ten years ago, one dollar would buy a gallon of milk, a newspaper, a coke and a package of gum. Today, it won't even buy a gallon of milk. Ten years from now, it might buy more or less of the same things.

The dollar itself doesn't change. It is still 4 quarters, 10 dimes, 20 nickels or 100 pennies. But what the dollar will buy does change. How does that change affect the foreign exchange rate and domestic interest rates? The explanation lies in inflation.

Inflation in a country weakens the domestic purchasing power of the currency for the consumer in that country. People on pensions and others on fixed incomes find that their dollars buy less. People with savings accounts find that inflation reduces the value of their savings.

The Inflationary Process

Monetary economists trace the inflationary process through as follows: First, a change in the rate of the growth in the money supply causes a change in people's incomes in the same direction about six to nine months later. This money "burns a hole in the pocket" and people rush out trying to spend their extra income. It usually takes about another six to nine months before this increased demand catches up with the available supply and prices start to rise. Thus, about a year to a year and a half after the money supply increases, one can expect to see a rise in prices. The Consumer Price Index reflects the general prices of things people buy and thus it becomes the most handy means of measuring inflation. The extent to which the money supply is increased, of course, will affect the extent to which incomes increase, which in turn will affect the amount of money people have to spend and their ability to bid up prices. So a small change in the money supply beyond the amount necessary to maintain economic growth, employment and stable prices, will probably result in small amounts of inflation.

153

Inflation and Interest Rates

Inflation rates become important in forecasting interest rate levels because the expectations about levels of inflation get built into the price for borrowing money. Look at it this way. Two years ago the dollar would buy a newspaper, a gallon of milk and a package of gum. Inflation (rising prices) has caused the domestic purchasing power of the dollar to decline so that today it takes two dollars to buy the same amount and quality of goods. So, if you loaned someone a dollar 10 years ago and if the average annual rate of inflation was 10%, when he pays it back today it is worth only about half as much as when you loaned it to him. If you had charged him 5% per year interest, you would have collected $.50 in interest and, counting that, would find your dollar worth only about three-fourths as much as 10 years ago.

Had you anticipated the 10% average annual inflation rate, you would have asked for at least a 10% interest charge in order to maintain your purchasing power over the 10-year period. More likely you would have asked for 15% interest, reasoning that you expect money to provide a 5% real rate of return after accounting for the 10% expected inflation. It is this latter way that businessmen and bankers react. Thus, expected inflation rates get built into interest rates. That is exactly what happened in the late 1960's and 1970's.

Inflation and Foreign Exchange Rates

Internationally, the purchasing power of the currency may be reduced if the inflation rate in the home country is greater than in other countries. So the important consideration from a foreign exchange trader's standpoint is the *relative* rate of inflation. If Italy inflates faster than the U.S., Italian products will become more expensive for Americans. Further, Italians will switch from the higher-priced Italian products to the lower-priced U.S. products. Thus, Italian exports to the U.S. will decrease and American exports to Italy will increase. All of this will reduce the demand for the Italian lira and increase the demand for the U.S. dollar.

Therefore, you should watch closely the relative rates of inflation in the U.S. compared to the other countries of the world. If you see that U.S. inflation, compared to Italian inflation, is consistently different and by a large amount, you can see that ultimately the exchange rate between the two currencies is going to have to change to reflect the reduced international purchasing power of the Italian lira. When they do ultimately change, the change may or may not (more likely not) reflect the exact changes in the relative purchasing power of the two currencies.

Of course, the relative rate of inflation is not the only factor to consider in forecasting exchange rates. It waxes and wanes, being a major factor at times, and at other times being a minor factor, overshadowed by other events. Certainly, in recent years, when the world was on a "fixed rate" system, the various governments' determination to maintain a fixed exchange rate overshadowed the impact of inflation rate differentials. The next chapter will discuss these and other basic elements of foreign exchange trading.

Thus, the money supply and rates of inflation become key elements in understanding and forecasting prices of foreign currency futures and interest rate futures. As early indicators of things to come in money supply trends, watch the action of the Federal Reserve Board and the Consumer Price Index.

16

Money, The Ultimate Commodity

If you buy a pound of cheese from Wisconsin or a gallon of California wine, you naturally pay for it in dollars. The cheese manufacturer and the wine producer expect to be paid in dollars because their expenses and living costs are all settled in dollars. Within the U.S such single currency transactions are made without a second thought.

On the other hand, if you wanted to buy an English topcoat directly from the British manufacturer, matters get more complicated. You must pay in British pounds (pound sterling) rather than in dollars. Similarly, an Englishman desiring Wisconsin cheese must somehow get U.S. dollars to pay the American producer, if he wants to buy the cheese directly. Most Americans have never seen a British pound note and would understandably be reluctant to accept it as payment if they could not be sure of converting it into U.S. dollars.

Clearly, then, if such transactions are to occur, there must be some means whereby the American who desires to get pounds sterling to pay for a topcoat can convert his dollars into British money and vice versa for the Englishman who wants to buy Wisconsin cheddar.

Simply stated, the conversion of one money into another is the sale of one currency for another. Money is treated like any other commodity. It is bought and sold at a price. This price is called the "foreign exchange rate."

Thus, when you read that the foreign exchange rate for the deutschemark is $.3300, this means that the price of one deutschemark is 33¢ in U.S. dollars.

Very often, you see headlines which announce the dollar is "weak" or some other currency is "strong." When the dollar is said to be weak, this means that people are selling the dollar and buying other currencies; that is, the dollar price of the other currencies has increased. For example, if the price of one deutschemark goes from 32¢ to 33¢, the dollar has weakened and te deutschemark has strengthened.

This chapter will explain some of the basic elements of the foreign exchange market, including why it exists and how it works. It will cover some of the fundamental aspects of foreign exchange, including a discussion of the recent history of the international monetary system, the development of the futures market in foreign exchange, the economic indicators that help you analyze the relative strength or weakness of a particular country's currency, and some very basic introductory concepts about hedging in foreign exchange.

The Price of Money

Foreign exchange transactions are usually done through a foreign exchange trader located at a bank. Modern-day foreign exchange dealings became common with the development in 11th century Europe of the Champaigne fairs where merchants bought and sold goods in their counterparts' currencies. Bankers attended the fairs to act as money changers, the modern day equivalent of the foreign exchange trader.

The price of a currency is determined in the same way you determine the price for any other commodity — by the forces of supply and demand. If the people in the U.S. begin to demand more English-made products, the demand for pound sterling goes up; as the demand for pound sterling increases, Americans will have to pay higher prices in order to induce holders of sterling to sell. Conversely, if the British developed an overwhelming taste for U.S. goods, they would have to sell more and more pounds sterling for the U.S. dollars to pay for the products they bought.

This increase in the supply of sterling being offered for sale would cause the price to drop relative to dollars.

Recent History of International Monetary System

Of course, all of the above sounds quite simple and straightforward, but the basic forces of supply and demand are not always allowed to operate freely in the foreign exchange market. The Persians in the 6th century attempted to thwart the basic forces of supply and demand by fixing an immutable gold/silver ratio. It failed.

A more recent attempt to fix prices was made in 1944 when a group of economic and finance experts from 47 Western nations met in a New Hampshire resort town called Bretton Woods. Their purpose in meeting was to develop a post-war plan for reconstruction of world trade and national economies. Out of that meeting came a plan for an international monetary system. It had four key points:

1. The establishment of a super-national agency called the International Monetary Fund whose purpose was to oversee the international monetary system and to assure its smooth functioning.
2. The establishment of par values or fixed exchange rates for currencies and an agreement among the countries that they would manipulate the supply and demand for their currencies in such a way as to maintain that rate. They did this by entering the market to buy their currency when its price fell 1% (in practice, ¾ of 1%) below the declared par and by selling their currency when the price rose 1% (in practice, ¾ of 1%) above the par value.
3. Agreement that the U.S. dollar would be the king pin of the system and other countries would accept and hold it for payment of international debts.
4. Agreement that the U.S. dollar was as good as gold and that any time a foreign government wanted to exchange its dollars for gold it could do so at the U.S. Treasury at the rate of $35 an ounce.

This system was in effect from 1944 to 1971, and world trade did indeed expand during those years. It expanded largely because the U.S. was willing to run its international business affairs at a loss. The U.S. continually imported more than it exported. It paid for its imports by running the printing presses and printing dollars. As long as others were willing to accept paper dollars, the U.S. received fine wines, nice automobiles, radios, televisions, etc., in return.

Ultimately, however, there were a lot more dollars held by foreigners than the U.S. held gold. Foreigners had from time to time turned in their dollars for gold and gradually the U.S. gold supply had disappeared until clearly the dollar was overvalued in terms of gold.

On Aug. 15, 1971, President Nixon declared that the U.S. would no longer abide by the Bretton Woods agreement of 1944. Accordingly, he said that the dollar was no longer convertible into gold; that is, that foreigners would no longer be able to turn their dollars in to the U.S. Treasury and obtain gold. Further, he said that the exchange rate for the dollar would no longer be fixed, instead it would be allowed to "float;" that is, it would be determined by free market forces.

The dollar floated just like a rock — straight down. It was devalued. Since that time, except for a brief period in 1972 when fixed rates were again reinstated, the value of the dollar has been determined more or less by free market forces.

The result of the devaluation of the dollar was that the relative purchasing power of the U.S. dollar was changed dramatically. Imports into the U.S. suddenly cost more (it took more dollars to buy the same amount of deutschemarks), and exports from the U.S. were lower priced (fewer deutschemarks would equal the dollar price). For example, between 1972 and 1973 the value of a bushel of wheat at Rotterdam increased by 122% in U.S. dollars, 117% in yen, 185% in deutschemarks, and 129% in sterling. Thus, it took about one-third fewer deutschemarks to buy the same bushel of U.S. wheat in 1973 than it took in 1972. Put another way, the same number of deutschemarks would buy one-third more U.S. wheat in 1973 than in 1972.

The Spot Market

The buying and selling of spot currencies (for immediate delivery or use) is accomplished through banks. Banks all over the world have accounts with each other in order to serve their customers, many of whom are multi-national companies which deal in many different currencies. Every day these banks make deposits and withdrawals for their customers. These deposits or withdrawals result in transfers of funds from one country to another and, therefore, the conversion of one currency into another. Hence, banks worldwide are constantly buying and selling currencies and providing a ready spot market.

This buying and selling is done by telephone and teletype. If a dealer in Frankfurt, Germany, wants to buy dollars and sell deutschemarks, he will probably call several New York banks and ask each for its rate. When he finds a bank with a rate that suits him, they agree to the trade and exchange specially coded telegrams confirming the transaction. The bank in Frankfurt will then credit the account of the New York bank with the proper amount of deutschemarks.

If a businessman desires to convert dollars into deutschemarks to pay a bill, he can simply notify his banker and, after receiving proper information, the banker will see that the proper German bank account is credited. For example, if a businessman imports German bicycles and needs deutschemarks to pay for them, he simply notifies his banker who, in turn, contacts other bankers in Germany or elsewhere in the world to buy the deutschemarks for the importer and have them deposited in the German bank account of the bicycle manufacturer. The U.S. bank will then deduct the dollar cost of the deutschemarks from the U.S. account of the importer. The importer will never see the deutschemarks; the bankers will simply debit and credit the appropriate accounts.

Evaluating Foreign Exchange Rates

What makes foreign exchange rates fluctuate from day to day? Why does the U.S. dollar buy less in Germany in 1976 than it did in 1966? Would an increase in the general level of interest rates in England be bullish or bearish? For whom?

These questions and many more are of great importance to anyone dealing in foreign exchange. And, as you may have guessed, the answers are not easily determined. Fundamental analysis of the money markets is more difficult than fundamental analysis in other commodities. There is a definite lack of good data, and the markets are highly sensitive to political elements. Yet, over the long run, fundamental economic factors will be the dominant considerations in determining the value of currency. In the short run and intermediate term, technical analysis can be very helpful. Indeed, the currency markets may be best suited to chart analysis.

It is not possible to cover all of the factors in detail here; however, we will touch on some of the highlights of each of them. For those who would like to dig deeper, there is a considerable amount of literature available at no cost from the International Monetary Market and from a number of its member firms.

International Trade and Capital Balances

The single most important long-run indicator of impending exchange rate changes today is the country's trade balance, also called the balance of goods and services. It reflects the relative value of merchandise imports and exports.

If exports are greater than imports, there is a trade surplus. This is a sign of currency strength. A shift in the trade balance to a deficit (imports greater than exports), on the other hand, is an indication of currency weakness.

A second important indicator is the official monetary reserves of a country, including gold, special drawing rights (SDR's) on account at the International Monetary Fund and foreign currency holdings. These reserves indicate the ability of the country to meet its international obligations — for example, its ability to repay loans, to finance imports and to intervene in the foreign exchange market to support (manipulate the value of) its currency. Official reserves should be building up when there is a trade surplus. Official reserves may, but not necessarily will, be falling when there is a trade deficit.

A third important international economic indicator is the capital balances of a country, including the direct foreign investment and the short-term speculative funds that flow to or from a country. Capital movements are very sensitive to short-term interest rates.

With the almost instantaneous speed of the world's financial system, funds may be transferred nearly anywhere in the world. These funds move in response to changes in the interest rates. Capital flows can have tremendous impact on short-term exchange rates. If three-month interest rates in Canada increase to 1% over U.S. rates, people will send their money to Canada. As they do so, they must sell U.S. dollars and buy Canadian dollars. An increase in a country's capital account reflects an increase in demand for assets denominated in that currency, such as time deposits or Treasury bills. This increased demand indicates fundamental strength in the currency. Conversely, a deficit in capital accounts indicates a weakening in the demand and an expectation that the price of the currency will fall.

163

Domestic Economic Factors

The underlying influences of the balance of trade, official reserves, and capital flows are the domestic interrelationships between income, prices and interest rates.

Among the factors to consider in evaluating the domestic health of a country are:

a. The rate of real (after adjustment for inflation) growth in gross national product. Steady growth is an overall indicator of good economic health for an economy.

b. The rate of growth in money supply and interest rate levels. These are important indicators of future economic conditions. The short-term interest rate differential is important in short-term capital flows. Such flows directly affect the demand for a currency.

c. The rate of inflation relative to the index of industrial capacity utilization. Differing rates of inflation in different countries is another very important factor affecting the price of a particular currency. The end result of inflation is an erosion of purchasing power, which ultimately means a weakening of the currency if other countries are not experiencing the same amount of inflation. High inflation with high utilization suggests that inflation is likely to stay high because "the machine" is already working at capacity, yet the people are demanding more goods. This would suggest a weak currency.

The general price level of a country affects the exports of that country. The U.S. is a good example. It has nearly priced itself out of the international market in some goods while Japan, on the other hand, making many similar goods, is able to sell them at lower prices. This reduces the exports of the United States and increases the imports to the U.S. from Japan, creating an outflow of dollars and what economists call an "unfavorable" balance of trade.

Each country should be studied individually and then one country compared against another. Since the IMM futures contracts reflect other currencies relative to the U.S. dollar, other countries' expected and actual economic conditions should be compared to the U.S. If the conditions seem more favorable to other countries

164

relative to the U.S., sell the futures. If the conditions favor the U.S., buy the contract.

Political and Governmental Influences

Political and governmental activities affect exchange rates by helping or hindering the international trade of a country and thus its balance of trade. Study carefully such things as import taxes, negative interest rates (a favorite of the Swiss, this means you pay them interest on savings accounts instead of the other way around), interest equalization taxes, embargoes, etc.

The internal political stability of a country also bears on the issue. Even in the more well-established industrial nations of the world, the unsettling influence of political elections is reflected in the foreign exchange market. Major economic policy changes, as well as revaluations or devaluations, are often made with an eye to the next election. A change in the political party in power very often brings a change in economic policy. Even the anticipation of a new party being elected to power can affect exchange rates. Which leads us to the significance of what people think is going to happen.

Expectations

Timing is all important. Expectations about changes in price level and the timing of such changes can have a great impact on the market. Many observers, for example, expected the British pound to be devalued toward the end of 1972, just before Britain entered the Common Market. Early in the year numerous money interests began to act in anticipation of the event and the British government was forced to float the pound in early summer, probably months before they would have liked to. Similarly, many people expected the Mexican peso to be devalued during the latter part of 1982 because a change of political administration would make it a convenient time to do so. The market anticipated the event, although not the exact magnitude, long in advance. The peso was devalued three times by about 90% during 1982.

Interest Rate Arbitrage

How would you like a deal where you borrow money at 10%,

invest it at 8%, and make a profit on the deal? Sounds impossible, doesn't it? It's not. In fact, it's done regularly in the foreign exchange market.

To demonstrate, let's suppose your mother-in-law lends you $100,000 in order to get started on an investment on your own so you can support her daughter in the style she and her mother are used to being supported. Let's say also that your mother-in-law isn't completely benign, and she charges you a rate of interest that is ½% over the bank's prime rate. Assume that would have been 10% (9½% plus ½%).

First you talk to your brother-in-law who suggests you send the money to Canada to be invested in three-month commercial paper (Prime Finance Company) at 8%. You suggest that he must be crazy since you're borrowing at 10%. You wanted something conservative but not that conservative! Brother-in-law suggests you watch your tongue and let him finish his plan. This is what he plans.

He'll sell your U.S. $100,000 for spot Canadian dollars, assume a rate of $.9944. The U.S. $100,000 will provide you with $100,563.15 Canadian dollars. He will then immediately buy an equivalent amount of Canadian commercial paper, due in 90 days, paying for it with the Canadian dollars, returning an annualized rate of 8%. You will hold the commercial paper for 90 days at which time it will mature and be redeemed for Canadian dollars again.

Now comes the important point. If you wait until the Canadian commercial paper matures to sell Canadian dollars and obtain U.S. dollars again, your net rate of return may be greater than, less than or equal to 8%, depending upon what's happened to the U.S./Canadian dollar exchange rate. If the Canadian dollar has increased in value to say $1.0232, a 2.89% increase, the net annualized return on the transactions will be 19.56%. If it has decreased in value, the 8% will be reduced accordingly because you'll be selling the Canadian dollars for less than you originally paid for them. If the spot rate hasn't changed, you'll reap the 8%, minus transaction costs, of course, which are usually quite small.

Of course, you tell your brother-in-law you don't want to take the risks that your Canadian dollars will change in value during the time of your investment. Your brother-in-law explains there is a way to avoid that risk and calculate your exact return before you ever buy the Canadian dollars. How's that, you ask. By hedging, he says. By selling a futures contract now, you set the price you will receive for the Canadian dollars in 90 days and establish, therefore, the exact net rate of return on your investment.

He explains that at the present time a 3-month futures for Canadian dollars is selling at a 2.49% annualized premium over the spot. Thus, you can buy the spot Canadian dollars today, immediately resell them for delivery in 90 days on a futures contract, and make a 2.49% annualized return on that transaction. The Canadian dollars you buy today will not be delivered in fulfillment of the futures contract for 90 days, so you invest them in 90-day commercial paper, which yields an 8% annual return. The net on all the transactions then turns out to be 10.49%.

Now obviously in the scenario described above, the young man is not going to get rich very fast, mostly because he's paying such a high rate of interst to his mother-in-law. If his mother-in-law were a little less greedy and would give him the money for a reduced interest rate, he'd obviously be doing better.

The procedure just described is referred to by foreign exchange traders as interest arbitrage. It's the purchase and sale of spot and futures in money in order to take advantage of differences in interest rates between the two countries. This illustrates a very important principle in using the foreign exchange markets. That is, there's a very strong relationship between exchange rate movements and interest rate movements in different countries. The basic rule of thumb is, "At equilibrium, the currency of the higher (lower) interest rate country should be selling at a forward rate discount (premium) in terms of the lower (higher) interest rate country's currency."

Thus, if interest rates in Canada tend to be 3% below U.S. interest rates, you would expect a forward U.S./Canadian exchange rate to reflect a 3% discount for dollars. Market forces will assure this result (assuming certain other factors to be discussed below) because if the exchange rates don't reflect interest rate differentials (plus transactions costs) exactly, arbitragers like our friend above can make money by borrowing funds in the high interest rate country, transferring them to the low interest rate country, and hedging them on a transaction in the forward exchange market. If enough money moves from one country to another in this manner, the spot prices of the two currencies will change relative to the forward price until the spread between spot and futures exactly reflects the differences in interest rates between the two countries. At that point, the profit opportunities in transferring funds from one country to another will have disappeared and the exchange rate between the two countries will be at what is called "interest rate parity."

As noted above, some important assumptions have been made in order to show how interest rate arbitrage is conducted. It works only under certain conditions:

a. Free flows of funds between the two countries concerned must be possible. In recent years, more and more countries have been instituting certain barriers and controls on the movement of capital into or out of their country. Obviously, if the controls are effective, great disparities between interest rate differentials and exchange rates may exist for long periods of time and interest arbitrage will not be possible nor will exchange rates reflect interest rate differentials.

b. Expectations of a devaluation, revaluation or of the imposition of capital controls on the currencies must be such that they do not outweigh the interest rate differential factor. Sometimes, people hold such strong expectations of changes in the exchange rate due to factors other than interest differentials that interest rate parity considerations are simply overwhelmed.

Hedged interest arbitrage transactions, like those described above, are virtually risk-free. The only major risk you take in those transactions is that a country will introduce strong capital controls which could prevent the fulfillment of the futures contract or the repatriation of the funds.

Opportunities for interest rate arbitrage appear frequently. People who are managing large sums of money, whether for corporate accounts or for personal investment, should become knowledgeable about interest arbitrage. In the years ahead, investment managers and advisors will need to be skillful at moving funds around the world to various security markets and financial centers. That sort of operation will require an understanding of foreign exchange markets and the concept of interest arbitrage.

Hedging in Foreign Currency

In earlier chapters we discussed the concept of hedging and demonstrated its application to some of the traditional agricultural commodities. These same concepts apply to the foreign currency hedger.

The following examples illustrate some potential hedging situations available to different sectors of the economy.

The buy hedge. Assume a Chicago tractor maker has a Swiss plant which is doing very well and has access to funds in the form of Swiss francs. It has no need for those funds until Swiss taxes are due in six months. At the same time, assume that the Chicago tractor maker has an engine plant in Milwaukee that is in need of a short-term loan to meet operating expenses. The best move for the tractor maker may be to transfer those funds from the Swiss plant to the Milwaukee plant for six months. In the transaction, the hedger would sell the spot Swiss francs for dollars and buy Swiss francs for future delivery, thus establishing a buy hedge. The summary of the transaction would look like this:

Cash Market	Basis	Futures Market
March 1		
Sell 500,000 Swiss francs for $.50000/SF = $250,000	100	Buy 4 September Swiss franc futures, 125,000 SF each at $.49900 = $249,500
September 1		
Buy 500,000 Swiss Francs at $.50300/SF = $251,500	10	Sell 4 Swiss franc futures contracts, 125,000 SF each at $.50290 = $251,450
Loss = 300 points ($1,500)	90	Gain = 390 points ($1,950)

In this example the hedger had a $1,500 loss in the cash market that was more than offset by a $1,950 gain in the futures market. His basis declined from 100 points to 10 points for a net decline of 90 points. Each point is worth $1.25 or $112.50 for each contract or a total of $450.

The sell hedge. Assume a Chicago bank has excess funds to invest in the short term, and the highest short-term interest rate currently is being paid in Canada. Let's say 91-day Canadian Treasury bills are yielding 8.5%, and U.S. Treasury bills are yielding 7.5%. The Chicago banker will buy Canadian dollars in the spot market, transfer them to his Canadian banking correspondent and direct him to purchase 91-day Canadian Treasury bills. At the same time, he will sell Canadian dollars in the futures market for delivery three months hence. The amount of the Canadian dollars he sells in the futures market will include the original number plus enough to cover the interest that will accrue.

The advantage of this hedge is that the banker will have fixed his selling price for the Canadian dollars 91 days from now. This way he can be assured that the interest in Treasury bills will not be lost in the conversion back to dollars, if the price of Canadian dollars goes down during the period. The transaction may be summarized as follows:

Cash Market	Basis	Futures Market
December 1		
Buy 191,000 Canadian dollars at $1.00000= $191,000	100	Sell 2 CD contracts, March delivery, $100,000 each at $1.00100 CD= $200,200
March 1		
Sell 191,000 CD at $.98000 CD=$187,180	10	Buy 2 CD March futures delivery at $100,000 each at $.98010 CD=$196,020
Loss=2,000 points ($4,000)	90	Gain=2,090 points ($4,180)

Interest Accrued $8,423.10

In this example, if the banker had not hedged, he would have lost nearly half of his interest income ($8,423.10) when he changed his Canadian dollars back to U.S. dollars because the spot price of the CD went down. However, by hedging in the futures market he actually recovered all of his interest income in the futures transaction and made an overall profit of $180 on the hedge as well ($4,180 − $4,000 = $180). He could just as easily have lost a small amount. The important point is that the hedge protected his interest income from the exchange risk. His basis declined from 100 points futures over cash to 10 points futures over cash, a net decline of 90 points. Each point for each contract is worth $1. Since he had two contracts, each point is worth $2 for a total of $180.

To Hedge or Not to Hedge

In any hedging decision the manager must answer three very important questions:
1. What is the net exposure?
2. What is the probability of a loss as a result of this risk exposure?
3. Which of the alternative methods available to me for managing this risk will provide the most complete coverage at the least cost?

What is the Net Risk Exposure?

Net risk exposure refers to the amount of money that would be lost if the exchange rate for a currency changes. It is an objective measure of the impact a devaluation or revaluation will have on the value of a firm's assets and liabilities. If a currency is devalued, any liability (such as loans) a foreign firm owes in that currency can be paid back with cheaper money. Conversely, if it has been revalued, the currency needed to pay back that loan will cost more.

There are a variety of ways by which the net risk exposure can be calculated. Current assets minus current liabilities is one very simple but probably incomplete way. Most firms today use a more sophisticated procedure which takes account of such things as receivables booked, liabilities incurred, and the method by which the balance sheet values are converted from one currency to

171

another. This is a very complex topic on which whole books can be and have been written. Suffice it to say, before you venture into this area, get your accountant's advice. A thorough understanding of accounting rules and tax laws is of key importance here.

What is the Probability of Loss on Net Exposure?

This is a subjective evaluation that should be based on an analysis of the economic and political information available about a country. In making this determination, the manager should first estimate the probability that there will be a change in the exchange rate. Is there a 50% chance that the peso will be devalued this month? this year? An 80% chance? And, second, estimate the probability of the size of change in the exchange rate. Will it be 10%? 20%? 30%? or even 40%?

Hedge Yes, Hedge No

Armed with these three pieces of information — net exposure, probability of loss and probability of size of loss — you can then calculate the expected value of a loss to the firm by multiplying the probability of a loss times the probability of the size of the loss. See Steps a, b, c, and d in Table 1. Once you have that answer, you are then in a position to compare the expected value of the loss (this is calculated by mutliplying the probability of a loss by the probable size of the loss) to your cost of hedging.

To estimate the cost, a manager needs to ask, "Which of the alternative methods available, singly or in concert with another alternative, will provide the most complete coverage of the risk at the least cost?" Generally, he has a number of alternatives available to him. He can self-protect through various management techniques; he can hedge by going to his bank and obtaining a forward contract; or he can hedge on a futures contract on the International Monetary Market of the Chicago Mercantile Exchange. In making this determination, he must examine the cost of each alternative.

To the foreign exchange trader, the cost of the hedge includes not just the commission cost, the interest on the margin for the futures contract and the bid-ask spread but also any premium or

172

discount that is reflected between the futures contract and the expected spot price. For example, if your expected spot price is 3% under the six-month forward price, the "cost of the buy hedge" includes that 3% premium. If the cost of the hedge is less than the expected loss, hedge. If that cost is greater, do not hedge.

To demonstrate, assume that the manager of a firm calculates his net exposure is $10 million based on an expected devaluation of the U.S. dollar relative to the German deutschemark. Secondly, assume that given his evaluation of the economic situation in Germany, he expects the probability of a loss to be 50%. In other words, he believes that there is a fifty-fifty chance that the devaluation of the U.S. dollar relative to the deutschemark will occur by the next year. Assume also that he calculates the probability of the size of the devaluation to be 10%.

Here's a summary of the situation and a way to determine whether to hedge:

a. **Net exposure** **$10,000,000**
b. **Probability of loss** **50%**
c. **Probable size of loss** **10%**
d. **Mathematical expectation of loss (b x c)** **5%**
e. **Cost of hedge** **3%**
f. **Decision — compare d to e. If d is greater than e, hedge. If d is less than e, do not hedge.**

In the example above, the firm would make the decision to hedge because the mathematical expectation of a loss exceeds the cost of hedging — 5% vs. 3%. If those expectations are correct, the firm would gain 2% by hedging. Note that the key to the decision of whether or not to hedge is found in correct calculation of the probabilities. If the probabilities were different, the mathematical expectations would be different also.

A caveat — one should not enter into a hedging transaction without considering the tax implications and the effects on cash flows. Any business firm that is engaged in foreign exchange transactions would do well to integrate its hedging transactions and its accounting decisions in order to assure it gets the maximum *net* benefit of its risk management efforts.

Delivery Points for the Futures Contracts

Delivery of a currency contract can be made to any bank selected by the buyer located in the country which issued that currency. The seller of the futures contract instructs its bank to contact and follow the instructions of the buyer's clearing member at the exchange regarding the bank and the name of the account to which the delivery is to be made. Choice of the delivery point, specific bank and account is the responsibility of the buyer.

To Sum Up

In summary, the world monetary system is in a continual state of transition. As a result, the risk of doing business internationally is increasing right along with the increased demands for international trade. As more and more businesses and banks seek means of protecting themselves from currency losses due to exchange fluctuations, the role of the foreign currency futures will undoubtedly grow in importance.

The currency futures markets can be used by a wide variety of commercial interests. The following are just a few categories in which futures hedging could be helpful:

1. Companies building plants abroad.
2. Companies financing subsidiaries.
3. Manufacturers importing raw materials and exporting finished products.
4. Exporters taking payment in foreign currency.
5. Companies dealing in goods bought and sold into foreign countries.
6. Companies abroad financing operations in Euro-currencies.
7. Stock purchases or sales in foreign countries.
8. Purchases or sales of foreign securities.

The possibilities are virtually limitless. Everyone who deals in or with foreign countries has a need for a hedging mechanism to avoid major losses due to exchange fluctuations.

Additionally, through the open, competitive futures market, the general public has an opportunity to make known its hopes, fears and beliefs about the value of a currency. And with daily reports from a futures exchange of trading volume and price fluctuations, there is a public weathervane providing daily signals of the true value of a currency — giving the public a clearer insight into the effect that political actions, monetary policies, balance of trade and other factors have on the economics of world commerce. All of this, of course, provides for differences of opinion and trading opportunities.

17

The Treasury Bill Contract

One of the most exciting new futures market developed in recent years is the Treasury bill contract which began trading Jan. 6, 1976, at the Chicago Mercantile Exchange. No other contract represents such an important "commodity" and no other commodity is so universal in its importance. There is no business enterprise and no borrower, lender or investor who is not affected by short-term interest rates.

At the same time there is no more "pure" indicator of short-term interest rates than 90-day Treasury bills issued and sold by the U.S. government. The Treasury bill market is a focal point for many other interest rate movements.

T-bills, as they are called, are direct obligations of the U.S. Treasury. They are sold to investors through the Federal Reserve System, acting as an agent for the Treasury. In this way the Treasury borrows money to help pay the cost of running the government. The Fed sells T-bills, usually having a life of 90 or 180 days, through a weekly auction. Competitive bids are accepted by the Treasury from Thursday until shortly after mid-day Monday when the auction is held. T-bills are sold on a discount basis and are redeemed at par value on maturity — 90 or 180 days later. For example, a $10,000 bill yielding a 4% rate of return with 90 days to run would be purchased for $9,900 and 90 days later would be worth $10,000 as the interest is added on daily to the purchase price. If the interest rate were 6.0%, the value of the 90-day bill would be $9,850. It would accrue $150 in interest and be worth $10,000 at maturity.

Trading Treasury bills is distinctly different from trading other commodities. One of the most important differences is that, when interest rates go up, the value of the contract goes down and vice versa. To the initiate in finance and to the seasoned futures trader, this seems quite curious. Normally, it would seem that, if the price of something went up and you owned it, you should have a profit on your position. The reason this is not true is because T-bills are traded on a discount basis; the higher the interest rate, the more earnings will accrue over the life of the bill.

The Contract Terms

The futures contract for U.S. Treasury bills calls for par delivery of T-bills having a face value of $1,000,000 at maturity, which is 90 days after the delivery date. At the seller's discretion, he may substitute for the 90-day maturity 91- or 92-day bills of equivalent value. (New T-Bill contracts for one-year and four-year maturities were pending when this book was written. This chapter concentrates only on 90-day T-Bills.)

The "price" of the future is quoted in terms of an exchange-devised index representing the actual annualized T-bill interest yield subtracted from 100. Hence, if you want to know the annual interest yield being represented by a particular futures quote, subtract the quote from 100. For example, an index number of 94.5 represents an annual yield of 5.5%. In contrast to interest rates, the index goes down as the contract loses in value and vice versa. Almost all newspapers carrying T-bill futures quotes carry the interest yield price as well as the index price. Bids and offers in the trading pit at the exchange must be made in terms of the index, so be sure that you give your orders to your broker in terms of the index. The minimum price fluctuation of the contract is .01 of the IMM index or one basis point of annual yield. This is equivalent to $25 on a $1,000 contract.

As noted earlier, the Fed holds T-bill auctions every week. The last day of trading in T-bill futures for any particular month is the second day following the third T-bill auction of that month. Delivery is the following day.

Delivery is accomplished through Chicago banks that are registered with the exchange and are members of the Federal Reserve System. Through them you can have the T-bills delivered to your account in any other major city. It is a relatively simple procedure and mirrors the action taken when deliveries are made in the cash market.

The futures contract on Treasury bills calls for the delivery of bills having 90 days of life remaining. Thus, on delivery you will obtain an instrument that will earn interest over the next 90 days. At the time you buy it, you pay something less than its face value — its discounted value. The difference between what you pay and the face value will be equal to the accrual of the interest during the remaining 90 days.

Therefore, keep in mind as you consider trading in financial instruments that, if you expect interest rates to go up, take a short position in the market. If you expect interest rates to go down, take a long position in the market.

Volatility

Yields on T-bills can fluctuate rapidly as money market conditions change. What makes interest rates fluctuate from day to day? What economic factors can affect the money market? These questions and many more are of great importance to anyone dealing in interest rate sensitive instruments.

Among the most important economic factors affecting T-bill prices and money market interest rates are (1) Federal Reserve activities, (2) financial needs of the business community, (3) technical tone of the money market and (4) the general condition of the economy.

Federal Reserve Activity

By far the most important determinative of T-bill rates is the Federal Reserve System. In the previous chapter we explained the role the Federal Reserve plays in the overall economy; and we explained, albeit briefly and simplistically, that the Federal Reserve has essentially three tools available to it which affect interest rates. First, its Open Market Committee Operations, through which it buys and sells government securities, influences interest rates and the availability of credit. When the Fed buys securities from the commercial bank, it results in an increase in loanable funds and a decrease in interest rates. When the Fed sells securities, the buyer's reserve account is debited. This results in a reduction of credit and a firming of interest rates.

Secondly, the Fed has a far-reaching monetary impact through its control over member bank reserve requirements. It can set them anywhere between 10% and 22%. These reserves directly affect the availability of loanable funds and indirectly the interest rates.

Thirdly, the Federal Reserve sets an interest rate called the discount rate. This is the interest rate that banks must pay the Central Bank when a commercial bank decides to borrow money in order to maintain its reserves. Changes in the discount rate often are regarded as indicating fundamental shifts in the Fed credit policy. Such shifts are immediately reflected by the financial market, sometimes even anticipated by it. Changes in the discount rate set up a virtual chain reaction throughout the financial market. When the discount rate is increased, banks are generally inclined to sell government securities, especially Treasury bills, rather than expand their borrowings at the Federal Reserve discount window. The sale of securities reduces security prices while raising their yields, and higher yields in the Treasury bill market finally spread to other money market instruments and are reflected across the board in higher interest rates. The opposite occurs when the discount rate is lowered.

Business Needs

Industry's demand for cash has a strong influence on short-term interest rate movements. As the demand for loans increases, interest rates generally rise. On the other hand, if loan demand begins to lag because of a slowdown in the general economy, one would expect downward pressure on interest rates. Indicators of short-term business loan demand include new orders in durable goods industries, contracts and orders for new plants and equipment, changes in the book value of inventories, industrial production and levels of commercial and industrial loans outstanding.

Dealer Activity

Anyone who desires to trade Treasury bill futures should become familiar with the activity of dealers in government securities. At the present time there are approximately 35 active government security dealers. The activity and aggressiveness of dealers in bidding and offering Treasury bills does not affect the direction and volatility of all interest rates. These dealers are continuously interpreting the Fed's actions, the nation's economic well-being and social and political events to determine the impact that such things have on prices. One should watch closely what these cash market dealers are doing.

General Economic Condition

In the previous chapter we discussed some of the significant indicators of the condition of an economy. A stable economic situation would help create stable money market conditions while a period of economic uncertainty usually leads to wide interest rate fluctuations. Such measures of economic conditions as the rate of growth in GNP, balance of trade, levels of unemployment, inflation, housing starts, etc., help determine the strength or weakness of the economy. Some of these factors and an interpretation of them are encompassed in the preceding chapters. Unfortunately, space does not permit more detailed discussion of them here. For those who might be interested in a more sophisticated treatment of this very complex subject, a bibliography is appended at the end of this chapter.

Applications of an Interest Rate Futures Market

Any commitment in the money markets exposes both borrowers and lenders to the risk of interest rate changes for as long as the debt instrument is outstanding. To minimize these risks, money market participants could hedge in the T-bill futures market.

As noted earlier, hedging is a method by which a borrower or lender of money market funds buys or sells a futures contract as a temporary substitute for a borrowing or lending transaction to be made at a later date. Hence, the money manager or trust fund manager who knows he will be investing in T-bills in September may establish the yield on the September bills in July by entering the futures market and buying the T-bill contract for delivery in

September. The corporate treasurer who knows he will be borrowing money soon but needs time to work out his financial plan and actually get the loan arranged can hedge against higher rates by selling the futures.

Builders, developers and other users of short-term construction loans can use the Treasury bill futures market to establish in advance the cost of borrowed money. Interest rates on short-term construction loans generally fluctuate with the prime rate. An increase in the prime rate during the period of construction could push the cost of financing beyond the capacity of the borrower. This risk can be effectively removed by a short hedge.

Hedging can also be used to protect against changes in the rates of other money market instruments such as commercial paper, certificates of deposit, bankers' acceptances, etc. The effectiveness of the hedge will be determined by the extent to which the movements in the rates for Treasury bills parallel the movements in rates for the other instruments. For example, if a perfect correlation existed between movements in T-bills and commercial paper, then a hedge in the T-Bill futures would be a very efficient device for protecting against changes in commercial paper rates. The closer the relationships, the more perfect the hedge.

Even in instances where the correlation is not perfect and the basis is unstable but the volatility in both markets is high, an imperfect hedge will be much preferred over no hedge at all. For example, if it is normal for commercial paper to trade at a +25 to +150 point range over T-bills, one might think that a T-bill futures would be a poor hedge mechanism for commercial paper rates because a range of 125 points shows a significant amount of instability in the basis. However, if the volatility of T-bills and commercial paper is such that a 300-point change in absolute rates is a highly probable occurrence, one could easily see that the 125-point basis exposure that would accompany the hedge is to be much preferred over the 300-point exposure of the non-hedged position.

Since the T-bill market is the center of the interest rate movements from which all other movements emanate, you can see that a T-bill futures contract can be an efficient vehicle for hedging interest rate movements in other money instruments. You need only compare the volatility of the basis relationships to the relative volatility of the absolute rates for each instrument to determine the efficiency and value of the hedge.

Hedging Against Falling Interest Rates

A financial manager who anticipates having funds to lend (i.e., invest) in short-term money markets at a known time in the future can hedge against the risk that rates may drop in the interim. He does this by buying a Treasury bill futures contract. If interest rates go down between the purchase date and the delivery date, the contract will increase in value. The futures contract's appreciation in value should offset the investor's "opportunity loss" which resulted from the actual decline in interest rates during the period. A hedge minimizes both the downside risk and upside potential gain.

The Buying Hedge

Judicious and selective use of the T-bill markets can help the corporate money manager match interest rates on borrowings and investments. It can also provide him a view of market expectations on future interest rate levels. Such information is valuable in establishing the maturity mix in a portfolio.

Let's assume that on May 1 a corporate treasurer anticipating cash inflows for short-term investment during the month of June observes that the September T-bill futures is selling at 93.00 (IMM index) to yield 7.00%. He feels this rate will fall during the next month or so to about 6.50%. Since he feels that 7.0% is a very favorable yield and he wanted to "lock in" that yield for his antici-pated investment, he buys September futures. On June 15 when he has the cash available for investment, he buys T-bills maturing in December to yield 5.60% annually (IMM index of 94.40). This is 90 points lower than he expected. At the same time, June 15, he lifts his hedge by selling his September futures at 94.08 to yield 5.92%. The 108-point gain on the futures more than offsets the lower than expected yield on the bills. The corporation will realize an addi-tional .18% yield return ($450 per million) on their T-bill invest-ment as a result of the hedge. The futures provided flexibility in timing the forward pricing of their investment yields.

The table below explains the sequence of transactions:

Cash Market	Basis	Futures Market
May 15		
Anticipated Investment yield of 6.50% (93.50 index)		Buy 1 September Future @ 7.00% (93.00 index)
	50	
June 15		
Buy $1,000,000 T-bill maturing 12/14/76 @ 5.6% yield (94.40 index)		Sell 1 September future @ 5.92% yield (94.08 index)
	32	
−90	**18**	**+108**

Hedging Against Rising Interest Rates

Borrowers in the money markets also can use interest rate futures to protect themselves against increases in short-term rates with a "short" hedge by selling a T-bill contract for future delivery. If rates rise, the vale of the futures contract will drop and the hedger can make a gain by buying it back for a lower price. The gain from this futures contract will be available to offset the increased cost of cash borrowings. Of course, if borrowing rates drop instead of rising, the hedger's lower-than-anticipated cost of borrowing has been offset by a loss on the futures contract.

The Sell Hedge

Assume a borrower plans on May 1 to sell $10 million in 90-day commercial paper in September. He expects to sell the paper at 5.5%. The current rate on September futures is 5.2%. He can hedge that sale and assure himself in advance of the interest rate he will pay by taking a short position in the futures market. (See example at top of next page.)

In this instance, had the borrower not hedged, he would have paid 1.13% more in interest cost than he originally expected. As it is, he paid .26% less. The futures provided the flexibility in timing the date on which he fixed his cost. He did not have to wait until the day he came to market with the paper.

Cash Market	Basis	Futures Market
May 1		
Anticipates selling $10 million of commercial paper. Expected rate in September 5.5% (IMM index 94.50)	30	Sells 10 September T-bill contracts at 5.20% (IMM index 94.80)
Sept. 5		
Sells $10 million commercial paper at 6.63% (IMM index 93.37)	4	Buys (offset 10 September T-bill contracts at 6.59% (IMM index 93.41)
Loss: 113 points	**26**	**Gain: 139 points**

As another example of a selling hedge, assume a money manager on June 15 holds in inventory $5 million in Treasury bills maturing in September yielding 6% annually (IMM index of 94.00). He knows that before Sept. 15 he will need the funds and will sell these Treasury bills to someone else. He can protect the selling rate and reduce his risk exposure by selling September futures contracts. Assume the September futures is at 93.35 (6.65% yield) for a basis of 65 points.

Cash Market	Basis	Futures Market
June 15		
Inventory of $5 million Treasury bills maturing 12/14/76, yielding 6.00% (IMM index 94.00)	65	Sell 5 September futures contracts. T-bill maturing 12/14/76 at 6.65% yield (IMM index 93.35)
July 1		
Sell inventory of $5 million T-bills maturing 12/14/76 @ 6.2% yield (IMM Index 93.80)	55	Buy 5 September futures T-bills maturing 12/14/76 @ 6.75 yield (IMM index 93.25)
Loss: 20 points ($500)	**−10 points**	**Gain: 10 points ($250)**

On June 15 he protects his inventory by selling September T-bill futures at a 6.65% yield. Time passes and rates rise, causing his inventory to decline in value. On July 1, he decides to liquidate the inventory at a price to yield 6.2%. He buys back the futures at 93.25 to yield 6.75%. The basis narrowed from 65 to 55 points. (It did not converge to zero because the delivery period had not yet arrived.) The use of the futures reduced the $500 loss in the cash market to a net loss of only $250.

Reducing Basis Risk

The whole idea behind hedging is to minimize the risk of unfavorable basis movement. If you can do that, you will have a very successful hedging program. There are several concepts to keep in mind in minimizing such risks.

One way to hold it down is through proper selection of the contract month for placing the hedge. So many hedgers ask, "Which month should I use?" The answer has several parts:

1. Use the futures month that most closely coincides with the maturity of your cash position.

2. Select the futures price that seems most overpriced or under-priced relative to the cash market.

This involves some understanding of what causes futures prices for different months to take on different values. Basically, the price differences between two futures months are reflecting two things:

1. The cost-of-carry.

2. Expectations.

Cost of carry is the difference between the cost to borrow the money to buy the cash instrument and the return received while owning the cash instrument. Cost of borrowing is best reflected in the repo rate. If the cost of carry is positive, you would expect futures to be trading at a higher yield than the cash or a lower price. If the cost of carry is negative, you would expect futures to trade at a lower yield or a higher price than the cash.

Why? If you can make money by borrowing to buy a cash instrument, you will bid for the futures as an alternative investment until the futures price provides exactly the same yield. Because futures are not an earning asset until delivery, you will bid only until the two prices are identical after adjustment for time difference and the cost of money over the time difference. If it is a positive carry of 2%, you will give up no more than 2% on futures to get the 2% income.

186

Expectations sometimes become a more important price influence than the cost-of-carry. Instances arise where people expect the cost-of-carry to change, or they expect significant shifts in the level of interest rates. Those expectations usually get reflected in distant months more dramatically than in nearby months. Thus, you need to watch market fundamentals closely to determine which of a myriad of factors is influencing the market at any particular time.

Treasury Bonds and Treasury Notes

Treasury Bill futures were so successful that futures contracts in Treasury Bonds and Treasury Notes were also begun. Bond futures were an immediate success, largely because they covered the long end of the yield curve and were a natural complement to T-Bill and GNMA futures. With short, intermediate and long-term points covered on the yield curve, investors now could get decent hedges for an entire portfolio.

The par delivery unit on T-bonds futures contracts calls for a $100,000 bond with an 8% coupon and minimum maturity of 15 years. There is no maximum maturity. Prices are quoted in 32nds. Thus, each minimum price change is $31.25.

To convert futures prices to actual cash values, the CBT uses a factor method. The conversion factors which adjust each available government bond to an 8% coupon with 15 years to maturity are published regularly by the CBT. This method of calculation almost always results in the bond with the longest maturity (usually 30 years) being the cheapest for delivery.

Delivery is made through the Federal Reserve's book entry system in the same manner as for Treasury bills.

Treasury Bonds are auctioned by the Treasury in the same manner, but less frequently, as the weekly auctions for Treasury Bills. Bids, however, are denominated in yields instead of dollars.

Ten-Year Treasury Notes

U.S. Treasury Notes represent the largest and fastest growing segment of the federal government's marketable debt instruments. Like other debt instruments, these are sold to public investors to raise funds for financing government programs and to refinance other maturing debt of the U.S. government. Notes, like bonds, are sold at regular auctions and are issued with a coupon which bears interest semiannually.

There are a number of Treasury Note futures listed on the various commodity exchanges, but the Chicago Board of Trade's 10-year Treasury Note futures contract is the only one sufficiently active to be a trading alternative. The 10-year Treasury futures contract is based on a government security with a face value of $100,000, maturing in 6½ to 10 years with an 8% coupon.

Like other coupon issues, Treasury Notes are auctioned. With each auction of notes, the coupon associated with those note changes and, hence, the list of deliverable notes changes. Each eligible coupon has a different maturity and a different value. Hence, at delivery, the value of the various deliverable notes must be converted to the equivalent of an 8% coupon. This is accomplished through "conversion factors" provided by the CBT. A seller delivering any one of these eligible notes calculates the invoice amount for a particular issue by multiplying the futures price by the appropriate conversion factor and adding the accrued interest. These conversion factors also become the means for calculating the correct number of contracts to use when hedging.

All debt instruments with similar maturity and investment quality are affected by the same economic fundamentals. For this reason, one will find that many debt instruments move in unison with one another — their yields rise and fall together. Put another way, they have a high correlation. That high correlation allows one to use Treasury Note futures as a hedging tool for the hedging of related instruments.

To some extent, Treasury Notes, like other government-backed securities, become a price benchmark for the pricing of other securities. Corporate Bonds, Federal Agency Issues, and Municipal Notes are all priced at a spread to Treasury Notes when they trade in the cash market. The size of the spread or the difference between their yields reflects the market's perception of the creditworthiness of the security. A narrow spread indicates that the market judges the security to be closer in credit quality to the Treasury Note. A wide spread indicates the market believes the related securities are a more risky investment than a Treasury Note.

Summary

Money fund managers, cash management funds and mutual funds also are potential users of the T-Bill, Bond and Note futures. The manager of a money fund whose cash investments are in various types of money market instruments such as CD's, commercial paper, T-Bills, etc., can effectively use a futures contract in three-month T-Bills. By anticipating the size and approximate dates of investment in these and other money-marketing vehicles, the fund manager can buy the number of contracts necessary to cover some part of the future interest rate exposure and thereby lock in an acceptable return on at least part of his portfolio.

Just as pointed out previously in other chapters on hedging, there are certain key steps a manager should follow in determining his hedging strategy. First, determine what is the risk exposure. Second, study the economic factors (including seasonal and cyclical influences). Third, consider how much risk can be prudently taken by the corporate firm and whether the cost of the hedge is such that it is worthwhile to carry the risk internally or to hedge in the futures market. In calculating the cost, include your basic risk.

18

Mortgage Futures Market

In October of 1975 the Chicago Board of Trade opened an organized futures market in Government National Mortgage Association (GNMA) mortgage interest rates. The purpose of that futures market was to provide hedging opportunities for those who are exposed to the risk of changes in long-term interest rates, particularly those who are involved in the housing industry, one of the most important industries in the U.S. economy. Everyone needs shelter, and when a house is built, there will usually be a mortgage issued on it.

During the last decade in general and the last few years in particular, interest rates on home mortgages have fluctuated substantially. If you had been building a house in 1970, you would probably have obtained a mortgage for around 7½% interest. If you had built a house in 1982, you would probably have a mortgage at around 16% interest. That 8½% difference adds up to a lot of money when you consider it over 30 years on, say, a $50,000 mortgage. It can raise the cost of owning a home by hundreds of dollars a month.

The new Ginnie Mae futures market is not a place where you can hedge your individual home mortgage unless it is, of course, for $100,000. But it is a place where your builder and lender can hedge their interest rate risks and, to the extent that they are able to hedge successfully, they can pass those benefits on to you in the form of slightly lower mortgage rates.

What is the mortgage futures market all about? How does one use it? Those are questions we will discuss in this chapter.

"Ginnie Mae"

Assume you desire to buy a house. Undoubtedly you will go to your local savings and loan association for some money. They make a loan to you for the purchase of the house, and in return you agree to pay them so much per month interest and principal on the loan for the next 25 or 30 years. Should you default on your payments at some time in the future, they will have certain rights to take control of the property and sell it to someone else. This loan agreement is called a mortgage, and it is "owned" by the S & L that has loaned money to you.

Now in order to keep the housing industry growing and money available for others to purchase homes, the local S & L association may sell your mortgage. The new owner will receive the monthly payments on the principal and the interest. In return, the S & L association will have new funds to be made available to another buyer.

Several government organizations have been established in order to make the purchase of these loans attractive for ordinary investors. One of the ways in which they do this is by buying loans made to veterans and others who qualify for special treatment. After they purchase the loans, they then resell them again. This time, however, instead of selling the individual loan, they sell a piece of paper certifying that the owner of this piece of paper has certain equity rights in a "pool" of mortgages. These certificates, in contrast to mortgages, are all standardized, representing the average mortgage in the pool.

Instead of putting their money into their local savings account, a retired couple may decide to buy one of these certificates. Such a certificate guarantees them a monthly payment equal to the principal and interest on a $25,000 mortgage, with 12 years to run. The certificates may yield a higher interest return to the investor than would the ordinary savings account at the bank. These certificates are highly liquid and may be easily resold. Investors are encouraged to buy these certificates because the Government National Mortgage Assn. (GNMA) guarantees they will receive payment of the principal and interest. Hence, if the couple who have taken the mortgage should default on their payment or if for some reason there should be a default somewhere else in the system — say, by the local S & L — "Ginne Mae" assures that anyone who purchases one of these pass-through certificates will still get their monthly check. In one sense, it is like owning a house and collecting monthly rent on it.

It is these pass-through certificates guaranteed by GNMA that are traded on the mortgage futures market at the Chicago Board of Trade. GNMA, which is an agency of the Department of Housing and Urban Development (HUD), purchases mortgages of all kinds and sizes from loan originators (those who lend money to you so you can buy the house), pools the mortgages bought and then sells new pieces of paper (certificates) in uniform denominations backed by the mortgages. These certificates are issued in $25,000 denominations, and they represent ownership in a pool of Federal Housing Administration or Veterans Administration's guaranteed home mortgages. In addition to buying its own inventory of mortgages, Ginne Mae also guarantees timely payment of principal and interest on FHA and VA mortgage pools put together by others.

Anyone hedging in GNMA futures should spend time to carefully study contract specifications. At present, there are two different contracts traded, a CD contract and a CDR contract.

The CD contract refers to a "Certificate Delivery" while the CDR contract refers to a "Collateralized Depository Receipt." Under terms of the CD contract, you receive delivery of a GNMA certificate adjusted in price to the equivalent of an 8% coupon. With the CDR contract, you receive a receipt issued by a registered depository bank which has accepted a $100,000 pool of 8% (or the equivalent) GNMA certificates from a registered originator of such a pool. That receipt can be presented at the depository bank to obtain the pool of actual mortgages.

The CDR contract is a yield maintenance contract, which means that if coupons other than 8% are delivered, the price is adjusted to the equivalent of $100,000 in GNMA 8% coupons, calculated at par, assuming a 30-year certificate prepaid in the 12th year. Hence, a seller delivering a GNMA with a coupon of less than 8% would be required to deliver more than $100,000 in face value to meet the equivalency test.

The CD contract has an additional feature called the "par cap" provision, which prohibits the seller from delivering a unit at a price in excess of the par. Some of the CD futures contracts, however, provide for substitutions at higher prices if the coupons were issued within the 90 days immediately before the delivery date.

The CDR contract has been, by far, the more successful contract of the two. The CD contract with its par cap provision has attracted very little trading.

The costs of trading GNMA futures are not much different than they are for other futures contracts. They include commission, interest on margin and the spread between bid and ask prices.

Using the Mortgage Futures Market

Since the mortgage futures market represents long-term interest rates, any businessman involved in long-term borrowing or lending may find the mortgage futures market a valuable planning, risk-shifting and pricing tool. Among those groups that can make the most direct use of it are mortgage bankers, who function as loan originators for construction companies and home buyers; saving and loans associations; mutual savings banks, and commercial banks, who in addition to making construction loans make mortgages for home buyers. Insurance companies, trust funds and pension funds, which most frequently perform the role of permanent investor in mortgages, can also make important use of the Ginnie Mae futures.

Hedging with GNMA's

A short hedge in GNMA mortgage futures can be used to protect a commitment to buy mortgages. Or it can be used to protect the value of an existing inventory of mortgages held. A long hedge can be used to protect a commitment to sell mortgages or to fix the price of an expected purchase of mortgages.

The Short Hedge

Suppose that in April an S & L makes a commitment to a builder to buy, over the next nine months, $1 million in mortgages from him at 8.500%, i.e., make mortgages at 8.5% to buyers of his houses. The 8.5% yield translates into price of 96-03 or a value of 96 3/32 dollars per $100. The S & L will plan on reselling these mortgages by forming a mortgage pool and selling Ginnie Mae pass-through certificates to investors. Since the interest rates at which mortgages will be issued to home buyers are set today, and since mortgage rates may change considerably between now and nine months hence when the homes are all sold and the pool formed, the S & L has a risk that, if interest rates go up, they will have to sell the mortgages at a lower price than they purchased them, thus losing money.

To protect against such a loss, the S & L hedger sells 10 December Ginnie Mae futures contracts ($100,000 each) at a price of 97.00 ($97 00/32 per $100) to yield 8.371%. (See Figure 1.)

Now time passes. Assume that in November the last house is sold, the final mortgage is issued, and the pool is formed. Assume also that interest rates have risen, so that the $1 million of

FIGURE 1

Cash Transactions	Basis**	Futures Transactions
April	29/32	**April**
S&L makes mortgage commitment $1,000,000 @ 8.500 (96-03)*		S&L sells 10 December GNMA futures @ 8.371 (97-00)
November	10/32	**November**
S&L completes the mortgage pool and sells $1,000,000 GNMA's 8's @ 9.00% yield (92.22)		S&L buys 10 December GNMA futures @ 8.954 (93-00)
Loss 3-13 points	19/32	**Gain 4-00 points**

Net Gain 19 Points

*Prices are normally quoted in 32nds of 100 points. Thus 96-03 is read as 96 and 3/32 and is equivalent to a yield of 8.5% assuming a 30-year mortgage prepaid in the 12th year.

**The concept of basis is equally as applicable here as in any other contract.

Ginnie Mae-backed mortgages are sold to investors at a price which yields 9%. The S & L completes the hedge at the time the Ginnie Mae certificates are sold to investors by buying 10 December contracts at 93-00 to yield 8.954%, thereby offsetting the futures position taken earlier. Since the yield has gone up, the value of the Ginnie Mae futures position will have fallen, reflecting the changed market condition. Nevertheless, the gain of the futures position should approximately equal the loss from the Ginnie Mae securities sold to private investors in the cash market.

The transactions in the cash market result in a loss to the S & L of 3-13 points. Since each point is worth $31.25, that figures out to $3,406.25 per contract or $34,062.50 per million. The futures transaction, on the other hand, resulted in a gain of 4-00 points, or $4,000 per contract, $40,000 per million. The firm has successfully hedged its commitment from increases in interest rates because gains from futures have offset losses from the cash market and have even returned an extra $5,937.50 (19 basis points times $31.25 times 10).

If the interest rates had fallen during the April to December period illustrated above, the opposite situation would have occurred in each market. The cash transaction would have resulted in a financial gain to the lender while the futures transaction would have resulted in a slightly larger loss. In either event, the S & L would have protected itself from major losses while at the same time removing the potential for major gains. Gains and losses did not exactly offset each other because the basis did not remain exactly stable. It is important to note, however, that the basis was much less volatile than absolute prices.

In the above example, the basis narrowed but didn't quite converge to zero. The major reason for this was that the hedge was lifted prior to the delivery period. In theory, the cash market and the futures market should normally be nearly identical during the delivery period. Thus, had the hedge been held until December, the basis should have narrowed to zero. This should happen naturally because if the cash price is significantly above the futures price, those who bought futures contracts will take delivery and resell the commodity in the cash market, thereby making a profit. As they do that, they bring pressure on each market so that the gap between the two markets narrows.

On the other hand, if the futures price is significantly above the cash price during the delivery period, a profit can be made by buying the product in the cash market, selling futures and making delivery. This, too, causes the differences between the two markets to narrow. In practice, the futures prices and cash prices for Ginnie Maes will usually differ by small amounts during the delivery month of the contract due to different market conditions in futures and cash markets.

The Buy Hedge

Suppose the S & L in the above example made a commitment to sell the mortgage to an investor at a specific price before all of the houses had been sold and the mortgages originated. In such instances, the S & L bears the risk that market rates will decline, causing it to have to buy mortgages at a higher price than expected. To protect itself in this situation, the S & L could buy futures contracts at the time it makes the commitment to sell mortgages to the institutional investors. Then later when the houses are sold and the buying price of the mortgages is determined, the futures contract is offset by selling futures contracts. If this price closely reflects the Ginnie Mae pass-through market price, the firm will again succeed in protecting its profit.

The key to successful hedging in Ginnie Maes is the same as it is for any other commodity — namely, the price of mortgages in the cash market must be closely related to the price movement in the Ginnie Mae futures market.

Speculating in Ginnie Maes

Just as you can speculate in short-term interest rates on Treasury bills, so you can speculate in long-term interest rates, and the Ginnie Mae futures market has attracted a large number of speculators. If you are interested in speculating in long-term interest rates, study carefully the economic factors explained in the preceding chapters and some of the material listed in the bibliography.

Money markets are generally all tied together. They all react to the fundamental health of an economy, changes in the money supply and Federal Reserve activity. Frequently, however, long-term interest rates will move in divergent directions from short-term interest rates. For this reason, be wary of arbitrage or spread transactions between the Treasury bill market and the Ginnie Mae market. Do not do it unless you are quite confident of your ability to analyze the different factors affecting each market and the extent to which they will counterbalance each other.

19

Using the "Yield Curve"

If you want to do an intelligent job trading the financial instruments market, spend your time studying the yield curve.

In financial markets, yield refers to the annual rate of return on an investment: It is determined by relating the interest rate, the price paid and time (the remaining life of the investment).

For example, if you lend $100 for one year at 7%, the yield on that investment is 7%. If you invest $95 in a note that will mature at the end of one year and be worth $100, you have a yield of 5.26% (5 ÷ 95 = 5.26%).

Yields become important because they reflect interest rates in various money market investments. These interest rates reflect powerful linkages that connect the money market, bond market, stock market, mortgage market and commodity markets. Money moves rapidly from one market to another, seeking its best return. That return is reflected in the yield.

A "yield curve" refers to the shape of line you get when you plot yields of various Treasury securities — or any other homogeneous group of securities — against their various maturities. Normally, you plot maturity dates or time on the horizontal scale and yields on the vertical scale of the graph as in the accompanying illustrations.

When a number of issues are plotted on the graph, you will see that a sort of pattern emerges from the placement of the dots. Draw a line through the dots so that most of them fall on the line. Those that don't should be distributed nearly evenly on either side of the line. Now, you have a "yield curve" picture.

To demonstrate, consider the data in Figure I, which reflects yields on May 25, 1978, for government bonds and notes of various maturities.

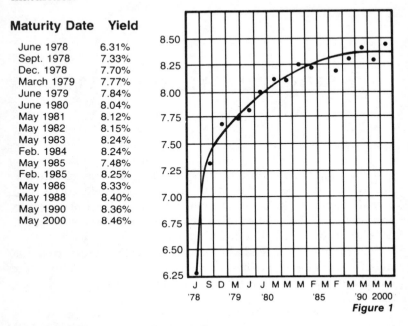

Maturity Date	Yield
June 1978	6.31%
Sept. 1978	7.33%
Dec. 1978	7.70%
March 1979	7.77%
June 1979	7.84%
June 1980	8.04%
May 1981	8.12%
May 1982	8.15%
May 1983	8.24%
Feb. 1984	8.24%
May 1985	7.48%
Feb. 1985	8.25%
May 1986	8.33%
May 1988	8.40%
May 1990	8.36%
May 2000	8.46%

Figure 1

Why Study Yield Curves?

You should study yield curves for several major reasons. First, it causes you to focus attention on the cash market, something which too few futures traders do. Cash market activity provides clues to price relationships in the futures market. Second, study of yield curves focuses attention on the concept of value, undervalue and overvalue. The yield curve becomes a general guide for measuring individual value.

As you can readily see in Figure I, not all the dots fall on the "curve." Those which do not fall on it are candidates to be investigated as possible buy/sell opportunities. Those represented by dots above the lines are relatively under-priced while those below the line are relatively over-priced. For example, the May 1985 notes seems to be over-priced, offering a lower yield than adjacent issues.

On the other hand, the May 1988 notes seems to be slightly under-priced, providing a slightly higher yield than adjacent issues.

Why the Differences?

Variations of this kind usually can be explained by several things:

1. Differences in coupon rates. For example, the May 1985 note carries a coupon of 3¼%, one of the lowest of any outstanding Treasury issue.

2. Difference in the supply of or demand for a particular issue. For example, the May 1985 bond is in short supply. It is what is called a "flower bond," which merely means it is eligible to be used to settle estate taxes at full value. There are only a few such issues around, yet the demand for them remains high. Thus, their price gets bid up and the yield falls.

3. Differences in the marketability of a particular issue. Trading in some issues is naturally more liquid than in others. Generally, short-term issues have much more liquidity than long-term issues.

4. Risks that the general level of interest rates will change in an adverse direction.

The Changing Shape of the Yield Curve

But it is not enough to know what yield curves are and how they are derived. You also need to know why they take on the shapes they do.

As noted previously, the so-called "normal" yield curve is an upward sloping curve to the right (Figure 2.) Near-term rates are

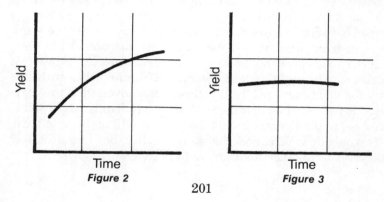

Figure 2   Figure 3

lower than far-term rates. Money market economists refer to this as a "positive carry" market. You can borrow short-term and lend long-term at higher rates.

Sometimes, however, the curve takes on a flat look (Figure 3). Rates are fairly even across the time spectrum.

Sometimes short-term yields are above long-term yields (Figure 4). This is referred to as a "negative carry" market.

And sometimes yield curves become humped (Figure 5) when short-term rates rise sharply at first, then fall sharply to a point where the curve for long-term rates becomes flat.

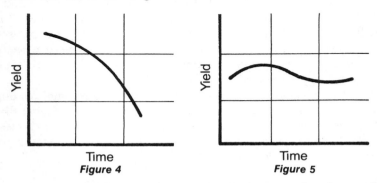

Time
Figure 4

Time
Figure 5

What does all this mean? Simply that knowing and understanding the yield curve, the shapes it takes on, and what those shapes mean can provide you with trading ideas. For example, you should expect that a downward sloping yield curve ultimately will return to a normal yield curve.

By studying economic fundamentals, you can begin to identify economic signals that indicate a fall in short-term rates. A logical trading strategy to take advantage of such a change would be a spread between long-term and short-term rates — buy the short-term instruments and sell the long-term instruments.

If the yield curve indeed does return to normal, this strategy is almost sure to be profitable. However, the risk in such a strategy is that the yield curve will become even more inverted. If that happens, losses could be enormous. A more prudent strategy would involve buying the intermediate-term and selling the long-term.

Not only do yield curves change shape, but they also shift from one level to another (as from A to B in Figure 6.)

202

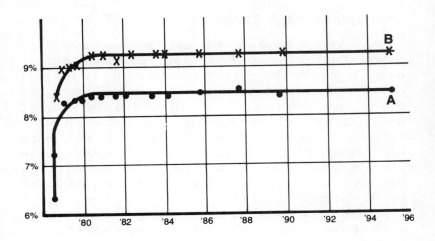

Figure 6

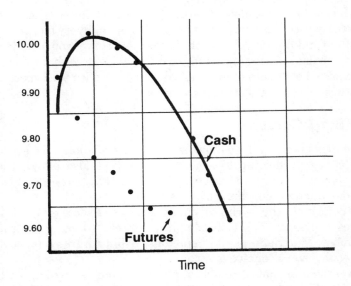

Figure 7

The Futures Yield Curve

Just as you can develop a yield curve for issues traded in the cash market, you also can develop a yield curve for the futures market (Figure 7). The process of constructing the futures yield curve is similar to constructing the cash market yield curve. The obvious major difference is that you use data from different futures contracts in a futures yield curve — i.e., 30-day commercial paper, 90-day T-bills, 1-year T-bills, 4-year Treasury notes. GNMAs (reflecting 12 years) and 15-year Treasury bonds. Just as in constructing the cash yield curve, you need to put them all on a bond equivalent basis, and you need to select issues of comparable quality and credit-worthiness.

This futures curve shifts and changes shape just like the cash market curve. Sometimes it anticipates changes before the cash market adjusts. At other times, it follows or moves in loose conjunction with cash market changes.

It's important to use the same contract months for each of the futures instruments for obvious reasons. Each different futures month represents a different future time period and, therefore, a different expectance curve. If you mix different delivery months — say, June and December — in the same yield curve, you would be mixing apples with oranges, comparing a yield curve that reflects the expected structure of interest rates in June with the expected structure of interest rates in December.

The Strip Curve

The existence of futures markets provides a whole new set of yield curves, reflecting expected rates. But it also allows the development of a third curve called "the strip curve," which provides another benchmark of value.

By definition, the "strip" is simply a series of successive T-bill futures contracts. For example, if you were to purchase the December, March, June and September T-bill futures contracts, you would own a one-year strip.

Ownership of that strip actually is the same as owning a 12-month T-bill because the series of futures provides you with rights to purchase a 90-day T-bill every 3 months. The four separate bills cover a total maturity span of 12 months. To obtain that coverage, you simply take delivery of the December futures, thus receiving a bill in December that matures in March. Money from the maturing March bill is then used to take delivery of March futures and receive another 90-day bill maturing in June and so on.

A major advantage of the strip is that you are completely flexible on the front end of the strip. Because you always are carrying an actuals position at the front end of the strip, you can move from T-bills to CD's to Bank Acceptances to Fed Funds or whatever instrument will provide the best short-term yield while keeping the latter part of the strip intact with the "locked in" yield. That flexibility provides the opportunity to increase the yield over the period.

Compounding Factor

The value of the strip is more than the average of each of the successive futures contracts because of the effect of compounding interest. Each time a T-bill matures, the interest earned during the life of that T-bill is available for re-investment during the next quarter. Thus, "interest-on-interest" increases the total return of the T-bill strip. The yield curves for both cash bills and for futures are best compared if converted to bond equivalents first.

There are, of course, some risks associated with this strategy. If rates change significantly, you could receive margin calls on the open futures position. The opportunity cost of such calls also needs to be considered.

Further, if you move from one cash instrument to another, transaction costs could get to be expensive. Last, if short-term rates on the cash instrument increase rapidly while the longer-term futures do not change or go down, you could get caught rolling from an instrument with a higher rate to one with a lower rate.

To use this strategy, you need to monitor the markets continuously and be able to make calculations instantaneously. Such opportunities, although regularly available, are not available all the time. That is particularly true during periods of an inverted curve.

In summary, the message is quite simple: Learn to understand the yield curve for futures as well as the yield curve for the actuals. Once you learn that, you will have the beginnings of a standard of value. The standard of value then becomes the means of identifying profit opportunities.

206

20

Some Practical
Hedging Applications
for Financial Futures

The preceding chapters on financial futures contain most of the basics you need to start understanding how financial futures markets work. Examples in those chapters also give you a general idea of how those markets can be used for hedging. This chapter provides a slight elaboration of some of the more practical applications of hedging, which will aid the interested reader in exploring these concepts further and in devising new means of application.

Dollar Equivalency Maturing Adjustment

As noted earlier, the value of a one-point move (1/100 of 1%) in the yield of a T-bill futures contract is $25. This is derived from the fact that T-bill futures represent a 90-day maturity. A one-year T-bill will have an equivalent value of $100 for each .01% movement in yield. Thus, the following value relationships hold:

$$.01\% \text{ for } 90 \text{ days} - \$25$$
$$.01\% \text{ for } 180 \text{ days} - \$50$$
$$.01\% \text{ for } 240 \text{ days} - \$75$$
$$.01\% \text{ for } 360 \text{ days} - \$100$$

The value of .01% over time becomes very important in hedging. For example, if you were trying to hedge a six-month loan by using 90-day T-bill futures, you would need to use twice as many futures contracts to get the equivalent movement in value between the cash position and the futures position. Each .01% movement in yield in the cash position would be worth $50 while each .01% movement in the futures position would be worth only $25.

Hedging the Funding of Loans Tied to the Prime Rate

During the first quarter of 1980, many banks issued six-month CD's to obtain funds to lend at a prime rate of 20%. By May of 1980, the prime rate had fallen to 14%, but the CD's still had several months to run. The profitability of these loans was reduced dramatically and remained that way until the CD's matured and new money could be obtained at the lower rates. A banker caught in such a profit squeeze could have protected his profit margin by hedging — by buying 90-day T-bill futures. As the prime rate falls, so should rates on 90-day T-bills because the two rates are correlated fairly closely (see table). In such a hedge, a long position in futures will yield a profit which can be used to offset the loss in loan income. As the cost of funding the loan comes in line with the prime rate, lift the hedge.

Correlation matrix **(Monday closing prices, Jan. 1, 1978 to May 23, 1980)**	
T-Bill Futures (nearby) vs. Prime Rate	88.5
T-Bill Futures (nearby) vs. Fed Funds (overnight)	94.4
GNMA Futures (nearby) vs. 10-year bonds	98.6
T-Bill Futures (4th month) vs. 2-year Government Notes	92.5

Hedging the Fed Funds Rate

Sometimes a regional bank has excess Fed Funds, so it sells them on a regular basis. When the Fed Funds rate is high, such sales can be a nice source of income. When Fed Funds rates fall, however, revenues fall. A bank can protect against this loss of income by buying T-bill futures. As rates fall, income from futures helps offset the loss of income from Fed Funds. Again, this hedge has a reasonable chance of success because the correlation between 90-day T-bill rates and the Fed Funds rate is quite high (see table).

208

Pre-Refunding or "Unlocking" a Portfolio

Suppose a bank has a liquidity portfolio with maturities in September and December. Assume it expects rates to be lower in those months than the rates currently reflected in futures. To protect against that fall in rates, the bank could follow several alternative courses.

If the bank has excess cash today, it could purchase replacement securities now for the securities maturing in September and December. It probably would not swap the securities in its current portfolio because it would have to reflect the loss on its financial statements. Such a loss would not have to be booked if the securities are kept to maturity when they will be redeemed at par.

Corporation Hedging Sinking Fund Obligations

Assume a corporation must purchase $5 million of its 8% bonds (six years to maturity) by Sept. 1 to fulfill a sinking fund obligation. The treasurer of the corporation believes there is at least an 80% probability that interest rates will be 1% point lower than current rates by September but does not have the cash available to buy the bonds at this time. That 1% fall on a six-year maturity would increase the costs to the fund manager by approximately $210,000.

He can hedge by purchasing 50 contracts of the 4 - 6-year Treasury note contract.

If rates indeed to decline by 1% AND if that 1% decline is reflected fully in T-note futures, then the manager will have an approximate profit of $210,000 in futures to offset the increased cost of his sinking fund bonds.

His transaction costs will include:

Commission on futures	$ 3,500
Interest lost on margin posted	$ 7,000
Total	$10,500

Bank Issuing CDs

Now, assume that on Friday, Oct. 5, 1979, a regional bank economic forecasting group concluded interest rates were headed sharply higher with a real possibility that the Fed might sharply tighten monetary policy. Assume that bank also was getting ready to issue $50 million in CD's but didn't have them issued yet.

How could the bank protect itself against the possibility that rates might rise before it got the CD's sold?

The answer is to hedge by selling T-bill futures. Here is how the hedge would have worked out:

Cash Market	Basis	Futures
Oct. 5, 1979		
Long $50 million CD's due April 1980		Sell $100 million March 1980 T-bill futures
12.80	2.61	10.19
Oct. 12, 1979		
$50 million CD's due April 1980		$100 million March 1980 T-bill futures
13.80	2.93	10.87
−1.00	−.32	+.68

Each basis point for futures = $25 × 68 × 100 = $170,000
Each basis point for CD's = $50 × 100 × 50 = $250,000
$ 80,000

Loss reduced from $250,000 to $80,000

Note: As the CD's are issued, the futures position should be liquidated proportionately.

This example teaches you several important points:

1. **The basis changed.** Rates in the cash position increased by more than rates in the futures market. Hence, gains and losses did not offset each other exactly. This emphasizes the importance of knowing the basis.

2. **This was a cross hedge.** The product being hedged in the cash market was not identical to the items represented in the futures contract. That is a major reason why the basis changed.

3. **Because the maturity of the cash item was different from the maturity of the futures instrument,** a .01 change in the rate for the two instruments was not equal. The value of .01 for the

210

90-day T-bill futures was $25. The value of .01 for the six-month CD was $50. Hence, to get "dollar equivalent" coverage, it was necessary that the futures position be double that of the cash position.

21

Commodity Options

The history of commodity trading in the U.S. is replete with stories of intrigue and conflict, of great fortunes gained and lost. None of the stories are more engrossing than those involving commodity options trading.

Commodity options trading has been conducted in this country on an intermittent basis since the early 1860's. At that time the Chicago Board of Trade passed a rule prohibiting its members from trading options. A few years later with a new Board of Governors the rules were changed again, this time permitting members to trade options. Throughout the rest of the 19th century, trading options on the CBT was a sometime thing as battles raged between the pro-options traders and anti-options people. They fought through the legislature, in the courts, in the board rooms and with other exchanges.

In 1936 it was charged that options played a role in a particularly blatant — and successful — attempt to manipulate the grain markets on the CBT. Congress held hearings on the matter and subsequently passed the Commodity Exchange Act, which barred all trading in options on commodities under the regulation of the Commodity Exchange Authority.

In 1974 during hearings to revise the Commodity Exchange Act, Congress once again addressed the question and at first seemed to lean toward extending the ban to all commodities. Ultimately, however, after a good deal of testimony extolling the economic virtues of commodity options, Congress decided to review the ban on options for all previously regulated agricultural commodities while leaving a decision on other commodities up to the discretion of the Commodity Futures Trading Commission.

That commission, after a good deal of study and debate, has decided to allow commodity options on futures and on physicals to be traded on organized exchanges in the U.S. for an initial test period. This pilot program, which began in 1982, is to provide a means by which the commercial usefulness of options and their impact on the underlying futures and cash prices can be studied. No matter which form (futures or physicals) the options trading takes, the basic principles outlined in this chapter are applicable. (For options currently authorized for trading, see Trading Facts and Figures at end of book.)

London Options

Commodity options have been traded in London for many years. The metal options market was particularly active prior to World War II. Since the early 1970's the markets have enjoyed a very strong growth, some of which was the result of efforts in the U.S. to sell London options to the man-on-the-street. Some of the firms selling London options were less than scrupulous, selling such options at extremely high mark-ups and charging exorbitant service fees.

Under the new CFTC regulations London options will continue to be sold in the U.S. but only by registered vendors operating under strict regulations. Before you get involved in London options consider carefully the points discussed later in this chapter under the section "Picking an Option Broker."

The Language

Although options may be written on actual commodities or on futures contracts, this section will focus on options on futures contracts. Trading strategies and concepts are basically the same, however.

Options trading has its own terminology, which is considerably different from that of futures trading. For example, a "call option" is an obligation of the grantor (seller) to provide a long futures position to the grantee (buyer) at a pre-determined price on or before the exercise date of the option contract, if and when the buyer chooses to exercise his right. Thus, a call option is a right to buy. It establishes a buying price for the buyer of the call.

A "put" option is an obligation of the grantor (seller) to provide a short futures position to the grantee (buyer) at a pre-determined price on or before the exercise date of the option contract, if and when the grantee chooses to exercise his right. Thus, a put option is a right to sell. It establishes a selling price for the buyer of the put.

A "double" option allows the purchaser the right to acquire *either* (not both) a long or short futures position at a specified price on or before a specified date if and when he chooses to exercise his right.

The "striking price" is the pre-determined price at which the futures position is transferred from the seller to the buyer if the option is exercised.

The term "exercise" refers to the buyer's decision to require the seller to fulfill the terms of the contract. If a call option is exercised, the option seller must provide to the buyer an underlying futures position at the striking price specified. When a put option on a futures contract is exercised, the seller of the option must provide a short futures position at the striking price specified.

The "premium" is the amount of money paid by the buyer of an option to the seller for the right to exercise the option at the striking price. The seller receives the premium regardless of whether or not the option is actually exercised. That is one-time payment to the seller. Irrespective of what happens to price, there are no further payments by the buyer unless he exercises.

The "exercise date" or "expiration date" is the last day on which the buyer of an option must decide whether to exercise or to abandon his right to exercise the option.

An option is said to be "at-the-money" if its strike price is equal (or approximately equal) to the current market price of the under-lying futures contract.

A call is said to be "in-the-money" if its strike price is below the current price of the underlying futures contract (i.e., if the option has intrinsic value). A put is "in-the-money" if its strike price is above the current price of the underlying futures contract (i.e., if the option has intrinsic value).

An "out-of-the-money" option is a put or call option which currently has no intrinsic value. That is, a call whose strike price is above the current futures price or a put whose strike price is below the current futures price.

The "intrinsic value" of an option is the dollar amount that could be realized if the option were to be currently exercised. (See "in-the-money.")

An option "margin" is the sum of money which must be deposited — and maintained — in order to provide protection to both parties to a trade. The exchange establishes minimum margin amounts. Brokerage firms often require margin deposits that exceed exchange minimums. In turn, they post and maintain customer margin with the clearing corporation. Buyers of options do not have to post margin since their risk is limited to the option premium.

"Margin calls" are additional funds which a person with a futures position or the writer of an option may be called upon to deposit if there is an adverse price change or if margin requirements are increased. Buyers of options are not subject to margin calls.

"Naked writing" of an option refers to writing a call or a put on a futures contract in which the writer has no opposite cash or futures market position. This is also known as uncovered writing.

An option "series" refers to all options of the same class having the same strike price and expiration date.

An option "spread" refers to a position consisting of both long and short options of the same class, such as having a long position in a call with one strike price and expiration and a short position in another call with a different strike price and/or expiration.

An option "straddle" is a combination in which the put and the call have the same strike price and the same expiration.

The "time value" of an option is the amount by which an option premium exceeds the option's intrinsic value. If an option has no intrinsic value, its premium is entirely time value.

The "writing" of an option refers to the sale of an option in an opening transaction.

Option vs. Futures

There are some important differences between an options

contract and a futures contract. A futures contract is a bilateral contract requiring action by both parties and obligating both the buyer and the seller to fulfill the conditions by delivery and payment. An option contract, on the other hand, is a unilateral contract. Unlike a futures contract, the buyer and the seller of the option do not have an equivalent obligation to perform. The purchaser of an option has the right but not the obligation to require the seller to perform under the contract, and the seller is obligated to do so only if the buyer exercises his right. The converse, however, is not true. The seller of an option cannot require the purchaser to exercise. Only the buyer has the right to require fulfillment of the contract terms.

Perhaps the most distinguishing feature of an option contract is the limited liability of the purchaser. The potential loss to an option purchaser is limited to the "premium" which he pays to the seller at the time of the purchase of the option. His potential for gain, theoretically, is limited only by the extent of the price movement of the underlying contract. In contrast, on the futures contract the holder of either a long or a short futures positions remains liable to margin calls as long as his position remains open.

In short, therefore, the purchaser of an option contract can lose at a maximum only the amount he pays for the option. This is so because, if the price does not move in his favor, he fails to "exercise" his option. Instead, he simply abandons it. An analogy can be drawn with an insurance contract. The writer of the insurance policy receives the premium for undertaking the risk but has to stand ready in the future to make any payments due the person who bought the insurance if that person submits a valid claim. If he does not submit the claim, the insurance company still keeps the premium.

One major advantage of options over futures markets for the businessman is that, when prices are extremely volatile, options can reduce the demands on cash flow. For example, if you have purchased a futures contract and it declines, you will have to pay in more margin, which, of course, must be paid in cash. If, on the other hand, you have purchased a call option, you will have a one-time payment; no matter how far price falls, you will not be asked to post more money. The converse of this is, of course, also true. If prices go up, the futures position will yield cash to you while no such thing will happen with the option. Options thus provide more certainty in planning cash flow exposure.

Options permit a range of investment and resource management strategies not available from futures. Options used in conjunction with futures and actual inventories of a product afford a wide range of strategies for a merchandiser, producer or processor in managing inventories. They can provide greater control with lower capital requirements than do futures alone.

To a large extent options are substitutes for stop orders on futures. You can attempt to limit your risk on a futures position by placing a stop loss order at whatever level you choose. Then, if the market touches that level, your broker would automatically offset the futures contract at the price stipulated or at the next best possible price.

In essence, the purchase of an option serves the same purpose as the stop loss order serves in the futures contract. They are both there to limit losses. The difference between the two, however, is:

1. A stop loss order may not always be exercised at the price stipulated so the loss cannot be absolutely fixed in advance. The size of the option premium, however, is fixed in advance, and the loss cannot exceed the size of the premium.

2. A poorly disciplined trader may decide not to use stop loss orders and to meet margin calls when he should not, thus sticking with a losing position in the hope that the market will reverse. This can lead to very large losses. An option, on the other hand, does not give that discretion to the holder. Once he buys the option, the marketplace decides whether it will be profitable to exercise it. The holder has no more decisions to make if the market moves against him or fails to rise to the exercise price.

3. One can get whipsawed in a market using stop loss orders. The market can set off a stop order, causing the offset of the futures contract, and then the market could turn around and go the opposite direction. Due to the offset, you would be without a position in the market and unable to take advantage of the rise.

In sum, the option is a more certain way of limiting losses. The value of this certainly has to be weighed against the size of the premium paid. It may be a very high price to pay for the luxury of not having to exercise the self-discipline in using stop loss orders or for the potential that you will get whipsawed.

Other differences between options and futures will become apparent as you read some of the strategies for trading options discussed in the next chapter.

Picking an Option Broker

An earlier section discussed selecting a broker for futures transactions. Chances are you will find that your futures broker also handles commodity options transactions for U.S. exchanges. In a few instances he may also handle London options.

Picking your option broker should be done with care. Shop around and find out:
1. What kind of services the firm offers and what kind of commission they charge for those services.
2. How much experience the broker has had in trading options and what is his track record.
3. Whether the broker is registered with the Commodity Futures Trading Commission and whether he is a member of any professional options organization or an exchange. If so, you can contact them for further information about the firm; e.g., is the firm in good standing? Are there any public records of past disciplinary action?

After you have picked your broker and before you decide to enter into any particular option transaction, check out the following:
1. What kind of contract is it? Is it a U.S. or a foreign option, and is it an exchange traded or a dealer option? The difference here can be substantial. A U.S. option is more easily monitored, and all parties to it are under the regulation and scrutiny of the Commodity Futures Trading Commission. An exchange option has a ready secondary market in contrast to most dealer options and, therefore, your option position can be easily offset. In addition, exchange traded options are standardized contracts with information readily and easily available about the underlying commodity.
2. Who guarantees the transaction, and what is the financial solvency of that party? In some instances the guarantor will be an exchange clearinghouse. If it is a U.S. exchange, the

federal government is monitoring the exchange's, the broker's and the clearinghouse's financial condition. That does not mean, of course, they couldn't still go bankrupt. If it is a foreign exchange, find out how the guarantee works and exactly how your account will be settled if there is a bankruptcy. The same care should be taken with an independent option dealer who is selling non-exchange options.

3. How much does the premium represent as a percentage of the value of the underlying commodity or futures contract?

4. The break-even point for your option. That is, how much will the price have to change before the option will become profitable?

5. How the option premium, if you are buying, will be passed to the seller and, if you are a seller, under what conditions you will receive the premium.

6. How much the premium is being marked up over what it cost at the time of origination. This is particularly important if you are not buying it directly on an exchange, such as would be the case with foreign options and dealer options.

7. How much commission you are paying and what services you are getting for the commission.

8. What research people in that firm, as well as other firms, are indicating the future prices of the underlying commodity will be. Remember, the premium represents the expected value of the expected volatility of prices. If most people expect very little price change, premiums should be quite low.

9. How you exercise your option and what you get when you exercise. Study the terms and conditions of the contract.

10. When and how your broker will notify you of the execution of your contract and the current status of your account.

11. Where to get regular information about the value of your option and the price of the underlying commodity.

In short, know as much about your broker as you do about your business partner and only deal with someone you know, trust and are comfortable with. He is using your money. Pick a professional who knows the business.

Other differences between options and futures will become apparent as you read some of the strategies for trading options discussed in the next chapter.

22

Strategies For Trading Options

The trading applications of options are numerous, and motives for buying and selling options are as varied as they are for trading commodity futures contracts. It is claimed, however, that in addition to the limited risk advantages options offer to speculators, they also perform certain economic functions and can be used for hedging purposes.

The potential for commodity options contracts to serve as a risk-shifting medium for individuals and firms dealing in a cash commodity is somewhat analogous to hedging in futures markets. A call option, by providing its buyer the right to acquire a commodity or futures contract at a fixed price, can provide price protection to a person who has a short position in the cash market, e.g., signed a contract to deliver a product. Buying a put option can also provide the same manner of price protection to its puchaser as can a short futures position. Both of them establish a sale price. In contrast to futures, however, options contracts provide price protection only to purchasers because only purchasers have the right to exercise an option. Sellers of options have a firm price for their product only if the buyer exercises, but they cannot require a buyer to exercise. Thus, the risk transfer is not as complete or as symmetrical in options as it is in futures.

Using Options in Business

Following are some examples of how the options market might be used for hedging. Concepts apply equally well to options on "actuals" or options on futures.

Purchasing a Put to Protect Profit Margin

Suppose a producer or processor of raw materials — a sugar refiner, a mine operator or an animal feed manufacturer — wishes to secure a manufacturing margin by selling his product forward but wants the right to cancel the deal should prices rise. He can achieve this by purchasing a put option for a forward delivery date. In the event that prices fall, he would exercise his option and, thus, have a secured sales contract. (If it is an option on a futures contract, he will have a short futures position which he can deliver upon or offset as a normal hedge. If it is an option on the actual product, he will deliver the product to the seller of the option.) But if prices rise, he could abandon the option and sell his product (either physically or through a futures hedge) at the higher level ruling in the market. The cost of this choice would be the option premium.

Buying a Call to Protect a Price

Exactly the reverse of this example would apply to someone who processes raw material and needs to buy those materials forward for delivery at a future date. The use of a call option to secure the purchases allows him the choice of abandoning the option of prices decline or of exercising his option if prices rise.

Buying a Put to Protect a Contingent Risk

Suppose a firm were preparing to make a sealed bid to buy large quantities of a product but wouldn't know for some time (perhaps weeks) whether its bid had been accepted or for how much. In such a situation the firm could buy a put on the product. If, in the interim between the submission of the bid and the acceptance of it, prices fall and the firm is awarded the winning bid, it will be able to exercise the put at the higher price, thus obtaining a sale price at the higher level and buying the needed supply at the new lower price. If, on the other hand, prices should rise and it should receive either no part of the bid or a partial fulfillment of it, the put can be abandoned and the product sold in the open market at the higher prices. In this latter instance the firm will have lost the premium paid for the put but will have gained protection from a price fall during the interim.

This same concept would be applied to any firm which sells largely by catalog or by direct mail. In such a situation, the pricing on the final product must frequently be done long in advance of manufacture and of shipment. If raw material costs change substantially during that time, profit margins can be adversely affected. Buying a call option on the raw material in such a situation provides protection against such dramatic price increases. If prices do increase, the firm can exercise the call at the lower price. If they fall, the call can be abandoned.

Buying a Call to Protect a Short Position

One further example. Suppose a merchant sold a quantity of sugar for deferred delivery to a food processor at a fixed price, but the merchant had not yet acquired sufficient sugar to cover the sale. He faces the risk that sugar prices may rise before he can make necessary purchases. Although he could hedge this risk with a long futures position, the merchant may be reluctant to lock in his profit margin in that manner because he suspects that sugar prices are more likely to fall than to rise, in which case he would have to meet margin calls. By purchasing call options rather than futures, the merchant can protect his short cash position, at the additional cost of the option premium, while still reserving the opportunity to take advantage of lower sugar prices should his expectations materialize.

Writing a Call Against Inventory

A holder of an inventory, such as a producer or a manufacturer, may use the options market to generate income on inventory by *selling a call* option on that inventory, thus giving the buyer the option to purchase the inventory. If the option is abandoned by the buyer because the price falls, the seller will still carry the inventory but his net cost of carry and ownership will be reduced because he has received the option premium and interest on it. This is a form of price speculation, and any businessman undertaking it should so realize. If prices rise and the option is exercised, then the seller must deliver the physical goods against the contract. This, of course, is an attractive procedure only if, at the time the option is sold, the striking price of the option is higher than the spot price, since the option seller obtains this differential together with the option premium and interest.

In short, options provide a businessman:

1. More flexibility in strategy than do futures contracts alone.
2. More certainty in planning cash exposure than do futures.
3. More control over the decision-making environment. This is particularly true when buying options because only the buyer may determine when and whether to exercise. Options allow the buyer to buy time during which he can wait for the future to be revealed. If the future turns out to his advantage, he exercises the option. If not, he abandons it, suffers the loss of at least part of his premium and makes his transaction through another channel.

Strategies for Speculating in Options

In general, the trading of options is a complex topic. Whole books have been written on the subject. All that can be done here is to introduce you to the topic and language to make you aware of some of the rich variety of ways in which options can be a part of your investment strategy.

If you expect prices to go up, you should buy a call or sell a put. If you expect prices to go down, you should buy a put or sell a call. Those two rules of thumb seem simple enough. But beware! If you sell a put expecting prices to go up but they actually go down, you run the risk that the put will be exercised. You do not have that risk buying a call. The same thing is true if you sell a call expecting prices to fall. If they go up, you have the risk of being called to fulfill your contractual obligations.

Buying a Gold Call

A call gives the purchaser the right to obtain a long position in the underlying futures contract. Hence, if you expect prices to rise, you would purchase a call, giving you the right to buy a futures contract at the strike price stated at any time before the call expires.

Suppose on Sept. 1 that December gold futures are trading at

$470 per ounce and that, after careful analysis of the market, you come to expect December gold to trade above the $500 per ounce level. There are two ways to take advantage of this expectation: (1) You can buy a futures contract for delivery in December. That will cost you approximately $2,000 in margin plus a $45 commission. If the price falls to $450 per ounce, you will have lost your entire $2,000 margin plus your $45 commission. If, on the other hand, the price does rise to the $500 level, you will have made $3,000 minus commission.

(2) An alternative to buying the December futures contract would have been to buy a call option on the December futures. Suppose you could purchase, for $20 per ounce ($2,000 − 100 ounces per contract × $20) a call option with the strike price of $470. You would then be potentially long one December futures contract at $470 with a break-even point of $490 ($470 + $20).[1] Now if the price rises to the $500 level, the option will be worth $1,500. If it is a tradeable option, you can sell (offset) the option to obtain the $2,000 profit. Or you can "exercise" (notify the person from whom the call was purchased that you wish to buy the December futures at $470 per ounce). You can sell the futures acquired by exercise and accept your profit of $30 per ounce ($1,000) on the transaction. If the price fails to rise to the $470 level, you will simply be out the amount of your premium, $1,000, plus commissions. If it rises to $475, the value of the option will fall to $500 and you will suffer a $1,500 loss.

The maximum loss to the call buyer can never exceed the premium cost — in this instance, $2,000. That maximum loss will occur only if the option is not exercised, which would happen if the market does not move above the $470 level. If the market does move above the $470 strike price but does not reach the $490 level before the expiration date, it is best to offset or exercise because the size of the loss decreases as the price rises to the break-even point. As the price rises above the break-even point, the option becomes profitable, and the profit increases as the price continues to advance.

---

[1] Some options are sold with a strike price equal to the immediate price of the future. This is true for most London options. Thus, the breakeven point is closer to the current price than would be true in the above example. In either event the breakeven point is still calculated by adding the premium and commission costs to the strike price.

Hedging a Profitable Call Option

As noted above, the major advantage is trading options is the unlimited opportunity it provides for gains with a fixed risk of loss. Another distinct advantage offered by options is the flexibility they provide for trading futures and options against each other at the same time. For example, if a taker has a profitable option position, he can "trade against it" (take an opposite position in the futures — the same as "hedge it"), thus opening many more possible opportunities for profit than simply through the exercise of the option. The following examples show how this can be done.

Hedging a Profitable Call By Selling a Future

Assume that on Oct. 15 the December futures contract advances to the $500 level. As a buyer, you can take advantage of this advance and "lock in" your profit on the option without exercise by selling a December futures contract at the $500 level. In effect, you hedge your option position. Now, if futures fall back to $460, the option will be "out of the money" (below the $470 strike price), but you will have a $40 gain on your short futures positions. You will realize the same profit as if you had exercised at $500 and then immediately offset.

The advantage of this technique over an immediate exercise on Oct. 15 when it reaches $500 is that the option is kept "alive" until the declaration date, thus providing you the opportunity to trade against it at a later time.

If, indeed, the market moves lower (say to the $470 level), the short futures contract can be covered by the purchase of a futures contract. This transaction will generate a profit on the futures side (remember that you went short the futures at the $500 level and bought it back at $470) and leave the original option position unchanged. Now, if the price goes back up (say to the $495 level) so that on the declaration date the market is above the striking price, the call can be exercised at a profit. Thus, you have made a profit on your option and also on your trade against the option. If on the declaration date the market is below the original striking price, the option would be abandoned, causing a loss of the premium. That loss, of course, would be offset by the profit made on trading against the option.

226

Hedging a Profitable Call By Buying a Put

Earlier, it was shown that you could "hedge" a profitable call by selling a futures against it. Another way to hedge a profitable call option is with the purchase of a put option. The maximum price for this protection is the premium on the put plus commissions. If the market does subsequently drop, the put can be profitably exercised. Even more importantly, if the market continues to rise, the maximum loss on the put is still only the premium plus commissions and the profit on the call will continue to accrue.

Note that when you hedge a profitable call position through the sale of a futures contract, you give up all potential benefits which might accrue from a continuation of a price rise and, in addition, you have to meet margin calls. Not so when you hedge with the purchase of a put. The other side of this coin, however, is that the cost of a futures hedge is usually far cheaper than the cost of the premium for the put option.

What happens to the call option if, on the declaration date, the futures contract is trading at a price higher than the striking price but below the breakeven mark. In such a case, it will always benefit the option holder to offset or to exercise the option even if the premium is not fully covered. In the above example, if December gold is trading at $475 on the declaration date, the call should be offset or exercised. Even though a net profit will not result, the cash thus generated will help reduce the total loss on the option. In this instance, had the call been abandoned, the loss would have been $20 per ounce. However, by exercising or offsetting it, the loss is only $15 per ounce.

Using the Futures to Convert a Call to a Put

If you sell a futures position short against the purchase of a call, it has the effect of converting the call to a put. (The opposite is also true. Buying a futures against the sale of a put has the same effect as buying a call.) Remember, a put gives the purchaser the right to sell the product at a later date at a price determined today. Thus, he has unlimited (down to zero price) potential for gain if prices fall and limited risk if prices rise.

Using the futures to convert a call into the equivalent of a put works like this. Assume that you buy a call for $20 with a strike price of $470 per ounce and that later you sell a futures at $490 per ounce. At that point you have a position equivalent to the purchase of a put; i.e., if prices rise, your call option position will become more valuable at the same time your short futures position becomes less valuable. They will offset each other, and you will have given up your premium. In effect, the financial result will be the same as it would have been if you had bought a put. If, on the other hand, prices fall, you will have a loss on the option position and a gain on the futures position — the same as if you owned a put. To the extent the price fall exceeds the cost of the call option, you will have a net profit on the transaction. The breakeven point, minus commission, will be $470, the same as if you had bought a put for $20 per ounce and a strike price of $490. The cost of the "put" is the premium for the call option plus interest on margins and commissions on the futures and the options.

Options on Financial Futures

Among the newcomers to the options scene are financial futures such as interest rates, stock indexes and foreign currencies. To further illustrate the rich variety of strategies available, this section focuses on options strategies for long-term U.S. Treasury Bond futures. These same strategies can be applied to currencies and stock indexes.

Rising Interest Rates — Declining Bond Prices

a. Buy put options.
Assume you are anticipating an increase in long-term interest rates and a corresponding decrease in futures price. To take advantage of your expectations, you could buy a put option on U.S. Treasury Bond futures. Assume you buy a March 76 put at a premium cost of $2,000, reflecting an interest rate on long-term bonds of about 11%. If, by expiration in March, the interest rate has increased to 12%, the futures price will have decreased to 70-00 and you should be able to sell the option at a difference in value of $6,000. Your profit on this transaction will be $4,000 ($6,000 less your $2,000 premium) minus transaction costs.

If, by the time March rolled around, interest rates had decreased to approximately 10.5%, the contract would be selling for about 79-00 and your put option with a strike price of 76-00 would expire worthless. You would have lost the entire $2,000 paid for the option.

In many cases, you might decide not to wait until expiration to close out your position. If, in the above example, interest rates started falling with expiration a month or so away, you might have decided to sell the option before it reached a value of zero. By selling the option at $500, for example, you would reduce your loss to only $1,500 ($2,000 premium minus $500) plus the transaction costs.

b. Sell futures and buy call options.

By selling a futures contract you can profit from any increase in long-term interest rates because as interest rates go up, U.S. Treasury Bond prices decline. The purchase of a call option in conjunction with a short futures position, makes it possible to limit the otherwise unlimited risk involved in selling futures contracts. In effect, the call option provides insurance against major loss.

For example, suppose you were expecting higher interest rates, and you sold a September U.S. Treasury Bond futures contract at the strike price of 70-00. At the same time, to protect yourself against major losses which could result if futures prices rise, you might decide to pay a $2,000 premium for the purchase of a September 70 call option. The most that you can now lose if futures prices rise instead of fall is the $2,000 cost of the call option. Shown below is a summary of how this transaction could turn out under various scenarios.

Scenario Summary of
Sell Futures - Buy Call Option

Sell Sept. T-Bond Futures @	70-00
Buy Sept. 70 T-Bond Futures Call @	$2,000

P or L at Expiration

Futures rise to 76-00

Buy Futures @ 76-00	$6,000 Loss
Sell Call @ 76-00	$4,000 Gain
	$2,000 Net Loss

Futures do not change

    Buy Futures @ 70-00   No Gain - No Loss
    Sell Call @ 0 $2,000 Loss
                                    $2,000 Net Loss

Futures fall to 68-00

    Buy Futures @ 68-00 $2,000 Gain
    Sell Call @ 0 $2,000 Loss
                                       0   Net

Futures fall to 62-00

    Buy Futures @ 62-00 $8,000 Gain
    Sell Call @ 0 $2,000 Loss
                                    $6,000 Net Gain

A major advantage of this strategy is the "staying power" it can provide. That is, these two transactions provide the ability to maintain a futures position despite adverse short-term price movements. One survives in order to maintain the potential that the position may still eventually become profitable.

In the absence of the protection provided by the call, you might be faced with a large margin call on your futures position. If such a margin requirement can't be met, you would be forced to liquidate the futures position at a loss. The call protects against that because, as the futures position loses value, the call increases in value. The call acts as a hedge against major losses.

c. A "bear" put spread.

If you expect rising interest rates and, therefore, declining bond prices, you could profit by purchasing a put option with a high strike price and selling or writing a put option with a high strike price and selling or writing a put option with a new low strike price. The maximum net profit is the difference in the strike prices less the net cost of the two options. The maximum loss is the net cost of the two options.

For example, suppose in June you expect rising interest rates through the month of September. Assume the September futures price is at 66-00. To profit from your expectations, let's say you buy a September 66 put for a premium of $2,000, and you sell a September 60 put and collect a premium of $400. Your net premium is $1,600.

If the futures price in September turns out to be 60-00 or lower, your profits will be the difference between the strike price of the options ($6,000 less the net premium cost of the two options), $1,600. The net profit will be $4,400. If, on the other hand, futures prices at expiration are 66-00 or above, both options will expire worthless and you will suffer your maximum loss of $1,600.

Summary of Option Strategies Under Various Price Scenarios

As is obvious from the foregoing, the number and variety of trading techniques that can be employed using options and futures, singly or in combination, is large. In general, you can now tailor a limited-risk trading strategy to almost any price trend (or non-trend) scenario that could occur. The table below has been compiled to help the reader better understand the variety of strategies available, and the situation in which they should be used. These strategies apply to price situations in all commodities, including stock index options and futures.

Summary of Option Strategies Under Various Price Scenarios

Interest Rate and Bond Price Expectation	Possible Strategy	Interest Rate and Bond Price Expectation	Possible Strategy
Declining Prices	Buy Put Options	Rising Prices	Buy Call Options
Declining Prices	Sell Futures and Buy Call Options	Rising Prices	Buy Futures and Buy Put Options
Declining Prices	A "Bear" Call Spread	Rising Prices	A "Bull" Call Spread
Declining Prices	A "Bear" Put Spread	Rising Prices	A "Bull" Put Spread

Steady to Slightly Lower Prices	Sell Futures and Write Put Options	Steady to Slightly Higher Prices	Buy Futures and Write Call Options
Steady to Slightly Lower Prices	Write Call Options	Steady to Slightly Higher Prices	Write Put Options
Relatively Flat Prices	A "Neutral" Calendar Spread	Prices will be highly volatile, could change in either direction	Buy a Put-Call Straddle
Relatively Flat Prices	Write a Put-Call Straddle		

NOTE: Interest Rates and Bonds, T-Bills, GNMAs, etc. move in opposite directions. So the above strategies for rising prices (falling prices) should be considered when interest rates are expected to fall (to rise).

Declining Interest Rates — Rising Bond Prices

a. Buy-call options

If you anticipate a decrease in long-term interest rates, your strategy should be to purchase call options on U.S. Treasury Bond futures. A call option, as noted above, gives you, the buyer, the right to buy the underlying futures contract at the specified strike price. You will realize a profit if the intrinsic value of the option at expiration is greater than the premium you paid for the option. For example, if it is now June and you expect interest rates to be lower in September, assume you pay a $2,000 premium to buy a September 70 call option reflecting an interest rate of about 12%. If, when September rolls around, the interest rate has declined to around 11%, the futures price should have increased to approximately 76-00. You should then be able to sell the call option at its intrinsic value of $6,000. Your profit would be $4,000 less the transaction costs.

Suppose, however, that when September arrives, the futures price was 70-00 or above. In that case your call would expire worthless and you would lose your entire $2,000. If, on the other hand, the futures price is at 72, your call would be worth the same price you paid for it. If the futures price has increased to 80-00, your call should be valued at 10-00, an $8,000 profit.

b. A "bull" call spread.

Perhaps a more conservative approach to a situation where you expect interest rates to decline and bond prices to rise would be one known as a vertical bull spread. With such a strategy, you would know in advance the exact maximum net profit you could possibly make, and the exact maximum net loss possible on the transaction.

Like all bull spreads, bull call spreads (meaning the investor is bullish on bond prices) involves buying one option and writing or selling another option. In this case, you would buy a call option with a low strike price and sell a call option with a high strike price.

Your maximum net loss potential is the net premium cost that is the difference between the premium you pay for the call you buy and the premium you receive for the call you sell.

The maximum net profit you can make in this transaction is the difference between the strike prices of the two options less the net premium cost.

For example, suppose in March you expect lower interest rates and higher bond prices, and you find that the June futures price is trading at 66-00. Suppose, further, you buy a June 66 call at a premium of $2,000 and sell a June 72 call at a premium of $500. The maximum net profit would be $4,500, the strike price difference of $6,000 less the net premium cost of $1,500, and your maximum net loss would be $1,500, the net premium cost. In order to realize maximum profit, the futures price at expiration must be equal to or above the strike price of the option written, in this case 72-00. If it isn't, the investor's resulting profit or loss will depend on whether the value of the purchase option at expiration is more or less than the premium cost.

What Option to Trade?

An important decision for an investor selecting among option

Scenario Summary
Bull Spread - Call Options

	Paid	Received
Buy June 66-00 call	$2,000	
Sell June 72-00 call		$500
Net premium	$1,500	

P or L Summary

Futures at 72-00

Sell June 66 call	+$6,000 Gain
Buy June 72 call	0
Net Premium Cost	−$1,500
	$4,500 Net Gain

Futures at 66-00

Sell June 66 call	0
Buy June 72 call	0
Net Premium Cost	$1,500
	$1,500 Net Loss

Futures at 60-00

Sell June 66 call	0
Buy June 72 call	0
Net Premium Cost	$1,500
	$1,500 Net Loss

Futures at 69-00

Sell June 66 call	$3,000
Buy June 72 call	0
Net Premium Cost	$1,500
	$1,500 Net Gain

---

strike prices and maturity dates is the determination of which option to select. Which is preferable: an option with a short period of time until expiration or an option with a long period of time until expiration? An option with a high strike price (an in-the-money option) or an option with a lower strike price (an out-of-the-money option)?

Generally, the premium costs will be higher the longer the time remaining until expiration. Such an option provides the buyer more time for his price expectations to be realized and, thus, a greater likelihood of his actually earning a profit. Generally, the longer time remaining until expiration, the lower the cost of each additional time unit. That is, a six-month option usually does not cost twice as much as a three-month option.

Decisions about purchasing an at-the-money or an out-of-the-money option are equally important. The option premium is usually higher for an at-the-money option than for an out-of-the-money option. An at-the-money option stands a greater chance of yielding a profit. However, an out-of-the-money option usually costs less to buy or to exercise, and involves a smaller potential loss, but also, a smaller potential profit.

Determining the Option Premium

It should be implicit in the foregoing that one needs to evaluate very carefully the factors that affect the value of the option premium. These include:
1. The current price level of the underlying commodity relative to the strike price of the option.
2. The length of time the option has left before it expires. The longer the life of the option, the more time you are buying and the greater time there is for the market to reach the strike price.
3. The volatility of the price for the underlying commodity. The more volatile the price, the greater chance that the market will reach the strike price within a given time period.
4. The expectations generally held that the commodity price will rise above the strike price. This is related to each of the three preceding elements.
5. Interest rates — higher interest rates generally mean higher premiums.

When trading options, it is wise to keep in mind some fundamental principles with respect to price behavior.
1. The value of the option is directly related to the expected volatility of the market and the probability that a particular price level will be reached during a given time period.
2. When trading options on futures, examine closely the price structure (relationships) between futures months. If the more distant months are at a higher price than the nearby months, a buyer of a put has, everything else remaining equal, a better

probability of a profitable trade. But, of course, everything else is not always equal. Price relationships may remain the same, but price levels which are the important element may change. The question is, will they change during the life of the option?

Calculating Return On Investment

In comparing transactions in the futures market with transactions in the options market, you should compare them on the basis of return on investment (ROI) which is calculated by dividing the dollar investment into net profit before taxes. Thus,

$$\text{ROI} = \frac{\textbf{Net income before taxes}}{\textbf{Total dollar investment}}$$

In the two gold examples earlier, the ROI would have been 50% for the options transaction and 150% for the futures transaction, assuming silver reached $5. An important reason for this is that the breakeven point on the futures is close to the purchase price. The futures market price needs to move only a small amount (commission plus interest on margin) to reach the breakeven point. On an option it has to move at least the amount of the premium and, if the strike price is above the current level, then it must move the amount of the premium *plus* the difference between the strike price and the current market level before the breakeven price is reached.

For example, in the earlier cases you would begin making money on your futures position as soon as it rose above the $492 level (the $45 commission interest on the margin at 10% for three months would equal approximately $2). The market would need to rise to only $497 to provide you a $500 profit, and if you were brave and fortunate enough to hold your position all the way up to $500, you would have realized a profit of $1,000 minus the commissions.

In the case of the option, the market has to move up enough to reach the strike price and then rise another $7 to yield the $500 net profit. Of course, the maximum loss on the downside was the $20 premium, or $2,000. The maximum loss potential on the downside with the futures was the entire value of the futures contract unless you entered a stop order and it was executed. At $470 per ounce the value of the futures contract was $47,000. For this loss to occur, the price of gold would need to fall to zero, an unlikely possibility.

Further, and just as importantly, has the size of the premium already accounted for any reasonable probability that they will not change?

Taxes and Options

Before you get too deeply involved in establishing an options trading strategy, you should evaluate carefully the impact of the tax laws on options transactions. That topic is too complex to study here, but it may be well worth your while to check with your tax advisor prior to entering into options transactions.

Summary

To summarize, when considering options relative to futures, remember:

1. Options provide you known and limited risk. Futures do not unless you use stop orders and then they do only if the stops actually are executed at or close to the stated level. This is sometimes hard to do if a market is fluctuating wildly and is locked in to limit moves.

2. To obtain this known and limited risk, you pay a premium. Weigh the size of the premium against the confidence of using stops and your desire to avoid being whipsawed. The size of this premium will be related to a lot of factors, the most important of which are price volatility, the remaining life of the option and the probability that the price will reach the strike price before expiration date.

3. The breakeven point on a futures transaction may be reached with a much smaller price move than in the case of an option.

4. Trading a futures against an option provides flexibility to an investment strategy and allows the holder of the option to make full use of all the "time" he paid for when he bought the option.

5. There are advantages to using a put option instead of a futures to hedge a profitable call option and vice versa.

6. There are a number of business uses for options. Many of them duplicate the advantages offered by futures contracts. Some of them, however, reflect advantages not available from ordinary futures hedges.

7. Before you open an account and make a trade in options, shop around and ask a lot of questions of your broker about the particular option deal being offered. There is no substitute for self-protection.

23

Stock Index Futures

Kansas City is famous for many things, some of which have been immortalized in song, but it now takes a place in the history of finance as the originator of stock index futures. Trading in stock index futures, specifically the Value Line Average (VLA), began in February 1982. The Kansas City Board of Trade worked actively on the concept of trading futures on stock indexes for five years before regulatory problems were overcome and trading actually began.

The last major regulatory hurdle was passed in mid-1981 when the Commodity Futures Trading Commission finally granted approval for the concept of cash settlement of futures contracts. Cash settlement means exactly what it suggests: At delivery time, the buyer and the seller exchange cash equal to the difference between the actual price of the product on that day and the price at which they had originally made their contract. Thus, in the case of stock indexes, there is no need for the seller to scurry around at delivery time collecting, in the correct proportion, the various shares of the companies that make up the index.

Since Kansas City inaugurated the trading, other exchanges have also listed stock index futures. The Chicago Mercantile Exchange (CME) offers futures on the Standard and Poor's 500 (S&P 500), and the New York Futures Exchange lists futures on the New York Stock Exchange (NYSE) Composite Index. The quick success of stock index futures has prompted plans for futures on a variety of other stock groupings, including some highly specialized selections in utility indexes and financial indexes.

What's Traded and When

The old Wall Street saying that you can't buy the market averages isn't true any more. Now if you have an opinion on the market as opposed to an individual stock, you can buy or sell the whole market — if you buy and the market goes up, the index will go up and you will make money. It will not be necessary to make an individual decision on each stock. In other words, index futures now allow you to get in on the price action of broad groups of stocks by buying or selling the futures contracts on those indexes.

Not all of the indexes are the same. The VLA index, the first stock index futures traded, reflects all of the stocks included in the Value Line Average of 1,700 stocks. The VLA is one of the most popular market indicators followed by investors. In the VLA, each company is weighted equally; thus, it represents one share of each of the 1,700 companies.

The S&P 500 stock index, a widely recognized representation of the stock market as a whole, is based on the equity prices of 500 different companies: 400 industrials, 40 utilities, 20 transportation firms and 40 financial institutions. The market value of the 500 firms is equal to approximately 80% of the value of all stocks listed on the NYSE.

The S&P 500 is a weighted index of the prices of the 500 firms. Each stock in the index is weighted so that changes in the stock's price will influence the index in proportion to the stock's respective market value. To determine the weight for the stock of any particular firm, the number of its shares outstanding is multiplied by its market price per share. In other words, a stock's market value determines the relative importance of the particular stock in the index; for example, General Motors accounts for approximately 1.35% of the S&P 500, while Rexnord accounts for only .01%.

The NYSE Composite Index reflects the value of the shares of all companies listed for trading on the NYSE. Similar to the S&P, the company shares are not weighted equally, but rather are included in the index according to the formula reflecting the stock's respective market value. The formula takes into account both the number of shares outstanding and the market price.

So both the S&P and NYSE attempt to measure the total value of the stocks included in their indexes, while the VLA attempts to measure average value. The NYSE measures every common stock on the NYSE. The S&P and VLA measure a designed market sample.

The contracts also differ in size (see tables, page 310) for further differences in contract specifications). On opening day, the VLA futures contract was valued at about $65,000, the S&P at about $70,000 and the NYSE at approximately $35,000. The size differences are also reflected in the margin requirements. Because the NYSE contract is about one-half the size of the S&P, margin requirements are likewise about half.

Computing a Stock Index

The best way to demonstrate the computation of an index is to actually show the computation. To illustrate, consider the S&P 500. That index is calculated using the base years 1941 to 1943 equal to 10. The price of each stock is multiplied by the number of shares outstanding for that company. In the case of the S&P 500, the value for each of the 500 shares is added, giving a total dollar value. To create the index, the total dollar value is then compared to the base value and the index is set according to the base index of 10. As a simple example, suppose the index was composed of only five issues:

	Outstanding Shares	Price	Value
Company A	100	30	3,000
Company B	500	10	5,000
Company C	200	50	10,000
Company D	400	4	1,600
Company E	300	20	6,000
	Current Market Value =		25,600

If the 1941-43 market value was $2,500, then 25,600 is to 2,500 what X is to 10.

Current Market Value $\frac{25,600}{2,500} = \frac{X}{10}$

1941-43 Market Value $256,000 = \$2,500\ X$

$$X = 102.40$$

241

To some extent, the indexes are substitutes for each other — i.e., they measure the same thing. The correlation coefficients in the table below demonstrate that the S&P and the NYSE are almost perfectly correlated (a perfect correlation equals 1.000); hence, they measure nearly the same thing and will be almost equally useful in hedging a portfolio. However, the VLA and the Dow Jones Industrial Average are not so highly correlated with the other two. Therefore, they would be less widely applicable as hedging devices.

Correlation Among Four Major Indices
2/1/71 to 4/1/82

	S&P	VLA	NYSE	DJIA
S&P	1.000	—	—	—
VLA	.882	1.000	—	—
NYSE	.989	.928	1.000	—
DJIA	.729	.507	.644	1.000

Volatility in Indexes

Like other futures contracts, index futures offer a way to play price movements with a lot of leverage. Leverage allows you to get more bang for your buck. Substantial movements in the value of your account will occur with small investments in the index. All of the exchanges have structured their contracts so that a one point move in the relevant index represents a gain or loss of $500.

The stock market, as represented by the various indexes, is highly variable when measured over long periods of time. For example, a study by the Index and Option Market (IOM), a subsidiary of the CME, shows that the average daily change in the S&P 500 was 2.58 points between Feb. 2, 1981, and March 12, 1982. In terms of futures contract value, that is equal to $1,290 per day (2.58 x $500). In addition, on at least one day during that period it changed by 5.26 points or $2,630.

Although futures prices move in the same direction as the underlying indexes do, the futures tend to be more volatile than the underlying indexes. When investors are bearish, prices frequently drop below, and fall faster than, the relevant index. In contrast, when investors are bullish, they tend to push futures prices above the index, and futures rise faster. This volatility tends to get accentuated in some of the more thinly traded months and the more thinly traded futures. As with most elements of volatility, these swings offer opportunities for making money and losing money.

In the long run, stock index futures will trade like all other futures: Prices for the futures will stay in close relationship with the current cash price, plus carrying costs. Generally speaking, when prices of futures stray away from their theoretical values, arbitrageurs push them back into line by buying when the price seems low and selling when the price seems high relative to its cash market value.

Trading the Stock Indexes

Investors or money managers may be interested in participating in stock index futures for a number of reasons. For example, they might have an overall opinion on the market direction and would buy or sell the market outright — thereby taking a position on market direction. They might want to sell stock index futures to protect an existing investment or in anticipation of a sale of all or part of a portfolio.

Traders may take both a long and short position in the market but in different delivery months. That technique of spreading one month against another works in stock indexes just as it works in other commodities. You can buy near-term futures and sell distant futures, or vice versa, hoping to gain as the price difference between the two months changes. You should be aware that such spreading techniques are not always low risk, particularly in stock indexes where there is not yet a good understanding of how to price these differences.

You may also be interested in integrating stock indexes into the overall management of the stock market portfolio. You could take 10% of your capital and place it in stock index futures, for example, putting the remainder in money market funds at a high yield. Assume you had $75,000 in money market funds in late 1982 and felt that the stock market was going up. However, you didn't have the time or resources to make the difficult decisions on individual stocks. Instead, you could have bought two NYSE contracts which would have been worth approximately $75,000. Approximately

20% of the capital would be necessary to margin those futures positions. The remainder of the money, $60,000, would stay invested in the money market fund at a higher rate of return than the dividend yield on the portfolio. This strategy would allow you to participate in the stock market while still maintaining a high yield on your funds.

Hedging Illustrated

As noted earlier in this book, a major use of futures markets is for hedging. In this instance, you may want to use the market to hedge your current market holdings or a portfolio of individual stocks. You may hold the stock investments and sell the stock index. If the market goes lower and the value of your individual investments declines with it, you will have a gain on the futures which can offset the loss on the value of the individual shares.

Suppose you owned a 10-stock diversified portfolio with a current market value of $35,000. In addition, suppose it generally reflected the value movements in the NYSE index. If the stock market generally declines by 10% as reflected in the NYSE index, your market loss would be about $3,500. You could protect against this loss by selling one NYSE index futures. Suppose at the time of the sale, it had an approximate value of $33,000. If you buy it back after the market has fallen, and if the index has in turn fallen by 10%, you will have made $3,300 on your hedge. That hedge will reduce your net market loss from $3,500 to $200.

While this may not work as an exact hedge, ways can be found to efficiently tailor (see the next section) a futures position to a particular portfolio to give you the most efficient hedge possible. Generally, you would not be well advised to use the futures market to hedge a portfolio unless it could be statistically demonstrated that the stocks which make up the portfolio do move in concert with the index used. If that can't be demonstrated in advance, the hedger might find himself in the unfortunate position of losing on both the stocks and the futures. If the portfolio is composed of small, little-known firms which are not included in the underlying index or, if included, are a very small proportion of the index, then it is unlikely that you will find efficient hedges. If, on the other hand, you have a portfolio that is composed of a small but diversified group of stocks that includes such big names as IBM or AT&T, you may indeed find the futures a reasonable hedge.

The Portfolio Manager and Hedging

A portfolio manager is one who takes responsibility for managing money invested in a group of assets usually including a range of securities. His objective is usually capital appreciation and income. In making investments, the manager must consider the risk or safety of the investment while attempting to achieve a reasonable return. Normally, the higher the risk, the higher the potential for return.

When a portfolio manager considers hedging, his objective with the hedge is akin to doing a balancing act with a scale. On one side of the scale, he has a group of investments with a particular risk associated with them. On the other side of the scale, he attempts to construct a futures position which will maintain a dollar balance with changes in the value of the portfolio. The success of his hedge will depend upon his success in constructing the proper futures position so that a dollar lost on one side of the scale will be offset by a dollar gain on the other side. He can construct that by selecting those futures contracts which are most closely correlated (as determined by statistical analysis) with the individual or groups of stocks in his portfolio.

Once he has identified the appropriate futures to use, he then must determine the number of futures contracts necessary to balance the scales. That calculation is usually accomplished through a statistical technique called regression analysis. Regression analysis is used to measure past price relationships for individual issues, or groups of related issues, relative to the underlying index chosen for the hedge. That volatility relationship will be expressed as a "beta" and is a statistical measurement reflecting the average relationship. Although this "beta" is based on past history, it is probably the best measure of future price relationships in the long run.

To determine the correct number of futures contracts to sell to balance the scale, the hedger should calculate a weighted beta for his portfolio. If the overall portfolio beta is 1.0 as measured against any of the indexes, it indicates that virtually all of the risk contained in the portfolio is accounted for, or eliminated, if an equal dollar amount of futures contracts are sold. If the portfolio beta is different than 1.0, the number of contracts sold must be adjusted accordingly.

For example, if a portfolio manager found a beta coefficient of 1.20 for his portfolio, he would determine the appropriate number of contracts to sell by dividing the value of the portfolio by the value of the futures contract and multiplying by 1.20. To illustrate, assume the manager's portfolio value is $20,000,000 and the manager intends to use the NYSE composite index, which we will assume is valued at $35,000. $20,000,000 divided by $35,000, multiplied by 1.2, equals 685.7 contracts. The manager would round that number up and would sell 686 contracts as the appropriate number for his short hedge.

Now, if past relationships hold and the market changes by 10%, the value of the portfolio should change by $2,000,000 and the dollar value of the change reflected in the index futures should be $2,000,000 as well.

It would be unusual if the hedge works out as perfectly as just illustrated. Even with all of the statistical techniques mentioned, it is likely there will be some variation in the total amount of gain or loss on the futures side compared to the total amount of the gain or loss in the portfolio. This variation will be due in part to the fact that the futures market may move more, or less, than individual stocks in the portfolio. Further, the timing of the two moves may not coincide exactly: One may move today and the other may move tomorrow or next week. This is referred to as basis risk. It must be noted that betas and other statistical calculations are based upon historical data, and futures seldom reflect past history exactly.

Before leaving this example, it would be reasonable to ask why a manager of a large portfolio would take a short futures position rather than simply sell the stock. One of the reasons may be liquidity. A highly liquid futures contract can absorb a hedge without significantly affecting the futures market price, while sales in the stock market of the same magnitude could pull down the price of those individual stocks to a much greater extent. Further, many portfolio managers do not find liquidation a feasible alternative because they are restricted to stocks of a particular kind. The cash generated from the sale of those stocks could not be immediately reinvested in other alternative areas. The futures market gives a manager the opportunity and the flexibility to make potential adjustments in his portfolio without going through complete liquidation.

The Long Hedge

Stock index futures can also be used by the portfolio manager as a means of pricing future acquistions of stock for his portfolio. Most managers receive periodic inflows of capital, resulting from contributions to pension funds, dividends received, etc. If in the portfolio manager's estimation the market is cheaper now than it will be at the expected time of the inflow, then he may wish to use the index futures to price the cost of his purchases now. Later, when he actually receives the funds and makes the purchase of the securities, he will offset his futures. In doing so, he protects himself from a rise in the market before he receives his funds for investment. Of course, should the market fall during that time period, he will have losses on his futures which will offset the opportunity gains he had from purchasing stock at a lower level. As with all properly constructed hedges, he gives up the opportunity to make windfall profits while at the same time protecting himself against substantial losses.

24

What To Look For —
And Where To Find It

Previous chapters of this book have set forth, in basic form, some of the *modus operandi* for analyzing futures price movements. What follows in this chapter provides a guide for selecting the type of information you should plug into a model for a particular commodity.

No attempt is made to be exhaustive in presenting the factors that may affect the price of a commodity. Nor are these data complete in covering all commodities traded on the various exchanges. Rather, the purpose is to be introductory only — to provide the new trader with an awareness of some of the kinds of information to seek out and where to find it.

You will still have to ask yourself these questions:

1. Which of these factors is most important?
2. Why is this particular piece of information important?
3. How does change in a certain factor affect prices?

You will note that sometimes the same factors appear on both the supply and demand sides of the price-making equation. This is because some factors interact to affect both sides. A worthwhile and fascinating — but frustrating — experiment is to take the supply/demand factors outlined for the commodities indicated on the tables that follow and arrange them in a schematic diagram to show their interaction and relationships to each other. Such an exercise would show you that there is no one interpretation of data, no single model that is "correct." In fact, the differences in interpretation of such information are what make a market. In the final analysis, the greatest satisfaction (aside from monetary gain) derived from commodity futures trading lies in interpreting the available facts better than anybody else and being "right."

Government Information

The U.S. government is probably the most important source of information for the commodity trader. And best of all, the information is usually available free. Virtually every major governmental agency or department collects information of some kind from the public at large or from the industry of its concern. Careful analysis of this information can be extremely helpful in developing a trading plan.

In addition to the general supply-demand data listed on the following pages, you should also try to understand the people who are trading the markets. To this end, it is suggested that you study the *Commitment of Traders Report* issued monthly by the CFTC. Each day the names of individual traders who have positions in excess of 40 contracts in the grains, 50 contracts in cotton and silver and 25 contracts in all other commodities are reported to the CFTC. This information, along with a good deal of other information concerning the cash market activities of the individual, is then used in the CFTC's market surveillance activity.

Once a month the accumulated data about these trader positions, their classification as hedger or speculator and the percent of the contracts owned by the largest four and largest eight traders is released to the public. Although the data is slightly out-of-date by the time it is released, it does provide some guidance as to whether hedgers or speculators are dominating any one side of the market and how they are changing their positions from month to month. When you couple that information with the price activity and trend, you can get a hint of what large speculators or large hedgers believe will happen to prices and how they are getting into a position to take advantage of it.

It would be misleading to place too much emphasis on the current value of this information. However, the CFTC is making some changes in the reporting system and expects to provide even more detailed analyses of the makeup of the market and to

provide it in a more timely fashion. When they do, you may find that to be some of the most valuable data available.

In addition to government reports on many topics, there are also a number of publications available from private sources or from commodity organizations. Daily newspapers and financial publications provide important information on a regular basis, and most exchanges also have a number of helpful publications available to the public. Although it would be impossible to list all of these sources, here are some of the key ones covering most commodities regularly:

Futures **Magazine, 219 Parkade, Cedar Falls, Iowa 50613**
Commodities **Report, 219 Parkade, Cedar Falls, Iowa 50613**
Wall Street Journal, **22 Cortlandt St., New York, N.Y. 10007**
Journal of Commerce, **99 Wall St., New York, N.Y. 10005**
Barron's, **22 Cortlandt St., New York, N.Y. 10007**
Consensus, **30 W. Pershing Rd., Kansas City, Mo. 64108**
New York Times, **229 W. 43rd St., New York, N.Y. 10036**
Commodity Yearbook, **Commodity Research Bureau Inc., One Liberty Plaza, New York, N.Y. 10006**

On the following pages you will find a breakdown of the most important factors to watch for each commodity as well as some other sources of information in each case.

Grains

Grain Sorghum, Wheat, Corn, Oats

Short-Term (less than 3 months)	Long-Term

Supply

Government programs	Producer technology
Imports/Exports of grains	Long-term yield trends
Current storage stocks	Long-term acreage planted trends
Amount in storage	Prices
Disappearance rate	Comparative past & present prices
Weather and growing conditions	Expected future prices
Acres planted	Competing land uses
Yield per acre expected	Relative return on investment
Seasonal supply influences	Government programs to encourage
	or discourage production
	Allotments
	Support prices
	Storage carryover
	Privately-held stocks
	CCC stocks
	Cost of production and marketing
	Expected long-term return on
	investment

Demand

Government purchases	Government programs
Prices of substitute grains	Imports/Exports
Numbers of livestock on feed	Trends in livestock production
Cattle	Size of calf and pig crops
Hogs	Number of cattle, hogs and poultry
Poultry	Growth in livestock and meat
Export shipments	industry
Cash bids (basis)	General economic conditions
	Industrial usage
	New product development

Sources of Information

Grain Market News — USDA*
The Feed Situation — USDA*
Crop Production — USDA*
Stocks of Grains in All Positions — USDA*
Cattle and Calves on Feed — USDA*
Hogs & Pigs — USDA*
Poultry Crop Reports — USDA*
Agricultural Prices — USDA*
Annual Report — Chicago Board of Trade, 141 W. Jackson, Chicago, Ill. 60604
Wheat Situation Report — USDA*
Chicago Mercantile Exchange Yearbook — 444 W. Jackson, Chicago, Ill. 60606
Corn/Bean Profit Alert — Professional Farmers of America, 219 Parkade, Cedar
    Falls, Iowa 50613

*USDA — Division of Information, Office of Management Service, USDA,
    Washington, D.C. 20250

Soybeans

Short-Term (less than 3 months)	Long-Term
Supply	
Weather and growing conditions	Producer technology
Storage Stocks	Long-term yield trends
Disappearance rate	Long-term acreage planting trends
Expected yield/acre	Prices
Acres planted	Present compared to past prices for
Government programs	soybeans, meal and oil
Import/Export programs	Expected futures prices for
Seasonal supply influences	soybeans, meal and oil
	Storage carryover
	Privately held stocks
	CCC stocks
	Competing land uses
	Relative return on investment
	Government programs to encourage or
	discourage production
	Allotments
	Price supports
	Cost of production and marketing
	Expected long-term return on
	investment
Demand	
Prices of substitute grains	Government programs
Numbers of livestock on feed	Export programs
Cattle	Trends in livestock production
Hogs	Size of calf and pig crops
Poultry	Size of breeding herds
Seasonal demand influences	Livestock feeding practices
Government purchases	New product development
Crushing rate	General economic conditions
	Industrial usage
	Crushing trends

Sources of Information

Weekly Grain Market News — USDA*

Fats & Oils Situation Reports — USDA*

Feed Situation Reports — USDA*

Crop Production Reports — USDA*

Stock of all Grains in All Positions Report — USDA*

Annual Report of the Chicago Board of Trade — 141 W. Jackson, Chicago, Ill. 60604

Statistical Abstract of the U.S. — Superintendent of Documents, Government Printing Office, Washington, D.C. 20402

Oil World Quarterly and Weekly — ISTA Mielke & Co., Langenberg, W. Germany

Soybean Digest — American Soybean Assn., Box 27300, St. Louis, Mo. 63141

Corn/Bean Profit Alert — Professional Farmers of America, 219 Parkade, Cedar Falls, Iowa 50613

*USDA — Division of Information, Office of Management Service, USDA, Washington, D.C. 20250

Potatoes

Short-Term (less than 3 months)	Long-Term

Supply

Current storage stocks	Producer technology
Disappearance rate	Long-term acreage planted trends
Weather & growing conditions	Long-term yield trend
Government programs	Government programs
Storage program	Production incentives
Import/Export programs	Storage programs
Acres planted	Competing land uses
Yield/Acre expected	Relative return on investment
Seasonal supply influences	Prices
	Comparative past & present
	Expected future prices
	Costs of production & marketing

Demand

Retail price of potatoes	Trends in per capita consumption
Prices of substitute products	Consumer tastes and preferences
Government purchase program	Consumer income
Seasonal demand influences	Consumer age distribution
	Number of consumers
	Retail prices of potatoes
	Prices of substitute products
	Import/Export programs
	New product development
	General economic conditions
	Government purchase program

Sources of Information

Irish Potatoes — USDA*

Potatoes — USDA — Statistical Reporting Service, Box 1699, Boise, Idaho 83701
    Production   Potatoes Processing
    Stocks   Acreage Yield & Production

Total Potatoes Stock — USDA*

Potatoes & Sweet Potatoes — USDA*

Acreage Marketing Guides — USDA*

Tabb Potato Service — Tabb Potato Service, Suite 300, One Gateway Center, Kansas City, Kansas 66101

The Potato & Onion Week — Tabb Potato Service, Suite 300, One Gateway Center, Kansas City, Kansas 66101

Fresh Fruit & Vegetables — USDA — Fruit & Vegetable Division, Box 166, Idaho Falls, Idaho

Chicago Mercantile Exchange Yearbook — 444 W. Jackson, Chicago, Ill. 60606

U.S. Crop Report (Eggs & Potatoes) — USDA*

Potato Sales — USDA*

*USDA — Division of Information, Office of Management Service, USDA, Washington, D.C. 20250

Eggs

Short-Term (less than 3 months)	Long-Term

Supply

Storage stocks	Prices
Disappearance rate	Present compared to past price of
Stocks of frozen eggs	eggs
Government programs	Expected future prices of eggs
Purchase programs	Trends in feed prices
Import programs	Poultry prices
Disease	Producer technology
Feed prices	Disease eradication
Seasonal supply influences	Higher yield chickens
	Capital costs
	Long-term return on investment
	Hatchery production

Demand

Government programs	Trends in per capita consumption
Purchase programs	Tastes and preferences
Export programs	Religious practices
Retail prices of eggs	Consumer incomes
Prices of substitutes	Trends in retail egg prices
Breaker demands	Population growth
Hatchery demands	General economic conditions
Seasonal demand influences	Availability of substitutes
	Trends in government programs
	Export programs
	Government buying

Sources of Information

Agricultural Prices — USDA*
Poultry & Egg Situation — USDA*
Chickens & Eggs — USDA*
Commercial Broilers — USDA*
Eggs, Chickens & Turkeys — USDA*
Feed Situation — USDA*
Poultry — USDA*
Egg Products — USDA*
Hatchery Report — USDA*
Chicago Mercantile Exchange Yearbook, 444 W. Jackson, Chicago, Ill. 60606

*USDA — Division of Information, Office of Management Service, USDA, Washington, D.C. 20250

Hogs

<table>
<tr><th>Short-Term (less than 3 months)</th><th>Long-Term</th></tr>
</table>

Supply

Short-Term	Long-Term
Shortage stock of pork	Prices
Disappearance rate	Present compared to past price of
Government programs	hogs
Imports of pork	Expected future prices of hogs
Government purchases	Feeder pig prices
Price restrictions	Trends in hog production
Prices of feed	Size of pig crop
Hog marketings	Number of feeder pigs
Number slaughtered	Number of hogs being fed
Weight of slaughter	Size of sow herds
Pounds of meat/animal	Trends in prices of feed
Number of hogs on feed in	Producer technology
heavyweight ranges	Diseases eradication
Weather & growing conditions	Higher yields
Seasonal supply influences	Availability of growth stimulants
	Alternative land uses
	Relative return on investment

Demand

Short-Term	Long-Term
Prices of substitutes	Trends in per capita consumption
Beef	Religious practices of consumers
Poultry	Tastes and preferences of consumers
Lamb & mutton	Geographic location of consumers
Government programs	Consumer income
Purchases program	Population growth
Exports of pork	Age distribution of consumer
Wholesale-retail prices of pork	General economic conditions
Seasonal demand influences	Trends in wholesale-retail prices of pork
	Availability of meat analogs

Sources of Information

Livestock and Meat Situation Report — USDA*
Hogs & Pigs Report — USDA*
Livestock Slaughter & Meat Production — USDA*
Livestock, Meat and Wool Market News — USDA*
Agricultural Prices — USDA*
Feed Situation — USDA*
Statistical Abstract of the U.S. — Superintendent of Documents, Government
    Printing Office, Washington, D.C. 20402
PorkPro — 219 Parkade, Cedar Falls, Iowa 50613
National Provisioner — 15 W. Huron, Chicago, Ill. 60610
Chicago Mercantile Exchange Yearbook — 444 W. Jackson, Chicago, Ill. 60606

*USDA — Division of Information, Office of Management Service, USDA, Wash-
    ington, D.C. 20250

Beef Cattle

Short-Term (less than 3 months)	Long-Term

Supply

Storage stocks of beef	Prices
Disappearance rate	Present compared to past prices
Government programs	Expected future prices
Government purchases	Feeder cattle prices
Import programs	Trends in price of feed
Price restrictions	Trends in cattle production
Cattle marketings	Size of calf crop
Number slaughtered	Feeder cattle numbers
Weight of slaughter	Size of cow herds
Pounds of meat/animal	Number of cattle on feed
Number of cattle on feed in	Availability of growth stimulants
heavyweight ranges	Range conditions
Weather & growing conditions	Alternative land uses
Seasonal supply influence	Relative return on investment
	Producer technology
	Disease eradication
	Higher yields

Demand

Prices of substitutes	Trends in per capita consumption
Poultry	Religious practices of consumer
Pork	Tastes and preferences of consumer
Lamb & mutton	Geographic location of consumer
Government programs	Consumer incomes
Purchase programs	Population growth
Export programs	Age distribution of consumer
Packer — profit margins	General economic conditions
Wholesale-retail prices of beef	Availability of meat analogs
	Trends in wholesale-retail prices of beef

Sources of Information

Livestock and Meat Situation Report — USDA*
Feed Situation Report — USDA*
Livestock, Meat and Wool — USDA*
Cattle and Calves on Feed — USDA*
Livestock Slaughter and Meat Production — USDA*
Statistical Abstract of the U.S. — Superintendent of Documents, Government
  Printing Office, Washington, D.C. 20402
National Provisioner — 15 W. Huron, Chicago, Ill. 60610
Chicago Mercantile Exchange Yearbook — 444 W. Jackson, Chicago, Ill. 60606

*USDA — Division of Information, Office of Management Service, USDA, Wash-
  ington, D.C. 20250

Feeder Cattle

Short-Term (less than 3 months)	Long-Term

Supply

Weather & growing conditions	Producer technology
Prices of feed	Disease eradication
Number of calves slaughtered for veal	Better forage
Number of calves at heavier	Prices
weight ranges	Present compared to past prices for:
Seasonal supply influence	Feeder cattle
	Fat catle
	Expected future prices for:
	Feeder cattle
	Fat cattle
	Trends in feed prices
	Range conditions
	Trends in size of cow herds
	Alternatives land uses
	Relative return on investment

Demand

Percent operating capacity of feedlots	Demand for fat cattle
Prices of fat cattle	Feed lot growth trends
Seasonal supply influences	Long term price trends of fat cattle
	General economic conditions

Sources of Information

Livestock and Meat Situation — USDA*
Livestock Slaughter & Meat Production — USDA*
Livestock, Meat and Wool Market News — USDA*
Calf Crop Report — USDA*
Cattle — USDA*
Cattle on Feed — USDA*
Statistical Abstract of the U.S. — Superintendent of Documents, Government Printing Office, Washington, D.C. 20402
Chicago Mercantile Exchange Yearbook — 444 W. Jackson, Chicago, Ill. 60606
National Provisioner — 15 W. Huron, Chicago, Ill. 60610

*USDA — Division of Information, Office of Management Service, USDA, Washington, D.C. 20250

Pork Bellies

Short-Term (less than 3 months)	Long-Term

Supply

Storage stocks	Prices
Disappearance rate	Present compared to past prices
Hog marketings	Expected future prices
Number of hogs slaughtered	Storage cost
Weights of hog slaughter	Producer technology
Seasonal supply influences	Hog yield trends
	Government programs
	Price restrictions
	Purchase programs (military, etc.)
	Cost of production and marketing
	Trend in hog production
	Number of hogs being fed
	Number of feeder pigs
	Size of pig crop (farrowings)
	Average size of litter

Demand

Prices	Trends in per capita consumption
Prices of other pork cuts	Consumer tastes and preferences
Egg prices	Religious practices
Retail prices of bacon	Consumer income
Government purchases	Number of consumers
Packer-profit margins	Consumer age distribution
Exports of pork bellies	General economic conditions
	Government purchase programs
	Technology and availability of high
	protein food substitutes
	Price trends
	Bacon prices
	Egg prices

Sources of Information

Livestock, Meat & Wool Market News — USDA*
Agricultural Prices — USDA*
Cold Storage Report — USDA*
Storage Movement — USDA*
Livestock Slaughter & Meat Production — USDA*
Hogs and Pigs Report — USDA*
Bacon Slicings Report — USDA*
Livestock and Meat Situation Report — USDA*
Statistical Abstract of the U.S. — Superintendent of Documents, Government
    Printing Office, Washington, D.C. 20402
Chicago Mercantile Exchange Yearbook — 444 W. Jackson, Chicago, Ill. 680606
National Provisioner — 15 W. Huron, Chicago, Ill. 60610

*USDA — Division of Information, Office of Management Service, USDA, Wash-
    ington, D.C. 20250

Lumber

Short-Term (less than 3 months)	Long-Term

Supply

Government programs	Forest technology
Import/Export programs	Fire control
Storage inventories	Improved seeding
Weather & terrain conditions	Higher-yield trees
Transportation costs	Land use management
Seasonal supply influences	Prices
	Present compared to past prices
	Expected future prices
	Stumpage prices on
	Government-owned lands
	Availability of land
	Privately-owned land
	Government-owned land
	Terrain
	Weather trends

Demand

Prices of substitutes	Construction
Aluminum stud prices	Residential construction
Steel stud prices	Other new construction
Plywood prices	Material handling
Prices of plastics	General economic conditions
Government programs	Trends in per capita consumption
Export programs	Geographic location
Repair and remodeling	Tastes and preferences
Seasonal demand influences	Population growth
	Consumer incomes

Sources of Information

Barometer — WWPA — 1500 Yeon Building, Portland, Ore. 97204

Western Lumber Facts — WWPA — 1500 Yeon Building, Portland, Ore. 97204

Lumber Price Trends — WWPA — 1500 Yeon Building, Portland, Ore. 97204

Lumber Price Trends — WWPA — 1500 Yeon Building, Portland, Ore. 97204

Statistical Yearbook — WWPA — 1500 Yeon Building, Portland, Ore. 97204

Forest Service of USDA — U.S. Government Printing Office, Division of Public Documents, Washington, D.C. 20402

  Housing Starts (Construction Rep. C 20)

  Lumber Production & Mill Stocks (Cur., Ind. Reps. Ser. MA24T)

U.S. Department of Commerce, Bureau of the Census — U.S. Government Printing Office, Division of Public Documents, Washington, D.C. 20402

  Timber Trends — (Forest Resource Rep. 17)

  Pacific Northwest Forest and Range Experiment Station, Portland, Ore.

Random Lenghts — Random Lengths Publication, Inc., Box 867, Eugene, Ore. 97402

Crow's Weekly Letter — C.C. Crow Publications, Inc., Terminal Sales Building, Portland, Ore. 97205

Mercantile Exchange Yearbook — 444 W. Jackson, Chicago, Ill. 60606

Interest Rate Futures

Federal Reserve actions
T-Bill auctions to increase or decrease bank reserve amount sold and
yields realized.
Federal Open Market Committee Trading Activity
Adjustments in bank discount rate

Other governmental agencies
FNMA auctions
Market activity by FNMA and GNMA
Government housing policies

Market activity
Recent volatility pattern
Volume of trading in the cash market
Aggressiveness of market dealers in buying and selling
Housing starts and general demand for mortgages
Demand for loans (major N.Y. banks)
Industry production trends
General economic condition
Interest rates on other instruments like commercial paper, certification of
deposit, etc.

Sources of Information

Monetary Trends — Federal Reserve Bank of St. Louis, St. Louis, Missouri
National Economic Trends — Federal Reserve Bank of St. Louis, St. Louis,
Missouri
Survey of Current Business — U.S. Department of Commerce Bank, Washington,
D.C.
Federal Reserve Bulletin — Federal Reserve Bank of New York, New York
International Monetary Market Daily Bulletin 444 West Jackson Boulevard,
Chicago, Ill. 60606
Chicago Board of Trade Statistical Department — LaSalle & Jackson, Chicago, Ill.
60604

Currency Futures

Not every country has the following information available, and those that do have it may each provide it in a different measure and with slightly different meaning. Nevertheless, if you are going to trade currencies, try to obtain the following information about each country:

Level of international monetary reserves
Balance of trade data
Consumer price index
Wholesale price index
Industrial production index
Unemployment
General economic indicators
Money supply
Import/export volume index

Sources of Information

U.S. Department of the Treasury — Washington, D.C.
U.S. Department of Commerce — Washington, D.C.
Federal Reserve Bank of New York — New York, New York
International Monetary Fund — Washington, D.C.

The Economist — 527 Madison Avenue, New York, New York 10022
Euromoney — 14 Finbury Circus, London EC2, England
Financial Times of London — 75 Rockefeller Plaza, New York, New York 10019

Sugar

Short-Term (less than 3 months)	Long-Term

Supply

Storage stocks	World Sugar production
Carryover stocks (near-	Sugar cane
term)	Sugar beet
Disappearance rate	Storage stocks and storage cost
Season supply influences	Cost of production & marketing
Quantity of cane & beet sugar	Spot price compared to past prices
Produced domestically	Price expectation
Nearby import levels of	Political & economic conditions
Foreign cane sugar	Government programs
	Price supports
	Import quotas
	Tariffs
	Inter-Government purchases
	Trends in sugar production
	Number and size of sugar mills
	Yield per acre
	Sugar content

Demand

Prices and quantities of	Trends in per capita consumption
Complements	Consumer tastes and preferences
Substitutes	Consumer income change
Export of sugar and by-products	Consumer expectations
Manufacturers inventories	U.S. & world economic conditions
Disappearance rate	Government purchase programs
	Technology & availability of
	sugar substitutes
	Price trends in products that use sugar

Sources of Information

Outlook for U.S. Agricultural Exports — USDA*
Foreign Agriculture Circular — USDA*
Foreign Agriculture — USDA*
Annual Report — New York coffee and sugar Exchange, 79 Pine Street, New York,
  New York 10005

*USDA — Foreign Agricultural Service, USDA, Washington, D.C. 20250

263

Coffee

Short-Term (less than 3 months)	Long-Term

Supply

Storage stocks
  Inventories
  Disappearance rate
Seasonal supply influence
Marketing of coffee products

World coffee productions
Storage cost
Storage stocks — long-term
Cost of production & marketing
Prices
  Spot price compared to past prices
Political and economic conditions
Government purchases
Government programs
  Price supports
  Import quotas
Tariffs
  Payments to growers
Migration of farmers and workers
  to urban centers
Change in cultivation and technology

Demand

Prices and quantities of
  Complements
  Substitutes
Export of coffee products

Trends in per capita consumption
  Consumer tastes and preferences
  Consumer income changes
  Consumer expectations
  Population change
U.S. & world economic conditions
Inter-government purchase
  programs
Technology & availability of coffee
  substitutes
Price trends

Sources of Information

Annual Report — New York Coffee & Sugar Exchange, 79 Pine Street, New York, New York 10005

Foreign Agricultural Trade of the U.S.A. — ERS*

Foreign Agriculture Circular — USDA**

Foreign Agriculture — USDA**

Structure and Prospects of the World Coffee Economy — World Bank Staff, Working Paper No. 208, June 1975, World Demand Prospects for Coffee in 1980 — USDA**

* ERS — Economic Research Service, USDA, Washington, D.C. 20250

**USDA — Foreign Agricultural Service, USDA, Washington, D.C. 20250

Cocoa

Supply

Short-Term (less than 3 months)	Long-Term
Storage stocks	World cocoa bean production
Producer and manufacturer inventories and disappearance rate	Available land suitable for cocoa cultivation
Seasonal supply influences, mid-July to early October	Renovation programs
West Africa crop development	Number of older trees vs. number of young trees
January to March cocoa shipments from West African producing countries	Shoot disease & capsid damage
Marketing of cocoa products	Price that marketing boards pay producers
Logistic difficulties of nearby shipments	Growing conditions
	Tariffs
	Political & economic conditions
	Influence of government marketing boards
	World cocoa bean grindings: Import vs. export countries
	Storage cost
	Trends in cocoa production
	Tree count per producing country
	Number of pods per tree
	Average yield per tree
	Change in producer's technology
	Cost of production & marketing
	Quantity of substitutes
	Prices of substitutes
	Present price vs. past prices

Demand

Short-Term (less than 3 months)	Long-Term
Price of Complements Substitutes	Trends in per capita consumption
	Consumer tastes & preferences
Costs of chocolate candy ingredients — sugar, nuts, fruits, milk	Consumer income
	Population change Seasonal customs
Exports of cocoa products	Consumer expectations
Manufacturer profit margin	U.S. & world conditions
	World cocoa bean grindings
	Price trends of products that use cocoa

Sources of Information

Foreign Agriculture — USDA*
Gill and Duffus Inc. — 130 John Street, New York, N.Y. 10038
International Cocoa Inc. — London, England
General Cocoa Company Inc. — 160 Water Street, New York, N.Y. 10038
*USDA — Foreign Agricultural Service, USDA, Washington, D.C. 20250

Metals
Copper, Silver, Platinum, Palladium, Mercury, Gold

Short-Term (less than 3 months)	Long-Term

Supply

Storage stocks	Prices
Disappearance rate	Present compared to past prices
Labor disputes & negotiations	Expected future prices
Political and social upheavals	Government programs
Government purchase programs	Price restrictions
	Import programs
	Storage costs
	Environmental obstacles
	Discovery and exploitation of new
	sources
	Producer technology
	Lower cost of production methods

Demand

Price of substitute metals	Trends in industrial consumption
International situation	Automotive industry
Political happenings	Chemical industry
Exchange rates	Jewelry industry
Balance of payments	Electronics industry
Foreign exchange reserves	Medical industry
	Agricultural industry
	Government programs
	Export programs
	Government coinage
	Hoarding
	Social customs
	Trends in per capita consumption
	Age distribution
	Consumer income levels

Sources of Information

Minerals Yearbook U.S. Bureau of Mines, Washington, D.C. 20240

Mineral Industry Surveys — U.S. Bureau of Mines, Washington, D.C. 20240

Statistical Abstact of the U.S. — Superintendent of Documents, Government Printing Office, Washington, D.C. 20402

Engineering & Mining Journal — McGraw Hill Book Co., 330 W. 42nd St., New York, N.Y. 10036

Iron Age — Chilton Way, Radnor, PA 19089

Metal Statistics — 576 5th Ave., New York, N.Y. 10036

Modern Metals — 919 N. Michigan Ave., Chicago, Ill. 60611

25

Historical Development of Commodity Futures Trading

Mention commodity futures trading to someone not actively engaged in the market and the first — and often only — reaction you get is that it is a high-risk form of financial speculation. True, speculation is a major aspect of futures trading as we know it today, but underlying current speculative activity is a sound economic purpose that has its roots in ancient times and has evolved slowly over centuries. Marketing practices naturally change with the basic economic needs of people involved in the pricing and handling of goods. Our current system did not miraculously appear.

If you were to select any single commodity from among those traded on exchanges today and trace its market development, you would find it has passed through five distinct stages: gift-giving, barter, cash (or spot) markets, contract (or forward) markets and last, futures markets.

Thus, the establishment of a futures market in a given commodity is only the current stage of a natural evolutionary process. It's a process which never ends and could very well lead to an as yet unknown sixth stage in decades ahead.

When did it all begin? Surely, gift-giving and barter, the first two stages, are as old as civilization itself. The third stage — cash markets — can be considered the true beginning of organized commodity markets.

Emergence of Organized Markets

Until about the early 1600's, trade throughout most of Europe and Asia was not heavy enough to support resident merchants or local markets. Periodic market fairs served as the trading outlets for large geographic areas. These fairs originated with the movements of itinerant merchants, who bartered their local goods for exotic things in distant lands. Coin was very scarce and the majority of transactions involved simple barter. Fairs were popular in ancient Greece and during the Roman Empire, and Marco Polo brought back to Europe accounts of the gigantic Kinsai Fairs in China.

Gradually, a network of highly specialized and well-organized fairs emerged. Fair rules confined traders to the fairgrounds, and specified times were designated for trading various commodities. In addition, they required that bids and offers be made publicly with every participant guaranteed an equal opportunity to accept bids and offers. Rules also banned traders from contracting outside the fairgrounds in attempts to corner a supply of a given commodity and thereby control its price.

Eventually, guilds (trade associations) were organized to promote the interests of the emerging merchant class. Business disputes were settled in courts especially established by the merchant class for that purpose, and a merchant code of law evolved from decisions handed down in these courts.

As trade grew, pieces of paper called "fair letters" came into being as a medium of exchange. These letters had the effect of postponing settlement in cash to a later date, actually providing an extension of credit. Traders were now free to travel from fair to fair settling their accounts by canceling debits and credits with the fair letters, leaving any remaining balance due to be settled eventually by payment in coin. As this medium of exchange was born, so was the cash (spot) market. Frequently, merchants would display samples of their wares, taking payment in coin or letter upon delivery when the title passed to the purchaser.

Early Futures Trading in Japan

Although the roots of futures trading can be traced to the

Medievel fair systems, it remained for Japan to develop sophisticated forward markets and the organized system of futures trading as we know it today. The Japanese experience carried

them through stages four and five of market development, completing the five-stage evolutionary process.

Japan holds claim to the first recorded use of modern futures trading concepts — in the year 1697 — approximately a century and a half before the common use of forward contracts in the United States.

During the 17th century, Japanese noblemen were forced into

the position of being absentee landlords. This was the result of the ruling shogunate's decree that these noblemen spend at least six months of every year in residence in the capital city so that the shogunate could keep a watchful eye on his noblemen in an effort to prevent the possibility of their conducting a revolt or uprising against him.

In keeping with the custom of the times, the noblemen maintained very high standards of living. They depended heavily on their rice crops for income, but rice was harvested during only a brief portion of the year, and they often ran short of cash while living it up away from home. This was understandable. They were maintaining dual households, entertaining lavishly and indulging in extravagant wardrobes.

As a solution to their cash shortage problems, the nobles began the practice of issuing receipts against their rice crops stored either in the country or in rented warehouses. Wholesale and retail merchants who eventually needed the rice would buy the tickets against anticipated needs. Eventually, these tickets became a form of currency. It soon followed that merchants began to extend credit to the nobles in advance of ticket sales. Some of the merchants were successful in manipulating the market and, in the process, became quite wealthy. One of the wealthiest of merchants in the city of Osaka set his house up as a center for rice market transactions. This was actually the world's first futures market. Later, this first exchange moved to the Dojima district in Osaka and became known as the Dojima Rice Market.

In many ways, this early exchange was strikingly similar to the modern futures exchange of today. The market functioned under legal sanction of the national government, and trades were executed in an orderly, well-disciplined manner according to rules established by the exchange. Transactions were cleared through a clearing house, with each trader establishing a line of credit with the clearing house of his choice. These clearing houses were non-profit organizations which did, however, charge commissions for their services.

The major difference between this first futures market and those which were to develop later was the fact that no physical deliveries could be made. This, of course, relegated the trading to gambling, and the government closed all exchanges for a brief period in the early 17th century. Later, after government regulation of the market was expanded and physical delivery was made acceptable in lieu of a cash settlement, trading was restored.

Development of Futures Trading in the U.S.

Although following at a much later date, a pattern of market development evolved in the United States similar to that experienced by Japan. The use of forward contracts, which arose in response to marketing needs as commodity markets became larger and more complex, ripened eventually into organized futures trading.

As the population in this country grew and spread westward — and the economy became more highly industrialized, with increased production capabilities — it became evident that an economic system based on local self-sufficiency was no longer viable. There were new economic needs to be filled — needs for additional capital, additional credit, and a means to absorb increased price risks caused by longer time periods between production and sale, expanded market areas and ever-increasing competition.

Stock exchanges took care of the capital needs. The national banking system answered the demand for expanded sources of new credit. Initially, the use of various forms of forward contracts represented an attempt on the part of commodity handlers to avoid increased price risks.

The midwest grain market and the development of commerce in Chicago provided the impetus for the evolution of modern commodity futures trading in the United States. The use of actual, full-fledged futures contracts was preceded by approximately 25 years of merchants' dealing in what were then referred to as "to-arrive-contracts" or what are now commonly called "forward contracts."

Soon, speculators outside the grain trade began participating in the bidding and holding of these contracts, passing them on to other parties before the delivery date. Bear in mind that this trading was taking place prior to the opening of any exchange. By the mid-1850's, contracts frequently changed hands several times before settling with a person interested in taking delivery of the actual commodity.

Midwest Grain Market

During the 1830's and 1840's prior to the opening of the railroads, grain farmers in the Midwest faced severe marketing problems. Every year at harvest time, grains arriving in Chicago created a market glut. Farmers had to take whatever they could get for their grain because the quantity available far exceeded the current demand of the market. Lack of adequate storage facilities made it impossible to store the grain to hold it for future sale. As a result, it was not an uncommon sight during the height of the grain hauling season to see thousands of tons of spoiled grain dumped into Lake Michigan.

As could be expected, the exact opposite of the above situation took place in late spring and early summer. All the harvest stocks

were gone. Available grain was in great demand and short supply. Anxious millers competed with one another to buy the available grain at astronomical prices.

As a result, farmers began to arrange prior sale of their crops. These forward sales involved a firm commitment on the part of the farmer to deliver a specified amount of grain at a future time period — say 10, 20, 30 or 60 days later. This left the farmer free to concentrate his attentions on the harvesting of his crop, assured that it was already sold. In this way, many of the producer's and user's problems resulting from alternate over-supply/under-supply situations were solved through the use of forward contracts.

Now buyers could take advantage of scheduling grain deliveries at designated intervals, which in turn enabled them to program grain arrivals and outbound shipments. Grain elevator operators and owners were able to plan with maximum utilization of their storage facilities in mind, thereby assuring themselves of a more profitable enterprise. In like manner, processors could count on having available a steady supply of the commodity for processing forward sales.

With the opening of the Illinois-Michigan Canal in 1848, and the expansion of railroads, Chicago rapidly became a grain terminal supplying the East Coast and export trade. Processing facilities developed quickly to support local livestock feed demands as well as for shipment east.

But those involved in the handling of these commodities found that the "to-arrive" contracts did not solve all their problems. For example:

1. Qualities were not standardized and deliveries were unreliable.
2. Terms of payment varied.
3. Prices were not common knowledge.
4. Contracts were not easily resalable.

Refinements were made in the contracts to meet specific marketing needs. Eventually, these evolved into our modern futures contracts.

Development of Chicago Commodity Markets

The first commodity exchange in the United States was the Chicago Board of Trade, organized in early 1848. Rather than an organized marketplace for trading, however, the early exchange functioned more as a meeting place where grain merchants could discuss their mutual problems. As the volume of grain trade increased in the city, confusion reigned supreme. Trades were made everywhere, even on street corners and in saloons. It finally became apparent that trade was going to have to be conducted in a single location — the Board of Trade.

273

The Board developed a set of standards for wheat and began a system of weighing and inspecting grain. The substitution of weight for volume measures made possible the issuance of warehouse receipts, useful in change of title and as collateral in trade financing.

Gradually, as the problems inherent in the original forward contracts were overcome, a smaller and smaller number of market participants actually entered into contracts with the intent of taking delivery.

In the late 1850's and early 1860's, there was still considerable contracting taking place outside the Board of Trade, for it wasn't until October of 1865 that the Board adopted its general rules. By that time, all the essential ingredients of futures trading had been incorporated in its rules. October 1865 should more realistically serve as the actual date for the origin of modern futures trading. Today, the Chicago Board of Trade deals in billions of dollars worth of commodities annually. In 1976, nearly 19 million contracts traded, worth several hundred billion dollars.

Chicago Mercantile Exchange

Another of the giants among modern commodity exchanges is the Chicago Mercantile Exchange (CME), which got its start toward the end of the 19th century. Like the Board of Trade in grains, it developed in response to the distribution and pricing problems inherent in the egg industry around the turn of the century. With the development of refrigeration techniques, Chicago became a forwarding market for eggs. As a result of large seasonal accumulations, egg dealers and storers of eggs found themselves faced with increasing problems of financing and price risk.

The exchange, known first as the Chicago Produce Exchange and later as the Chicago Butter and Egg Board, was initially established to determine price quotations, define grades for butter and eggs and establish regulated trade practices. By 1916, trading in time contracts in these commodities was firmly established within the exchange. Trading was temporarily halted, however, with the imposition of the Food Control Act during World War I. After the resumption of trading in 1919, there was widespread dissatisfaction because of the non-fulfillment of contracts, caused primarily by sharp price advances. The butter and egg men within the Butter and Egg Board felt that insufficient attention had been given to establishing rules for organized trading in their commodities.Their solution was to reorganize the Board and eventually form a separate organization which they named the Chicago Mercantile Exchange, also looking toward an expansion of well-regulated and organized futures trading in commodities other than butter and eggs.

The real impetus to CME growth was the establishment of meat futures contracts in 1961 and financial futures in 1972. Both have been highly successful.

Today, actively traded commodities on the CME also include a large number of meat and livestock products as well as eight foreign currencies, T-bills, Certificates of Deposit and Eurodollars on the exchange's International Monetary Market division and stock index futures and options on the exchange's Index and Options Market division.

Other Exchanges

In addition to the CBT and the CME, other exchanges have developed over the years, each specializing in certain areas. Some exchanges have traded for a few years and then closed due to lack of volume, but at present there are 10 major futures exchanges in the U.S. — five in New York, three in Chicago and one each in Minneapolis and Kansas City. The New Orleans Commodity Exchange still exists but trades on the floor of the MidAmerica Commodity Exchange in Chicago rather than in New Orleans. London is also a major center for futures trading; other exchanges are located in Paris, Winnipeg, Toronto, Hong Kong, and Singapore. Policies on some foreign exchanges may vary considerably from U.S. practices, and the following sections deal only with U.S. exchanges.

Characteristics of Organized Futures Trading

Although organized futures trading differs significantly and substantially from other forms of trading, the concept of futurity or deferred performance in transactions is not new or unusual, nor is it the key element in distinguishing futures trading from other forms of trading.

Elements of a transaction (pricing, payment, title transfer and delivery) can be arranged in any order of time sequence. Hence, one can agree today on the price of a new car, receive the car and title to it two weeks from now and pay for it six weeks later when the credit card bill arrives. The element of futurity, then, is a necessary though not sufficient condition for a futures contract. Futurity is not what really distinguishes organized futures trading from any of a number of trading arrangements.

Organized futures trading, as it exists on several exchanges in the United States and abroad, may be distinguished from the widespread trading that involves other elements of futurity in the following respects.

1. Futures trading is conducted on an organized exchange, with a common set of rules governing all the transactions. Although a car dealer may contract to sell an automobile for delivery in three months, this is *not* futures trading. This is a customized contract or forward contract between one buyer and one seller, usually done in accordance with standard trade practice and subject to contract laws in the various localities but not under uniform exchange rules.

2. Futures have specific rules governing trading. Most important of these (which do not apply to most forward dealings) are:

   a. Trading must occur at one place (the trading pit or ring) by open outcry within specified hours. All bids and offers are thus known to all participants, and all transactions are public knowledge.

   b. Various anti-competitive practices are forbidden, e.g., no member may fill or match a customer's order without first offering it openly in a pit.

3. Futures contracts are standardized with respect to size, date, delivery location and delivery procedure. Only price is negotiated at the exchange. In ordinary forward dealings, of course, any peripheral terms and conditions can be negotiated.

4. Futures trading is impersonal. The exchange clearinghouse becomes a party to every contract that is negotiated at the Exchange—buyer and seller do the negotiating, but once the deal is struck, each has reciprocal obligations with the clearinghouse —

not with one another. In other forward dealings the parties continue to rely on their personal relationships for fulfillment.

5. Futures contracts are legally cancelled by offset. A member who sells one July pork belly futures contract incurs an obligation to deliver 36,000 pounds of pork bellies to the clearinghouse during July. This he may ultimately do to fulfill his contractual obligation. But if he buys a July contract prior to the completion of trading in late July, he then has equal and offsetting obligations to the clearinghouse so he is out of the market with no obligation.

6. The exchange clearinghouse acts as a common guarantor of all contracts. Members of the clearinghouse must maintain minimum amounts of working capital and must deposit funds to "margin" their outstanding trades. Exchange members who are not clearing members must affiliate with clearing members for purposes of verifying and guaranteeing all contracts. No credit is extended in this process; the margin deposit is a performance bond — not a down payment. When delivery occurs in satisfaction of a futures contract, full cash payment is required as the title is transferred. Prior to delivery, no title has been transferred and no credit is extended.

The term "futures contract" then is applied to a special type of forward contract bought and sold under the rules of organized exchanges having a clearinghouse. It is a legally binding contract to buy or sell a stipulated amount of a carefully specified product or service, during an agreed future period, subject to the rules and regulations of the exchange where the contract is made, and with price determined by public auction on the floor of the exchange.

Commodity Futures Trading and The Law

From its earliest beginnings in the form of forward contracts and even following the opening of organized commodity futures exchanges, futures trading repeatedly faced attack from hostile legislators. Among the earliest of such attacks was a proclamation in 1610 which prohibited short-selling in Holland. Almost always, general laws prohibiting organized futures trading on exchanges have been repealed within a short time after their passage. However, one such bill, banning futures trading in onions, did become law in the U.S. in 1958. It is still in effect, although recent studies by the U.S. government have shown that arguments used to persuade Congress of the need for the legislation were invalid and incorrect.

The general public's mistrust of futures trading stemmed in part from a misunderstanding of the concepts, particularly short selling, and in part from abusive practices on the part of exchange members who had little regard for the public welfare during the early stages of commodity futures trading. The uninformed, therefore, quickly equated speculation in futures with gambling, an unfortunate equation which still persists today, though to a lesser extent.

From 1884 to 1953, Congress introduced some 330 bills with the intent to restrain futures trading in one way or another. From 1890 to 1924, at least 30 separate investigations were undertaken in the grain trade. The Hatch Bill, which passed both houses in 1891 and almost became a law, would have imposed a tax upon all futures contracts in specified commodities. Fortunately, exchange officials recognized the need for getting their houses in order and so tightened internal controls and effected reforms in their organizations and the trading.

In 1916, the Cotton Futures Act and, in 1922, the Grain Futures Act were passed, bringing trading in these commodities under government regulation for the first time. Although widely bemoaned by the exchange community at the time, these acts proved beneficial to both the exchanges and the public. The Grain Futures Act was subsequently amended in the 1930's and renamed the Commodity Exchange Act. This legislation outlawed certain manipulative practices and established rules for safeguarding customer funds held by brokers. The act, which covered a broad range of commodities, was administered by the U.S. Department of Agriculture's Commodity Exchange Authority.

Not all commodity futures trading in the United States fell under the aegis of the Commodity Exchange Authority. Only trading in those commodities specifically mentioned in the Act were within its jurisdiction. The Act has been amended from time to time to include additional commodities and to broaden its scope. The most recent amendment occurred with the passage of the Commodity Futures Trading Commission Act of 1974.

The Commmodity Futures Trading Commission

The Commodity Futures Trading Commission Act was passed in October of 1974 largely as a result of high price levels reached in 1972 and 1973 when so many raw materials were in short supply. The furor that grew out of the Russian grain deals and the scandals that enveloped commodity options trading in the United States during the early 1970's also caused Congress to feel that the operation of the futures markets had become a matter of great public importance.

The CFTC Act amended the Commodity Exchange Act and established federal regulation over all commodities, rights and services traded on futures contracts.

Basically, the CFTC Act recognizes that properly functioning futures markets are in the best interest of the United States. The objectives of the CFTC Act are: (a) to foster competition in the marketplace and (b) to protect people who participate in the markets from fraud, deceit and abusive practices.

To administer the newly amended Commodity Exchange Act, an independent regulatory commission called the Commodity Futures Trading Commission was created. The Commission consists of a chairman and four other commissioners, each appointed by the President with the advice and consent of the Senate and each serving five-year terms. The Commission is headquartered in Washington, D.C., and has branch offices in New York, Chicago, Kansas City, Minneapolis and Los Angeles.

The new Act strengthens the exchanges' role as quasi-public institutions and brings almost all of their activities under regulation of the federal government. Every contract market (exchange) has to be specifically approved by the Commission. Everybody involved in execution of futures contracts and in dealing with the public has to be registered with the Commission and has to pass examination and fitness requirements established by the Commission. The new Act extends materially the concept of the public interest to be protected by including not only farmer interests but the interests of all people — producers, processors, merchants, other market users and consumers.

All contract markets must demonstrate that the futures contracts for which they seek designation for trading are not contrary to the national public interest and serve an economic function. All bylaws, rules, regulations and resolutions which relate to the terms and conditions of the contracts and other trading requirements must be submitted by the contract market to the CFTC for

approval. In addition, the Commission has the authority to go directly into court to enjoin any contract market or any person from violating the Act or restraining trade in a commodity for future delivery. The Commission has the authority, in emergency situations, to direct contract markets to take such actions as are necessary to maintain or restore orderly trading. Penalties can be assessed up to $100,000 in fines.

The Commission has established a number of operating programs to achieve the objectives of the Act. Among those programs are:

a. Market surveillance, which refers to the continual monitoring and analysis of the people who trade the various markets, the prices generated by the trading and the supply/demand elements affecting the prices. The purpose of the surveillance is to maintain orderly markets which are free of manipulation.

b. Rule reviews. The Act requires the CFTC to approve all rules, regulations, procedures and bylaws of the exchanges. Basically, they are reviewed for their equitability, their effect on competition, the extent to which they further the objectives of the Act and the degree to which they reflect normal commercial practices.

c. Registration and audit. All persons acting as futures commission merchants, floor brokers, associated persons, pool operators, trading advisors and options dealers must register with the Commission. Each of them is subject to independent financial audits conducted by CFTC or its legal designate.

d. Research. The Commission has established a research program designed to assess the status and role of competition in the industry and seek out ways of improving it. In addition, the research effort serves to systematically investigate the functioning of the market and market users.

e. Education. The Act authorized the Commission to establish an education program to inform people about the important functions performed by futures trading and the role of the CFTC in overseeing trading to assure that it furthers the objectives of the Act.

f. Enforcement. The enforcement program is designed to secure compliance with the law by the conduct of investigations to uncover violations of the Act and the prosecution of wrongdoers. In addition, the enforcement program administers the reparations program of the Commission.

g. Reparations. The Act authorized the commission to establish a procedure for receiving and reviewing claims for damages which arise from various violations of the Act by any person or

281

firm registered with the CFTC. Reparation claims may be filed for any amount, but the claim must be filed within two years after the alleged violation occurs. Reparations procedures are intended as an alternative to arbitration or court proceedings and not as an additional procedure if others are in process or completed. The CFTC encourages arbitration between the disputing parties.

To file a reparation claim, reparations complaints should be filed with:

Commodity Futures Trading Commission
Reparations Unit
2033 K Street, N.W.
Washington, D.C. 20581

When the complaint is filed, it should include the name and address of each person alleged to have violated the Act; the specific violations claimed; all relevant facts concerning the alleged violation, including dates, places and circumstances; and any documentation which supports the amount and manner of damage suffered by the claimant. The complaint should be notarized and should include a statement that no arbitration proceeding or civil court proceeding is underway.

The CFTC will review the complaint, and if action is warranted, each person complained against will receive a copy of it. Such persons have 45 days to answer the complaint. Counterclaims are allowed.

If the parties do not settle their differences, formal proceedings will begin, and the case will be assigned to an Administrative Law Judge for oral hearings. After the Administrative Law Judge rules on the case, either side may appeal the verdict to the Commission for review. The Commission decision may also be appealed to the U.S. Court of Appeals.

Although less government intervention in the marketplace is a desirable goal, the existence of a governmental agency to oversee exchange activities and to assure the enforcement of exchange rules is certainly healthy. In addition, such an agency, particularly if it is a strong agency using its power wisely, aids in establishing the credibility of the exchanges and the valuable economic functions they perform. It also assures the public that an independent entity is mindful of their interests.

CFTC Organization Chart

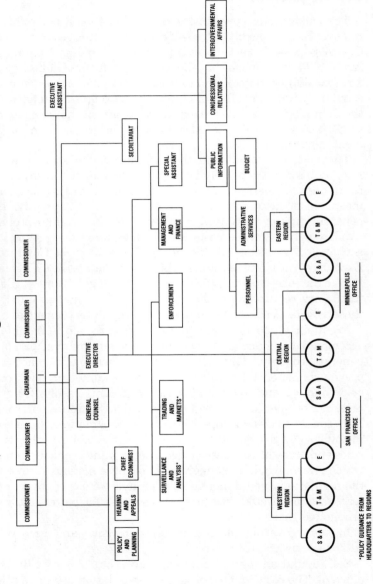

COMMISSIONER — COMMISSIONER — CHAIRMAN — COMMISSIONER — COMMISSIONER

EXECUTIVE ASSISTANT

SECRETARIAT

CONGRESSIONAL RELATIONS

INTERGOVERNMENTAL AFFAIRS

PUBLIC INFORMATION

POLICY AND PLANNING

HEARING AND APPEALS

CHIEF ECONOMIST

GENERAL COUNSEL

EXECUTIVE DIRECTOR

SPECIAL ASSISTANT

MANAGEMENT AND FINANCE

ENFORCEMENT

BUDGET

ADMINISTRATIVE SERVICES

PERSONNEL

SURVEILLANCE AND ANALYSIS*

TRADING AND MARKETS*

WESTERN REGION — S&A — T&M — E

SAN FRANCISCO OFFICE

CENTRAL REGION — S&A — T&M — E

MINNEAPOLIS OFFICE

EASTERN REGION — S&A — T&M — E

*POLICY GUIDANCE FROM HEADQUARTERS TO REGIONS

283

Self-Regulation

The existence of government regulation should not reduce or remove the responsibility for self-regulation. It is clear that when Congress passed the Commodity Futures Trading Commission Act of 1974, it intended that the commodity futures industry have a responsibility to itself and to the public to perform certain self-regulatory functions. It is also clear that Congress intended that the Commission require the exchanges to accept that responsibility. This is good. Self-regulation is more desirable than government regulation.

The motives behind and the net effect of most government regulations have generally been commendable and positive. Unfortunately, sometimes government regulations turn out to be incapable of achieving their intended goals. Frequently, they generate greater costs that resulted from the original problem. (And sometimes those costs are considerable.) One commodity exchange that spent $2,500 on legal fees to meet Commodity Exchange Authority requirements the year before the CFTC came into existence spent $75,000 on legal fees to meet CFTC regulatory requirements the year after. The long-run impact of these effects needs to be analyzed by regulatory agencies.

Frequently, government regulations are too inflexible to accommodate changes in the business environment and the general economy. Thus, they stifle innovation. Sometimes a previously beneficial regulation becomes outdated or even counter-productive and yet remains in effect. This results from the pressure of special interests. Historically, business enterprises have sought to avoid competition and have sometimes been aided in doing so by government or even self-regulation. At other times rules and procedures create vested interests and economic benefits which reform would endanger. In all of these instances, reform of the regulations would increase the productive use of government resources and would free private resources for better and more productive tasks.

In short, government regulation is expensive, and many of the costs to society are hidden.

Self-regulation may also be expensive, but it is usually more efficient. The costs and benefits of self-regulation usually acrue to the proper people — those most directly affected, instead of the general populace.

Regulatory agencies need to do more to identify the scope and seriousness of the actual problems they are trying to solve and to consider the total cost and total benefits of their actions. Only those regulations for which benefits outweigh costs should be instituted.

Regulators need also to consider the "why" test more often than the "why not" test when reviewing proposed regulations. They should seriously ask "why" particular regulation is needed and whether there are a number of alternative solutions to the problem other than establishing another regulation. Conversely, in order to create an environment conducive to encouraging innovation and experimentation in the marketplace, regulators should consider a "why not" test when reviewing proposals for new contracts and new types of business arrangements at the exchanges.

Perhaps most importantly, regulatory agencies, regulatees and private citizens need to pass the message that there is no substitute for self-protection and that government regulatory agencies cannot protect all people from all things. Citizens ought to be expected to put forth a reasonable amount of effort toward self-protection. Perhaps in trying to determine whether a particular regulation is necessary or not, regulatory agencies should apply an "ability to self-protect test" which would determine whether a reasonable individual exercising prudence and common sense in a particular situation could be reasonably expected to be able to protect himself without the need for government regulations. Every person has a responsibility to himself and to his fellow citizens to protect himself as much as possible.

To facilitate self-protection efforts, the CFTC should require full disclosure of all relevant aspects of commodity futures and commodity options transactions. In this way, natural forces of competition, which are the most effective means of regulating, will flourish.

26

The Commodity Futures Exchange

It is said that in the early 17th century, when futures trading was just emerging in Japan, traders wore the long, flowing, classic Japanese robes with very wide sleeves. As a trade was consummated, each trader allowed the opposite trader to put an arm up his sleeve. This was a sign of good faith, conveying to the opposite party that there were no tricks "up his sleeve" in the transaction.

As business increased and clothing styles changed, no doubt the Japanese found this a cumbersome or needless process. At any rate, in modern commodity futures trading the signs of good faith and contract guarantees are much more tangible. They now take the form of cash, and contract guarantees are provided by a clearing house, the heart of any commodity futures exchange.

The commodity futures exchange of today is a meeting place for buyers and sellers of futures contracts. Its role is to provide the facilities through which futures trading can be conducted; to establish trading rules; to supervise business conduct on the trading floor, and to collect and disseminate information about the market. The exchange itself never enters into the trading. It does not influence or establish prices. Market participants and economic forces influencing the market do that.

Nature of the Organization

The internal structure of all exchanges is basically similar. Therefore, the following discussion of exchange organization and operations, although primarily descriptive of the Chicago Mercantile Exchange, adequately describes virtually all commodity futures exchanges.

Most commodity exchanges are not-for-profit organizations. The shares in the corporations are called memberships. The total number of memberships varies from exchange to exchange and is generally fixed by the exchange governing board.

Membership on the exchange, which is an individual privilege, allows the member, among other things, to appear on the exchange trading floor, to act as a floor trader, to pay reduced commission on his trades and to participate in the management of the exchange.

Changes in membership occur only as privately-held exchange seats become available for purchase on a bid-and-offer basis. The actual price for a membership may fluctuate considerably from time to time. For example, in 1982 a seat on the Chicago Mercantile Exchange sold for a high of $160,000. These same memberships were being bid and offered in the $60,000-$70,000 range through 1971.

Applications for membership are submitted to the exchange, which then conducts a thorough investigation of the applicant's financial background and character. An applicant who meets financial and other requirements must then receive the approval of the Board of Governors.

Exchange Administration

The exchange is governed by a Board of Governors elected from a slate of nominees selected from its membership and, on most exchanges, from several non-member candidates who represent the public-at-large or the various commodity interests affected by the contracts traded on the exchange — e.g., banking, farming, etc. The Board is responsible for establishing major policies and making and amending exchange rules. In addition, it may act in a judicial capacity in conducting hearings involving member misconduct. The responsibilities and broad powers of an exchange governing board may differ slightly from one exchange to another, but they are generally pretty much alike.

Exchange Staff

Daily administration of the exchange is in the hands of an appointed and salaried president, employed with the approval of the exchange board. The president, as chief executive officer of the exchange, is assisted by such other officers and staff as he deems necessary. Generally, the major departments are: audits and investigations, education, public relations, quotations, research, and statistical.

The most important functions of these departments include:

Audits and Investigations — (a) monitoring the financial status of member firms and uncovering financial weakness early enough to enable corrective action to be taken; (b) market surveillance, including the review of all discretionary and omnibus accounts, which must be registered with the exchange; (c) aiding the Clearing House Committee by providing information gleaned from its review of all applications for clearing-house privileges, broker applications and solicitor applications, and (d) screening applicants for membership and reviewing applications from member firms to open branch offices.

Statistical Department — maintained by all major commodity futures exchanges, it reports and disseminates daily market price data and such information as may become available from governmental and other sources about supply and demand factors.

Quotations Department — responsible for supervising the

instantaneous release of market price quotations over national and international wire services, as well as supervision of all price data posted on the exchange floor.

Research Department — conducts or assists in making feasibility studies with respect to new contracts that might be traded and also in the analysis and implementation of changes to be made in existing contracts.

Education Department — charged with the responsibility of providing educational materials and services to various segments of the public concerned with or interested in the function and operation of the markets. The groups the department attempts to reach include commercial hedgers, bankers, speculators, the commodity brokerage industry and the academic community.

Public Relations Department — supervises and administrates all matters concerning the public relations function of the exchange. Its primary function is to promote public awareness of the vital economic role fulfilled by the modern commodity futures exchange and its place in our society as a financial institution of integrity and responsibility.

Exchange Committees

The exchange members themselves play an important role in the functioning of the market through a member committee system employed by most commodity futures exchanges. The Board chairman, with the approval of the Board, usually selects members of the various committees to serve during his term of office.

Certain committees are common to most major exchanges; though they may go by different titles, their functions are almost identical. These include an arbitration committee, membership committee, rules committee, business conduct committee, public relations committee, floor practices committee, clearing house committee, pit committee, floor brokers qualification committee, and contract specifications committee.

Arbitration Committee — reconciles controversies arising between two or more members through arbitration proceedings.

Membership Committee — reviews all applications of prospective members, investigates their qualifications and makes reports and recommendations on their findings to the Board.

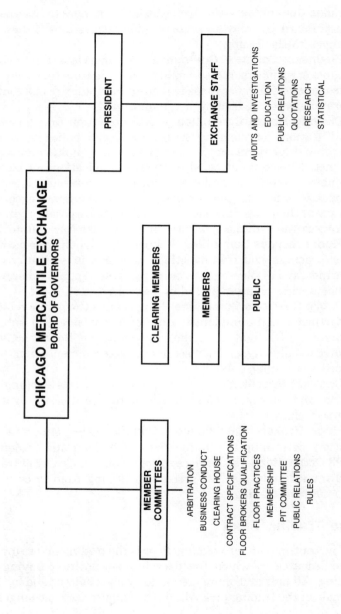

CHICAGO MERCANTILE EXCHANGE
BOARD OF GOVERNORS

PRESIDENT

EXCHANGE STAFF

AUDITS AND INVESTIGATIONS
EDUCATION
PUBLIC RELATIONS
QUOTATIONS
RESEARCH
STATISTICAL

CLEARING MEMBERS

MEMBERS

PUBLIC

MEMBER COMMITTEES

ARBITRATION
BUSINESS CONDUCT
CLEARING HOUSE
CONTRACT SPECIFICATIONS
FLOOR BROKERS QUALIFICATION
FLOOR PRACTICES
MEMBERSHIP
PIT COMMITTEE
PUBLIC RELATIONS
RULES

Rules Committee — drafts new rules or changes to rules passed by the Board and may also refer or offer suggestions for new rule changes to the Board.

Business Conduct Committee — supervises the business conduct of members. It also conducts investigations and may take action against member firms to assure that integrity of a contract and orderliness of trading are maintained.

Clearing House Committee — sole discretion in determining qualifications of clearing house member applicants and in adopting those regulations setting forth what qualifications must be met. This committee also reviews applications of clearing members, associate brokers, registered representatives, and applications for assignment of member rates. Some exchanges maintain their clearing house as a separate corporation. In such instances these duties are performed by that corporation.

Floor Practices Committee — supervises all matters relating to floor practices and trading ethics, conducts investigations and hearings, and resolves any errors or price discrepancies discovered either during or after a trading session.

Public Relations Committee — supervises the public relations department in the implementation of advertising and publicity activities; investigates, at the request of the Board, activities related to publicity, and advises or makes recommendations to the Board concerning publicity.

Contract Specifications Committee — reviews existing contracts and makes recommendations to the Board regarding contract changes.

Floor Brokers Qualification Committee — supervises all matters pertaining to qualifications of brokers and traders.

Pit Committee — supervises the opening and closing of trading and immediately resolves grievances arising from price infractions during trading.

The Trading Floor

The central point of a trading floor is the trading pit or ring — a specified area in which the floor brokers do their buying and selling. All bids and offers are made by open out-cry and by hand signals in the trading pits. Although computerized exchanges are not in existence yet, the CFTC Act requires the Commission to study the feasibility of such. Preliminary study has begun and in the not too distant future do not be surprised if an attempt is made to substitute a computer on the current trading floors.

As bids and offers are made and trades are consummated, prices are recorded by an observing reporter (an employee of the market) and reported on the quotation boards adjoining the pits. This information is also wired instantaneously to other markets and trading centers throughout the country and abroad.

Most floor brokers have telephone, telex and other communication lines adjacent to the trading area from which they receive customer orders for trades and confirm executed trades. Also on the floor, adjacent to the trading pits, are a bulletin board for posting important information and news tickers. The latter carry the most up-to-date information and commentary from financial centers such as New York and London, as well as pertinent news of the day.

Execution of Trades

When someone decides to trade on the exchange (having first opened an account with a member firm — a simple procedure which is explained in Chapter 4), he places his order with a registered representative of the member firm. A proper order should specify whether to buy or sell, what commodity, the number of contracts, at which price and the length of time the order is to run. When the account representative accepts the order, he confirms it orally and also in writing through the mail. This enables the customer to double-check the accuracy of the order and also signifies that the representative has accepted responsibility for it.

The order is immediately sent to the wire room of the firm's office where it is recorded and time-stamped upon receipt. (The order is electronically time-stamped at each relay point except at execution — see next section — so that a full record can be kept of its progress.) Then it is telephoned from the wire room to a company phoneman on the exchange floor. The phoneman relays the order in written form, via a runner, to the floor broker in the pit. Upon execution, the floor broker endorses the price on the order form, returns it via runner to the floor phoneman, who in

ORDER EXECUTION PROCESS

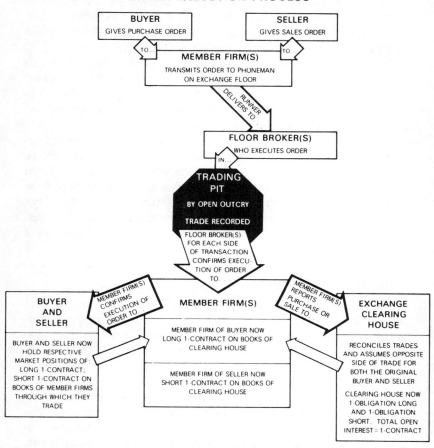

BUYER
GIVES PURCHASE ORDER

SELLER
GIVES SALES ORDER

TO...

TO...

MEMBER FIRM(S)
TRANSMITS ORDER TO PHONEMAN
ON EXCHANGE FLOOR

RUNNER DELIVERS TO...

FLOOR BROKER(S)
WHO EXECUTES ORDER

IN...

TRADING PIT
BY OPEN OUTCRY
TRADE RECORDED

FLOOR BROKER(S)
FOR EACH SIDE
OF TRANSACTION
CONFIRMS EXECU-
TION OF ORDER
TO...

MEMBER FIRM(S)
CONFIRMS
EXECUTION OF
ORDER TO...

MEMBER FIRM(S)
REPORTS
PURCHASE OR
SALE TO...

BUYER AND SELLER

BUYER AND SELLER NOW
HOLD RESPECTIVE
MARKET POSITIONS OF:
LONG 1-CONTRACT;
SHORT 1-CONTRACT ON
BOOKS OF MEMBER FIRMS
THROUGH WHICH THEY
TRADE

MEMBER FIRM(S)

MEMBER FIRM OF BUYER NOW
LONG 1-CONTRACT ON BOOKS OF
CLEARING HOUSE

MEMBER FIRM OF SELLER NOW
SHORT 1-CONTRACT ON BOOKS OF
CLEARING HOUSE

EXCHANGE CLEARING HOUSE

RECONCILES TRADES
AND ASSUMES OPPOSITE
SIDE OF TRADE FOR
BOTH THE ORIGINAL
BUYER AND SELLER

CLEARING HOUSE NOW
1-OBLIGATION LONG
AND 1-OBLIGATION
SHORT. TOTAL OPEN
INTEREST = 1-CONTRACT

DELIVERY PROCEDURE

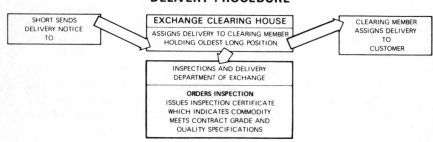

SHORT SENDS
DELIVERY NOTICE
TO...

EXCHANGE CLEARING HOUSE
ASSIGNS DELIVERY TO CLEARING MEMBER
HOLDING OLDEST LONG POSITION

CLEARING MEMBER
ASSIGNS DELIVERY
TO
CUSTOMER

INSPECTIONS AND DELIVERY
DEPARTMENT OF EXCHANGE

ORDERS INSPECTION
ISSUES INSPECTION CERTIFICATE
WHICH INDICATES COMMODITY
MEETS CONTRACT GRADE AND
QUALITY SPECIFICATIONS

turn relays it to the wire room. As soon as the registered representative is informed of the trade execution by the wire room, he provides the customer with verbal confirmation and later confirms it in writing. If the order is a market order, this entire process—from the time the customer enters the order until it is executed in

the pit and confirmation is relayed back to the customer — can take less than one minute. The diagram on the facing page illustrates this order execution process.

At the end of each trading day, member firms report all transactions to the clearing house which reconciles (or matches) the trades and assumes the opposite side of the trade for both the original buyer and seller. This facilitates the offsetting of futures positions by the traders and greatly simplifies the settlement and delivery process.

Time Stamping

One of the issues that Congress discussed extensively in its deliberations over the CFTC Act of 1974 had to do with dual trading — i.e., the practice of a floor broker, FCM, associated person, etc. trading for his own account at the same time that he solicits and executes orders for customers. Such a practice seemingly has some inherent conflicts of interest.

Congress directed the CFTC to study this issue and make a determination on whether to allow the practice, and if so, under what conditions. The Commission has tentatively decided not to ban the practice but rather to require all exchanges and registered persons to institute a record-keeping system which will ultimately lead to a record of execution times. Such a time record will make it easy for the exchange, the CFTC or any customer who believes that a broker has taken advantage of his order by trading ahead of it or by some other abusive practice to reconstruct a sequence of events to determine with a high degree of certainty whether the complaint is valid. Such a time-stamping system will protect the broker as much as the customers.

Although a complete time-stamping system is not yet in effect on any exchange, all exchanges are experimenting with a variety of time-stamping procedures and intervals and improved record-keeping systems. The CFTC expects that in several years a highly efficient and effective system will be developed and adopted by all exchanges and registered entities dealing with the public.

The Clearing House[1]

Most of us are familiar with the clearing house operations our nation's banking system uses to expedite the flow and transfer of funds from one bank to another within the system. In the case of a futures exchange, the clearing operation exists to perform a similar function in that it facilitates the flow and transfer of funds resulting from its member firms' execution of trades. As is true in the case of the bank depositor, the individual commodity trader has no direct contact with the clearing organization; it serves as a central point for depositing and dispensing funds to be credited or debited to the accounts of member firms.

An additional function served by the exchange clearing house is as guarantor of contract performance. In other words, the fulfill-

---

[1]Exchanges in many other parts of the world do not use clearing houses. This is risky, and most such exchanges have very little public business.

ment of contract obligations of a clearing member is guaranteed through the collective financial resources of all clearing members, regardless of what happens to the other clearing-member party to the contract. There is no direct comparison here with banks' clearing operation, as the responsibility of guaranteeing transactions rests solely with the individual bank with regard to each of its customers.

The exchange clearing house performs a third important function which is in no way comparable to the banking system's clearing operation — namely, its role in the assignment and overseeing of contract deliveries.

The formal relationships between the clearing house and the exchange may differ from one exchange to another. For example, the International Commodities Clearing House in London is a privately owned clearing house, separate from ownership of any exchange. It provides clearing services for a number of independent exchanges in several countries. On both the International Monetary Market and the Chicago Mercantile Exchange, the clearing house is an integral part of the exchange, operating under the direct jurisdiction of the exchange's Clearing House Committee. At the Chicago Board of Trade, the clearing house is a separate corporate entity with its own board of directors. No matter what formal arrangements exist, however, all commodity exchange clearing houses in the U.S. operate in a similar fashion and perform nearly identical functions.

Membership in the clearing house is normally confined to exchange members, although the majority of exchange members are not clearing house members. Those exchange members who are not clearing house members must still have their trades cleared (verified and guaranteed) by a clearing house member. To put it another way, each member must either be a clearing member or be affiliated with a clearing member.

Clearing members do not pay commissions for trades executed, but do pay clearance fees and floor brokerage fees if an independent floor broker is used for trade executions. They also collect a fee from exchange members who clear trades through them.

The function of the clearing house begins as trading closes for the day. Clearing house members submit a trade confirmation card for each trade executed. Customers' names do not actually appear on these cards as buyer or seller, but only the name of the clearing house member in whose name the trade is executed for the customer.

Once these confirmation cards have been matched or verified, the original parties to the transactions — the member brokers — cease to deal with one another directly. They each deal instead exclusively with the clearing house. In effect, they are now long or short to the clearing house, as it has assumed the position of second party to each member's transaction. The liquidation of contracts is facilitated through this system, because a trader can now offset his contract without the necessity of obtaining the agreement of the original second party to the contract. The clearing house then merely notes that the original trader's obligation is cancelled.

The clearing member firm is ultimately responsible for fulfillment of a contract with the clearing house, not the individual customer. The customer's responsibility lies solely with his broker. The brokerage firm, after executing the trade, then deals exclusively with the clearing house.

Finance

Whenever a transaction is made in the market, both parties to the trade are asked to post a "good-faith" bond in the form of cash, Treasury bills, listed securities or Letters of Credit. This "good-faith" money is usually referred to as margin, although on some markets it is called "security deposit," a term which more accurately describe it and distinguishes it from margin in the securities market.

The clearing house establishes and maintains strict control over these minimum security deposits (margins), both for initiating and for maintaining positions. Member firms are required to collect these minimum amounts from customers. Brokers may, and frequently do, charge customers more than the minimum, but they may not collect less. Clearing member firms must, in turn, deposit and maintain a specified level of funds in the clearing house to back up their aggregate net market position.

The purpose for requiring these funds is to insure performance under the terms of the futures contract. It is a safeguard or surety to both buyer and seller (and to the carrying broker) that there will be funds available to make proper settlement when the contract is terminated. When the contracts are offset or delivered upon, this money is returned to the trader along with his profit on the transaction, or is applied toward his debits if he has lost money.

A trader who has a paper profit on his transaction may withdraw his gain over and above the minimum security deposit required at any time before he offsets his position. On the other hand, if his transaction shows a paper loss, his account will be debited accordingly, and he may be asked to deposit additional funds in order to maintain the value of his account at the required minimum amount.

The clearing house requires daily settlement in cash for all price variations in every contract traded. This means that each day the clearing house credits the account of clearing members showing a net gain due to favorable price movements during that day's trading and requires immediate payment from those members showing a net loss on their positions.

Since there is, of course, a buyer for every seller, the monies paid out must be equal the monies collected, and the clearing house must show neither a gain nor loss. It must balance before a new trading day begins.

Brokers use the cash payments received from the clearing house to pay out trading profits to customers. Conversely, they have to pay additional money to the clearing house to cover losses sustained by customers.

In summary, today's modern commodity futures exchanges have come a long way in developing managerial techniques for handling the tremendous explosion in volume of trading seen in recent years. The exchanges themselves are modern structures, which make use of the most modern data processing technology available. Over the years they have developed an unbroken record in maintaining the financial integrity of member firms, and assuring the safety of customer funds deposited with member firms.

The Trading Plan — Part I

**Am I Financially Suitable For Futures Trading And
How Much Money Can I Afford To Risk On Futures Trading?**

The Income Statement
(Average last 3 years)

Annual Income
    My salary   _____
    Spouse's salary   _____
    Investment income   _____
    Other income   _____
A.   TOTAL   _____

Annual Expense
    Mortgage payments   _____
    Insurance   _____
    Taxes   _____
    Education   _____
    Savings   _____
    Living Expenses   _____
    Vacations   _____
    Loan payments   _____
    Retirement account   _____
B.   TOTAL   _____
C.   Average annual net income available for investment (A - B):
     $ _____
D.   Percent of C to be committed to futures trading* _____
E. $C \times D = \$$____— amount of income available for futures trading.

---

*The maximum proportion of your available investment income which should be committed to
futures trading will vary depending upon individual circumstances. Nevertheless, a prudent
man would not exceed 25%.

Personal Balance Sheet

Major Fixed Assets
Home _____
Other real estate _____
Equity in business _____
Other (describe) _____
TOTAL _____

Major Liabilities
Mortgage on home _____
Other mortgages _____
Loans _____
_____
_____
TOTAL _____

Liquid assets
Cash in banks _____
Savings accounts _____
Securities owned _____
Other (describe) _____
TOTAL _____

TOTAL Assets ($ _____) — TOTAL Liabilities ($ _____)
= $ _____ Net Worth

Summary
Maximum amount available for futures trading:

Net worth $ _____ × _____ %* = _____
Liquid assets _____ × _____ % = _____
Net income _____ × _____ % = _____

Which of these you select as your maximum depends on how you think
a reduction in one versus another will affect achievement of your short-
and long-run goal. Generally, it would be prudent to select the smallest of
the three numbers.

---

* The maximum proportion of one's net worth liquid assets or net income that one should
commit to futures trading will vary with the individual's circumstances. Generally, however,
it would be prudent to commit no more than 20% of net worth, 10% of liquid assets, or 25% of
net income. Further, if you don't have a net worth of at least $50,000 excluding your home,
you probably should not speculate on commodity futures contracts. The exact amount that is
right for you depends on your family status, the extent to which the loss of the funds would
affect your long-run personal and family goals, your desire to take risks, your annual income
levels and your expected future income levels. For example, a man with $100,000 income and
a net worth of $200,000, two kids in high school and two in college, two homes and several
club memberships is probably less able to take risks than a 30-year-old bachelor earning
$35,000 per year and having a net worth of $25,000.

Trading Plan — Part II
Initiating A Position

I. **The commodity** I am interested in trading is: _____
  The contract month I like is: _____

II. **Market Analysis:**

	COL. I	COL. II	COL. III	SCORE*
Are the supply/ demand factors:	__Bullish	__Neutral	__Bearish	_____
Is the seasonal influence:	__Bullish	__Neutral	__Bearish	_____
In relation to historial price levels, is the current price:	__Low	__Average	__High	_____
Have recent government reports been:	__Bullish	__Neutral	__Bearish	_____
Are the chart patterns/technical analysis:	__Bullish	__Neutral	__Bearish	_____
			TOTAL**	_____

*Assign the following points for each column checked.
  COL I = 2 points, COL. II = 1 point, COL. III = 0 points.
**Use the following scale for assessing the expected market direction:

BULLISH	**NEUTRAL**	**BEARISH**
10 9 8 7	6 5 4	3 2 1 0
Consider buying	**Do nothing**	**Consider selling**

III. Expectations:

Expected Price Change	__10%	__5%-10%	__0%-5%
Probability of Occurring	__75%	__51%-75%	__10%-50%

If you expect less than a 5% change in price or if you think the probability of achieving the expected price change is less than 50%, you are probably better off not taking a position. If you feel you have more than a 75% chance of getting at least a 10% change in price, you

303

probably have a good possibility for a successful trade. In between those extremes it is your best judgment as to whether you think the risk is worth the potential reward.

IV. Action

Based on what I know about market factors, I will take the following position:

I will _____ (____) quantity_____
       (buy) (sell) (stand aside)   (month)

_____at _____and will enter a STOP at _____
  (commodity)   (price)   (price)

Trading Plan — Part III

Liquidating a Position

The Plan

I (will) (will not) maintain my position into the delivery month. Therefore, my maximum date beyond which I will not hold this position is
_____.

A. My target price(s) for liquidation is   ____contracts @_____
                                          ____contracts @_____
                                          ____ contracts @_____

B. If I achieve my target price(s), I
will have a net gain on the transaction of   _____

_____

_____

C. The probability of achieving the net gain is   _____

_____

_____

D. If the market moves against me
and my stop orders are executed,
I will suffer losses of   _____

_____

_____

E. The probability of my suffering such losses is   _____

_____

_____

Given these circumstances, the most I
could expect to gain on average over a long
run from these transactions is
    $(B \times C) - (D \times E) =$ _____ *

---

*If this number is not positive, do not make the trade. The greater this number, assuming the probabilities you assigned are correct, the greater the reward you can expect relative to the risk and the more certain you can be that the trade will be successful.

The Results

I did liquidate my position at:

_____ contracts @ _____
_____ contracts @ _____
_____ contracts @ _____

My gain on the transactions was: _____

I paid commissions of: _____

Interest not earned on my margin money was: _____ *

My net gain (loss) on the transaction(s) was: _____

This represented _____% return on my margin money.

*This is an opportunity cost. You could have invested the money in a savings account or some other investment.

Trading Plan — Part IV
Evaluation of Plan

Overall, my plan reflected what I actually did

_____ Quite Well   _____ Fair   _____ Poorly

The mistakes I made were _____

_____

_____

_____

Appendix II
Commodity Trader's Scorecard*

This scorecard is a practice trading exercise. It is designed to give you a basic "feel" for commodity futures trading. The more sophisticated kinds of futures trading transactions such as day trades, stradles and spreads have been eliminated in order to keep your practice trading as simple as possible. To best utilize the scorecard, first familiarize yourself as much as possible with all the aspects of commodity futures trading explained in this book. Then:

1. Develop a trading plan. Determine your financial suitability, select a commodity, its delivery month, the number of contracts you wish to "sell or buy," and your strategy for trading. This should be based upon your knowledge of the commodity's supply, demand and technical situation along with your best judgment of which direction prices will be moving in the future. Remember, it is just as feasible to sell first with the intention of buying later as is the opposite transaction.

2. To make the hypothetical trades, determine the price of your contracts on the initial date of the transaction. Look for the daily prices in the business section of your newspaper. All major newspapers carry this information. Use closing (sometimes called "settlement") prices. Remember that, while the value of a contract may be many thousands of dollars, the "earnest money" (margin) you have to put up is a much lesser amount. Thus, only a small change in price can provide a large change in your investment, either positive or negative. Your profit or loss in dollars is determined by the difference between the purchase and sales price.

3. Commodity futures prices are quoted in cents per pounds, dollars per hundredweight, cents per dozen, and dollars per thousand board feet, etc. To keep track of how much money you make or lose with each change in price, you need to know how large each contract is and what unit the price quote represents. For example, if the price of pork belly futures moves from 34.00¢ per lb. to 34.50¢ per lb., the price movement would be considered 50 "points." Since each pork belly contract is for 36,000 lbs., each movement of one "point" up or down is worth $3.60 and a 50-point move would, therefore, amount to $180.

4. Enter the information from items 1 and 2 on your scorecard. Obviously, you will not be able to fill in the net profit or loss until termination of the transaction. Assume a minimum commission per contract of $40. (Most brokers have negotiated commission rates for large orders and are committed to completely negotiated rates for all orders, irrespective of size, after 1978.)

This scorecard was originally developed by the Chicago Mercantile Exchange and is reprinted here courtesy of the CME.

5. To calculate your profit or loss, take the lower price and subtract it from the higher price after you have terminated your position. Multiply the difference by the value per "point" (see step 3 above) and then multiply that number by the quantity of contracts you sold or bought. If you bought for less than you sold, you have a profit and vice versa. Deduct your commission from the profits. Add it to your losses.

EXAMPLE: Buy (long)

Step 1:	$	31.62	bought 5 July bellies 9-16-76
		31.02	sold 5 July bellies 11-2-76
	$	.60	difference in points
Step 2:	1	3.60	price per point
	×	60	points
	$	216.00	loss
Step 3:	$	40.00	commission
	×	5	contracts
	$	200.00	total commission
Step 4:	$	216.00	loss
	−	5	contracts
	$	1,080.00	loss
	+	200.00	commission
	$	1,280.00	Net Loss

EXAMPLE: Selling (short)

Step 1:	$	31.62	sold 5 July bellies 9-16-76
		31.02	bought 5 July bellies 11-2-76
	$	.60	difference in points
Step 2:	$	3.60	price per point
	×	60	points
	$	216.00	profit
Step 3:	$	40.00	commission
	×	5	contracts
	$	200.00	total commissions
Step 4:	$	216.00	profit
	×	5	contracts
	$	1,080.0	profit
		−200.00	commission
	$	880.00	Net Profit

6. When you have terminated your position and calculated your net profit or loss, enter the results in the proper column of your scorecard.

7. Evaluate your plan.

8. Be honest. Don't cheat. You're not fooling others; you're fooling yourself.

(SAMPLE)
COMMODITY SCORECARD*

	BOUGHT				SOLD			COMMISSION	LOSS (Including Commission(s))	PROFIT (Including Commission(s))
Date	Qty	Commodity	Price	Date	Qty	Commodity	Price			
9-16-76	5	Pork Bellies July '77	31.62	11-2-76	5	Pork Bellies July '77	31.02	$200	$1,280.00	

*This scoreboard was originally developed and distributed by the Chicago Mercantile Exchange. It is reprinted here, with some slight modification, courtesy of the Chicago Mercantile Exchange.

Trading facts and figures

All futures contracts on U.S. and foreign commodity exchanges are listed on the following pages. However, some of these contracts are not being traded at this time. The list does not include new contracts awaiting CFTC approval.

Details of all contracts are current, to the best of our knowledge, but any one of the areas listed is subject to change. The daily limit figure given is the normal limit that prices can move up or down from the previous day's close. A number of exchanges have variable limit policies which can alter these limits in a volatile market. In a fast-moving market, you should check with your broker about limit changes.

Exchange	Commodity	Trading Months	Trading Hours (Local Time)	Contract Size	Minimum Price Fluctuation	Daily Limit
Chicago Board of Trade	Corn	Mar/May/July Sept/Dec	9:30-1:15	5,000 bu.	1/4¢/bu. = $12.50	10¢/bu. = $500
	Oats	Mar/May/July Sept/Dec	9:30-1:15	5,000 bu.	1/4¢/bu. = $12.50	6¢/bu. = $300
	Soybeans	Jan/Mar/May/July Aug/Sept/Nov	9:30-1:15	5,000 bu.	1/4¢/bu. = $12.50	30¢/bu. = $1,500
	Soybean Meal	Jan/Mar/May/July Aug/Sept/Oct/Dec	9:30-1:15	100 tons	10¢/ton = $10	$10/ton = $1,000
	Soybean Oil	Jan/Mar/May/July Aug/Sept/Oct/Dec	9:30-1:15	60,000 lbs.	1/100¢/lb. = $6	1¢/lb. = $600
	Wheat	Mar/May/July Sept/Dec	9:30-1:15	5,000 bu.	1/4¢/bu. = $12.50	20¢/bu. = $1,000

	Delivery Months	Hours	Contract Size	Minimum Fluctuation	Daily Limit
Crude Oil	Feb/June/July/Aug Sept/Oct/Dec	8:30-2:30	1,000 barrels (42,000 gal.)	1¢/barrel = $10	$1/barrel = $1,000
Heating Oil (No. 2)	Feb/May/June/July Aug/Sept/Oct/Dec	8:30-2:30	1,000 barrels (42,000 gal.)	0.025¢/gal. = $10.50	3.0¢/gal. = $1,260
Unleaded Gasoline	Feb/Mar/Apr/May June/Aug/Oct	8:30-2:30	1,000 barrels (42,000 gal.)	0.025¢/gal. = $10.50	3.0¢/gal. = $1,260
GNMA CDR	Mar/June Sept/Dec	8:00-2:00	$100,000 principal	1/32 pt. = $31.25	64/32 pt. = $2,000
U.S. Treasury Bonds	Mar/June Sept/Dec	8:00-2:00	$100,000 8% coupon	1/32 pt. = $31.25	64/32 pt. = $2,000
U.S. Treasury Bond Options	(See options on futures section)				
U.S. Treasury Notes (6½-10 yr.)	Mar/June Sept/Dec	8:00-2:00	$100,000 8% coupon	1/32 pt. = $31.25	64/32 pt. = $2,000
U.S. Treasury Notes (2-year)	Mar/June Sept/Dec	8:00-2:00	$400,000	1/128 pt. = $31.25	96/128 pt. = $3,000
Gold	Feb/Mar/Apr June/Aug/Oct/Dec	8:00-1:30	100 oz.	10¢/oz. = $10	$25/oz. = $2,500
Gold	Feb/Apr/June Aug/Oct/Dec	8:00-1:30	1 kilogram = 32.15 oz.	10¢/oz. = $3.22	$50/oz. = $1,607.50
Silver	Feb/Mar/Apr June/Aug/Oct/Dec	8:05-1:25	1,000 troy oz.	1/10¢/oz. = $5	50¢/oz. = $500
Silver	Feb/Mar/Apr/May June/Aug/Oct/Dec	8:05-1:25	5,000 troy oz.	1/10¢/oz. = $5	50¢/oz. = $2,500
Western Plywood	Jan/Mar/May July/Sept/Nov	9:00-1:05	76,032 sq. ft.	10¢/1,000 sq. ft. = $7.60	$7/1,000 sq. ft. = $532

Exchange	Commodity	Trading Months	Trading Hours (Local Time)	Contract Size	Minimum Price Fluctuation	Daily Limit
Chicago Mercantile Exchange	**Broilers, Fresh**	Feb/Apr/June/July Aug/Oct/Dec	9:10-1:00	30,000 lbs.	2.5/100¢/lb. = $7.50	2¢/lb. = $600
	Cattle, Feeder	Jan/Mar/Apr/May Aug/Sept/Oct/Nov	9:05-12:45	44,000 lbs.	2.5/100¢/lb. = $11	1.5¢/lb. = $660
	Cattle, Live	Feb/Apr/June Aug/Oct/Dec	9:05-12:45	40,000 lbs.	2.5/100¢/lb. = $10	1.5¢/lb. = $600
	Eggs, Fresh White	Jan/Mar/May June/Sept/Nov	9:20-1:00	22,500 doz.	5/100¢/doz. = $11.25	2¢/doz. = $450
	Hogs, Live	Feb/Apr/June/July Aug/Oct/Dec	9:10-1:00	30,000 lbs.	2.5/100¢/lb. = $7.50	1.5¢/lb. = $450
	Pork Bellies	Feb/Mar/May July/Aug	9:10-1:00	38,000 lbs.	2.5/100¢/lb. = $9.50	2¢/lb. = $760

Exchange	Commodity	Trading Months	Trading Hours (Local Time)	Contract Size	Minimum Price Fluctuation	Daily Limit
International Monetary Market of the Chicago Mercantile Exchange	Deutsche Mark	Jan/Mar/Apr/June July/Sept/Oct/Dec and spot month	7:30-1:20	125,000 DM	0.0001/DM = $12.50	0.01 = $1,250
	Canadian Dollar	Jan/Mar/Apr/June July/Sept/Oct/Dec and spot month	7:30-1:26	100,000 CD	0.0001/CD = $10	0.0075 = $750
	French Franc	Jan/Mar/Apr/June July/Sept/Oct/Dec and spot month	7:30-1:28	250,000 FF	0.00005/FF = $12.50	0.005 = $1,250
	Swiss Franc	Jan/Mar/Apr/June July/Sept/Oct/Dec and spot month	7:30-1:16	125,000 SF	0.0001/SF = $12.50	0.0150 = $1,875
	Dutch Guilder	Jan/Mar/Apr/June July/Sept/Oct/Dec and spot month	7:30-1:30	125,000 DG	0.0001/DG = $12.50	0.0100 = $1,250
	British Pound	Jan/Mar/Apr/June July/Sept/Oct/Dec and spot month	7:30-1:24	25,000 BP	0.0005/BP = $12.50	0.05 = $1,250
	Mexican Peso	Jan/Mar/Apr/June July/Sept/Oct/Dec and spot month	7:30-1:18	1,000,000 MP	0.00001/MP = $10	0.00150 = $1,500
	Japanese Yen	Jan/Mar/Apr/June July/Sept/Oct/Dec and spot month	7:30-1:22	12,500,000 JY	0.000001/JY = $12.50	0.0001 = $1,250
	Gold	Jan/Mar/Apr/June July/Sept/Oct/Dec and spot month	8:00-1:30	100 troy oz.	10¢/oz. = $10	$50/oz. = $5,000

Exchange	Commodity	Trading Months	Trading Hours (Local Time)	Contract Size	Minimum Price Fluctuation	Daily Limit
	Treasury Bills (13-week)	Mar/June Sept/Dec	8:00-2:00	$1,000,000	1 pt. = $25	60 pt. = $1,500
	Treasury Bills (1-year)	Mar/June Sept/Dec	8:15-1:35	$250,000	1 pt. = $25	50 pt. = $1,250
	Domestic Certificates of Deposit (3-mo.)	Mar/June/ Sept/Dec	7:30-2:00	$1,000,000	1 pt. = $25	80 pt. = $2,000
	Eurodollar Time Deposit (3-month)	Mar/June/Sept/Dec and spot month	7:30-2:00	$1,000,000	1 pt. = $25	100 pt. = $2,500
Index and Option Market of the Chicago Mercantile Exchange	Standard & Poor's 500 Stock Index	Mar/June Sept/Dec	9:00-3:15	500 × S&P Stock Index	5 pt. = $25	None
	S&P 500 Stock Index Options	(See options on futures section)				
	Lumber (random-length)	Jan/Mar/May July/Sept/Nov	9:00-1:05	130,000 bd. ft.	10¢/1,000 bd. ft. = $13	$5/1,000 bd. ft. = $650

Exchange	Commodity	Trading Months	Trading Hours (Local Time)	Contract Size	Minimum Price Fluctuation	Daily Limit
Coffee, Sugar & Cocoa Exchange, Inc.	**Cocoa**	Mar/May/July Sept/Dec	9:30-3:00	10 metric tons	$1/metric ton = $10	$88/metric ton = $880
	Coffee "C"	Mar/May/July Sept/Dec	9:45-2:30	37,500 lbs.	1/100¢/lb. = $3.75	4¢/lb. = $1,500
	Sugar No. 11 (world)	Jan/Mar/May July/Sept/Oct	10:00-1:45	112,000 lbs.	1/100¢/lb. = $11.20	1/2¢/lb. = $560
	Sugar No. 12 (domestic)	Jan/Mar/May July/Sept/Nov	10:00-1:45	112,000 lbs.	1/100¢/lb. = $11.20	1/2¢/lb. = $560
	Sugar No. 11 Options	(See options on futures sections)				

Exchange	Commodity	Trading Months	Trading Hours (Local Time)	Contract Size	Minimum Price Fluctuation	Daily Limit
Commodity Exchange (Comex)	**Copper**	Current calendar month, next two calendar months and Jan/Mar May/July/Sept/Dec	9:50-2:00	25,000 lbs.	5/100¢/lb. = $12.50	5¢/lb. = $1,250
	Gold	Current calendar month, next two calendar months and Jan/Mar May/July/Sept/Dec	9:25-2:30	100 troy oz.	10¢/oz. = $10	$25/oz. = $2,500
	Silver	Current calendar month, next two calendar months and Jan/Mar May/July/Sept/Dec	9:40-2:15	5,000 troy oz.	10/100¢/oz. = $5	50¢/oz. = $2,500
	Gold Options	(See options on futures section)				

315

Exchange	Commodity	Trading Months	Trading Hours (Local Time)	Contract Size	Minimum Price Fluctuation	Daily Limit
Kansas City Board of Trade	**Wheat** (hard red winter)	Mar/May/July Sept/Dec	9:30-1:15	5,000 bu.	1/4¢/bu. = $12.50	25¢/bu. = $1,250
	Value Line Stock Index	Mar/June Sept/Dec	9:00-3:15	500 times the futures price	0.05 = $25	5.00 pt. = $2,500

Exchange	Commodity	Trading Months	Trading Hours (Local Time)	Contract Size	Minimum Price Fluctuation	Daily Limit
MidAmerica Commodity Exchange	**Cattle, Live**	Jan/Feb/Apr/June Aug/Oct/Dec	9:05-1:00	20,000 lbs.	2.5/100¢/lb. = $5	1.5¢/lb. = $300
	Hogs, Live	Feb/Apr/June July/Aug/Oct/Dec	9:10-1:15	15,000 lbs.	2.5/100¢/lb. = $3.75	1.5¢/lb. = $225
	Corn	Mar/May/July Sept/Dec	9:30-1:30	1,000 bu.	1/8¢/bu. = $1.25	10¢/bu. = $100
	Oats	Mar/May/July Sept/Dec	9:30-1:30	1,000 bu.	1/8¢/bu. = $10	6¢/bu. = $60
	Soybeans	Jan/Mar/May July/Aug/Sept/Nov	9:30-1:30	1,000 bu.	1/8¢/bu. = $1.25	30¢/bu. = $300
	Wheat	Mar/May/July Sept/Dec	9:30-1:30	1,000 bu.	1/8¢/bu. = $1.25	20¢/bu. = $200
	Gold	Mar/June/Sept Dec	8:00-1:40	33.2 fine troy oz.	2.5¢/oz. = $0.83	$50/oz. = $1,660
	Silver (Chicago contract)	Current month and any subsequent months, up to 12-15 months ahead	8:05-1:40	1,000 troy oz.	5/100¢/oz. = 50¢	50¢/oz. = $500

316

Exchange	Commodity	Trading Months	Trading Hours (Local Time)	Contract Size	Minimum Price Fluctuation	Daily Limit
	U.S. Treasury Bonds	Mar/June Sept/Dec	8:00-2:15	$50,000 face value	1/32 pt. = $15.62	64/32 pt. = $1,000
	U.S. Treasury Bills (13-week)	Mar/June Sept/Dec	8:00-2:15	$500,000 face value	1/10 pt. = $12.50	60 pt. = $750
	Sugar (domestic refined)	Jan/Mar/May July/Sept/Nov	9:00-1:00	40,000 lb.	1/100¢/lb. = $4	1/2¢/lb. = $200 (None in two nearby months)
Minneapolis Grain Exchange	Spring Wheat	Mar/May/July Sept/Dec	9:30-1:15	5,000 bu.	1/8¢/bu. = $6.25	20¢/bu. = $1,000
	Sunflower Seeds	Jan/Mar/May July/Nov	9:25-1:20	100,000 lbs.	1/100¢/lb. = $10	1/2¢/lb. = $500

Exchange	Commodity	Trading Months	Trading Hours (Local Time)	Contract Size	Minimum Price Fluctuation	Daily Limit
New Orleans Commodity Exchange	Milled Rice	Jan/Mar/May Sept/Nov	9:45-1:40	1,200 cwt. (120,000 lbs.)	$0.005/cwt. = $6	$0.50/cwt. ($600)
	Rough Rice	Jan/Mar/May July/Sept/Nov	9:45-1:45	2,000 cwt. (200,000 lbs.)	$0.005/cwt. = $10	$0.30/cwt. ($600)
	Soybeans	Jan/Mar/May July/Oct/Nov	9:30-1:15	5,000 bu.	1/4¢/bu. = $12.50	30¢/bu. = $1,500
	Cotton	Mar/May/July Oct/Dec	9:15-2:00	50,000 lbs. (100 bales)	1/100¢/lb. = $5	2¢/lb. = $1,000
	Corn	Mar/May/July Sept/Dec	9:30-1:15	5,000 bu.	1/4¢/bu. = $12.50	10¢/bu. = $500

Exchange	Commodity	Trading Months	Trading Hours (Local Time)	Contract Size	Minimum Price Fluctuation	Daily Limit
New York Cotton Exchange	Cotton No. 2	Mar/May/July Oct/Dec	10:30-3:00	50,000 lbs.	1/100¢/lb. = $5	2¢/lb. = $1,000
	Orange Juice	Jan/Mar/May July/Sept/Nov	10:15-2:45	15,000 lbs.	5/100¢/lb. = $7.50	5¢/lb. = $750
	Propane Gas (liquified)	All months	10:45-3:15	42,000 gal.	1/100¢/gal. = $4.20	2¢/gal. = $840

Exchange	Commodity	Trading Months	Trading Hours (Local Time)	Contract Size	Minimum Price Fluctuation	Daily Limit
New York Futures Exchange	NYSE Composite Stock Index	Mar/June Sept/Dec	10:00-4:00	500 × Index	5 pt. = $25	None
	NYSE Financial Stock Index	Mar/June Sept/Dec	10:00-4:15	1,000 × Index	1 pt. = $10	None
	NYSE Composite Stock Index Options	(See options on futures section)				

Exchange	Commodity	Trading Months	Trading Hours (Local Time)	Contract Size	Minimum Price Fluctuation	Daily Limit
New York Mercantile Exchange	Palladium	All months	9:20-2:20	100 troy oz.	5¢/oz. = $5	$6/oz. = $600
	Platinum	All months	9:30-2:30	50 troy oz.	10¢/oz. = $5	$20/oz. = $1,000
	Potatoes	Feb/Mar/Apr Nov	10:00-2:00	50,000 lbs.	1/100¢/lb. = $5	1/2¢/lb. = $250

Exchange	Commodity	Trading Months	Trading Hours (Local Time)	Contract Size	Minimum Price Fluctuation	Daily Limit
	No. 2 Heating Oil (New York)	All months	10:30-2:45	42,000 gal.	1/100¢/gal. = $4.20	2¢/gal. = $840
	No. 2 Heating Oil (Gulf Coast)	All months	9:45-3:00	42,000 gal.	1/100¢/gal. = $4.20	2¢/gal. = $840
	Leaded Gasoline (New York)	All months	10:05-2:55	42,000 gal.	1/100¢/gal. = $4.20	2¢/gal. = $840
	Leaded Gasoline (Gulf Coast)	All months	10:15-2:50	42,000 gal.	1/100¢/gal. = $4.20	2¢/gal. = $840
	Crude Oil	Jan/Apr/July/Oct and next 6 months	9:30-3:30	1,000 barrels (42,000 gal.)	1¢/barrel = $10	$1/barrel = $1,000
Toronto Stock Exchange	**Canadian Bonds** (18-year)	Mar/June Sept/Dec	9:00-3:15	CD$100,000	1/32 pt. = $31.25	2 pt. = $2,000
	Canadian Bonds (3-5 year)	Mar/June Sept/Dec	9:00-3:15	CD$50,000	1/32 pt. = $15.63	2 pt. = $1,000
	Canadian T-Bills (13-week)	Mar/June Sept/Dec	9:00-3:15	CD $1,000,000	0.005 pt. = $50	0.150 pt. = $1,500
	Toronto Equity Futures Contract (10 TSE stocks)	Mar/June Sept/Dec	10:00-4:00	Sum of 100 shares of each	0.1 pt. = $10	25 pt. = $2,500

Exchange	Commodity	Trading Months	Trading Hours (Local Time)	Contract Size	Minimum Price Fluctuation	Daily Limit
The Winnipeg Commodity Exchange	**Domestic Feed Barley**	Mar/May/July Oct/Dec	9:30-1:15	100 metric tons	10¢/ton = $10	$5/ton = $500
	Alberta Domestic Feed Barley	Feb/Apr/June Sept/Nov	9:30-1:15	20 metric tons	10¢/ton = $2	$5/ton = $100
	Flaxseed	Mar/May/July Oct/Dec	9:30-1:15	100 metric tons	10¢/ton = $10	$10/ton = $1,000
	Domestic Feed Oats	Mar/May/July Oct/Dec	9:30-1:15	100 metric tons	10¢/ton = $10	$5/ton = $500
	Rapeseed	Jan/Mar/June Sept/Nov	9:30-1:15	100 metric tons	10¢/ton = $10	$10/ton = $1,000
	Rye	Mar/May/July Oct/Dec	9:30-1:15	100 metric tons	10¢/ton = $10	$5/ton = $500
	Domestic Feed Wheat	Mar/May/July Oct/Dec	9:30-1:15	100 metric tons	10¢/ton = $10	$5/ton = $500
	Gold	Mar/June/Sept Dec	8:25-1:30	20 oz.	10¢/oz.	$25/oz.
	Gold Options			(See options on futures section)		
	Silver	Jan/Apr/July Oct	8:30-1:35	200 oz.	1¢/oz. = $2	50¢/oz. = $100
	Treasury Bills (13-week)	Mar/June/Sept Dec	8:20-1:25	$200,000	One index point	Sixty index points
	Long-Term Bonds	Mar/June/Sept Dec	8:20-1:25	$20,000	1/32 of $1 per $100 face value	64/32 of $1 per $100 face value

Options on Futures

Options on futures have the same contract months, trading hours, limits, etc., as their underlying futures contracts.

Exchange	Underlying futures contract	Contract size	Strike price increments	Minimum fluctuation	Expiration date
Chicago Board of Trade	U.S. Treasury Bonds	$100,000	2 pt.	1/64 pt. = $15.62 (1.0 = $1,000)	Noon on Friday at least five business days before first notice day

Exchange	Underlying futures contract	Contract size	Strike price increments	Minimum fluctuation	Expiration date
Index and Option Market of the Chicago Mercantile Exchange	S&P 500 Stock Index	500 × S&P Index	5 pt.	0.05 pt. = $25 (1.0 = $500)	Third Thursday of contract month

Exchange	Underlying futures contract	Contract size	Strike price increments	Minimum fluctuation	Expiration date
Coffee, Sugar and Cocoa Exchange	Sugar No. 11	112,000 lb. (50 long tons)	Varies*	1/100¢/lb. = $11.20 (1.0 = $1,120)	Second Friday of month before futures expire

*1/2¢/lb. for two nearby options and 1¢/lb. for deferreds when futures price is below 15¢/lb.

Exchange	Underlying futures contract	Contract size	Strike price increments	Minimum fluctuation	Expiration date
Commodity Exchange Inc. (Comex)	Gold	100 troy oz.	Varies*	10¢/oz. = $10 (1.0 = $100)	Second Friday of month before futures expire

*$10/oz. below $300; $20/oz. $301-$500; $30/oz. $501-800; $40/oz. above $800

Exchange	Underlying futures contract	Contract size	Strike price increments	Minimum fluctuation	Expiration date
New York Futures Exchange	**NYSE Composite Stock Index**	500 × NYSE Composite Index	2 pt.	0.05 pt. = $25 (1.0 = $500)	Business day before futures expire

Exchange	Underlying futures contract	Contract size	Strike price increments	Minimum fluctuation	Expiration date
Winnipeg Commodity Exchange	**Gold** (Calls only)	20 oz.	$20/oz.	10¢/oz. = $2 (1.0 = $20)	Six business days before delivery month

323

Options on Actuals

New options were being introduced as this book was being put together so the following list may not be complete. Options on futures (see above) required Commodity Futures Trading Commission approval. U.S. options in the list below have gone through the Securities and Exchange Commission.

Exchange	Underlying instrument	Contract months	Contract size	Local trading hours	Strike price increments	Minimum fluctuation
American Stock Exchange (Amex)	**Major Market Stock Index** (20 stocks)	Mar/June/Sept/Dec	100 × Major Market Index	10:00–4:10	5 pt.	Premium less than $3: 1/16; above $3: 1/8 (1.0 = $100)
	U.S. Treasury Bills (13-week)	Mar/June/Sept/Dec	$200,000	9:00–3:00	1 pt.	0.01 pt. = $5 (1.0 = $500)
	U.S. Treasury Notes (10-year)	Mar/June/Sept/Dec	$20,000	9:00–3:00	4 pt.	1/32 pt. = $6.25 (1.0 = $200)

Exchange	Underlying instrument	Contract months	Contract size	Local trading hours	Strike price increments	Minimum fluctuation
Chicago Board Options Exchange (CBOE)	**S&P 100 Stock Index**	Mar/June/Sept/Dec	500 × S&P 100 Index	9:00–3:10	5 pt.	Premium less than $3: 1/16; above $3: 1/8 (1.0 = $100)
	U.S. Treasury Bonds	Mar/June/Sept/Dec	$100,000	8:00–2:00	2 pt.	1/32 pt. = $31.25 (1.0 = $1,000)

Exchange	Underlying instrument	Contract months	Contract size	Local trading hours	Strike price increments	Minimum fluctuation
	U.S. Treasury Bonds	Mar/June/Sept/Dec	$20,000	8:00-2:00	2 pt.	1/32 pt. = $6.25 (1.0 = $200)
	GNMA	Mar/June/Sept/Dec	$100,000	8:00-2:00	2 pt.	1/32 pt. = $31.25 (1.0 = $1,000)
International Options Market (IOM) Division of the Montreal Stock Exchange* (All times EST/EDT)	Gold	Feb/May/Aug/Nov	10 oz.	Amsterdam: 4:30-10:30 Montreal: 9:00-2:30 Vancouver: 2:30-7:00	U.S. $25 under $500; $50 above $500	10¢/oz. = $1
	Silver	Mar/June/Sept/Dec	250 oz.	Amsterdam: 4:30-10:30 Vancouver: 10:30-7:00 Not traded in Montreal	U.S. $1	5¢/oz.
	Canadian Dollar	Mar/June/Sept/Dec	CD $50,000	Montreal: 9:00-2:30 Vancouver: 2:30-7:00	U.S. $0.01	$0.0001/CD = $5
	Deutsche Mark	Mar/June/Sept/Dec	DM 25,000	**	U.S. $0.02	$0.0001/DM = $5
	Swiss Franc	Mar/June/Sept/Dec	SF 25,000	Montreal: 9:00-4:00	U.S. $0.02	$0.0001/SF = $5
	British Pound	Mar/June/Sept/Dec	£5,000	**	U.S. $0.05	$0.0005/£ = $5

	Contract months	Contract size	Local trading hours	Strike price increments	Minimum fluctuation
Japanese Yen	Mar/June/Sept/Dec	JY 2,500,000	**	U.S. $0.02	$0.000001/JY = $5
U.S. Dollar	Mar/June/Sept/Dec	$10,000	Amsterdam: 4:30-10:30	1 Guilder cent	DG 0.0001/$
Canadian Bonds	Mar/June/Sept/Dec	CD $25,000	Montreal: 9:00-4:00	CD $2.50	Premium under $2: 5¢; above $2: 1/8

*Some options also traded on the European Options Exchange at the Amsterdam Stock Exchange and at the Vancouver Stock Exchange.
**Not trading yet; expected to be introduced at all three exchanges by this summer.

Exchange	Underlying instrument	Contract months	Contract size	Local trading hours	Strike price increments	Minimum fluctuation
Philadelphia Stock Exchange (PHLX)	**Deutsche Mark**	Mar/June/Sept/Dec	DM 62,500	8:30-2:30	$0.02	$0.0001/DM = $6.25 (1.0 = $625)
	Swiss Franc	Mar/June/Sept/Dec	SF 62,500	8:30-2:30	$0.02	$0.0001/SF = $6.25 (1.0 = $625)
	Canadian Dollar	Mar/June/Sept/Dec	CD $50,000	8:30-2:30	$0.02	$0.0001/CD = $5 (1.0 = $500)
	British Pound	Mar/June/Sept/Dec	£12,500	8:30-2:30	$0.05	$0.0005/£ = $6.25 (1.0 = $125)
	Japanese Yen	Mar/June/Sept/Dec	JY 6,250,000	8:30-2:30	$0.0002	$0.000001/JY = $6.25 (1.0 = $625)

Glossary of Commodity Futures Terms

These definitions are not intended to state or suggest the correct legal significance or meaning of any word or phrase, but only to help in understanding the commodity and foreign currency futures markets and the nomenclature used in them.

Special thanks for help in putting together much of the material in this glossary must go to the Research and Education Department of the Chicago Mercantile Exchange.

(To) Accumulate — Buy futures contracts heavily in a specific commodity at regular predetermined intervals.

Acreage Allotment — Government limitation on planted acreage of some basic crops.

Allowances — The discounts (premiums) allowed the buyer for grades or locations of a commodity lower (higher) than the par or basis-grade or location specified in the futures contract. Also called differentials.

Annualize — To put on an annual basis. Usually pertains to interest rates, which are quoted on a yearly basis, or "per annum." A profit of $4 on a 3-month investment of $100 would, on an annualized basis, be 16%.

Appreciation — An increase in value. If the Deutschemark appreciates relative to the U.S. dollar, it will take more dollars to buys the same amount of Deutschemarks. See Revaluation.

Approved Delivery Facility — Any bank, stockyard, mill, store, warehouse, plant, elevator, or other institution that is authorized by the exchange for delivery of exchange contracts.

Arbitrage — The simultaneous purchase or sale of a contract in different markets in order to profit from discrepancies in prices between those markets. See Interest Arbitrage, Covered Interest Arbitrage, Spreads, Straddles.

At-The-Market — An order to buy or sell at the best price obtainable at the time the order is received. See Market Order.

Balance of Payments — a record, presented in balance sheet form, of the value of all the economic transactions between residents, business firms, governments, and any other institutions in a country and the rest of the world.

Basis — The difference between the spot price and the price of futures.

Basis Grade — The grade of a commodity used as the standard of the contract.

Bear — One who believes prices will move lower. See Bull.

Bear Market — A market in which prices are declining.

Bid — An offer to purchase at a specified price. See Offer.

Break — A rapid and sharp decline.

Broker — A man or firm who handles the actual execution of all trades.

Bull — One who expects prices to rise. See Bear.

Bull Market — A market in which prices are rising.

Buy In — To cover or close out a short position. See Offset.

Buy-On-Close — To buy at the end of the trading session at a price within the closing range.

Buy-On-Opening — To buy at the begining of the trading session at a price within the opening range.

CCC — Commodity Credit Corporation. A government-owned corporation established in 1933 to assist American agriculture. Major operations include price support programs, supply control, and foreign sales programs for agricultural commodities.

CEA — The Commodity Exchange Authority. An agency of the U.S. Department of Agriculture, which formerly administered the Commodity Exchange Act before being replaced by the CFTC in 1975.

CFTC — Commodity Futures Trading Commission established in 1975 to succeed the CEA and take over regulation of all commodity futures and options trading in the U.S. The Commission consists of a chairman, vice-chairman and three other members, all appointed by the President.

C & F — "Cost and Freight" paid to move a commodity to a port of destination.

CIF — Cost, Insurance, and Freight paid to move a commodity to a port of destination and included in the price quoted.

Call — An exchange-designated buying and selling period during which trading is conducted in order to establish a price or price range for a particular time. Also an option to buy a security or commodity at a pre-determined price within a given time period.

Car — A loose, quantitative term sometimes used to describe a contract, e.g., "a car of bellies." Derived from fact that quantities of the product specified on a contract often correspond closely to the quantity carried in a railroad car.

Carrying Broker — A member of the commodity exchange, usually a commission house broker, through whom another broker or customer, elects to "clear" all or some of his trades.

Carrying Charges — Cost of storing a physical commodity over a period of time. Includes insurance and interest on the invested funds as well as other incidental costs.

Cash Commodity — The actual physical commodity, as distinguished from a futures commodity.

Cash Market — Market for immediate delivery and payment of commodities.

Central Bank — A financial institution that has official or semiofficial status in a federal government. Central banks are the instruments used by governments to expand, contract, or stabilize the supply of money and credit. They hold reserves of other banks, act as fiscal agents for their governments, and can issue paper money.

Central Rate — Similar to par value, as established by the International Monetary Fund.

Certified Stocks — Quantities of commodities designated and certified for delivery by an exchange under its trading and testing regulations at delivery points specified and approved by the exchange.

(To) Clear — To be verified and guaranteed.

Clearing House — An adjunct to a commodity exchange through which transactions executed on the floor of the exchange are settled. Also charged with assuring the proper conduct of delivery procedures and the adequate financing of the trading.

Clearing Member — A member of the Clearing House or Association. All trades of a non-clearing member must be registered and eventually settled through a clearing member.

Clerk — A member's employee who has been registered to work on the trading floor as a phoneman or runner.

(The) Close — A short period at the end of the trading session during which the closing price range is established. Sometimes used to refer to the closing price. See Opening.

Closing Range (or Range) — The closing price (or price range) recorded during the period designated as the official close. See Settling Price.

Commercial Stocks — Commodity in-store in public and private elevators or warehouses at important markets and afloat in vessels or barges in harbors and port.

Commission — The fee charged by a broker to a customer when a transaction is made.

Commission House — A concern that buys and sells actual commodities or futures contracts for the accounts of customers. Its income is generated by the commissions charged customers. Often used synonymously with brokerage house.

Commitment — A trader is said to have a "commitment" when he assumes the obligation to accept or make delivery by entering into a futures contract. See Open Interest.

Commodity Exchange Act — Federal act passed in 1936 establishing the Commodity Exchange Commission and placing futures trading in a wide range of commodities under the regulation of the Government.

Contract — A term of reference describing a unit of trading for a commodity future, similar to "round lot" in securities markets. Also, actual bilateral agreement between the buyer and seller in a futures transaction.

Contract Grade — That grade of a commodity which has been officially approved by an exchange as deliverable in settlement of a futures contract. See Basis Grade, Par.

Contract Month — The month in which futures contracts may be satisfied by making or accepting delivery.

(To) Cover — The purchase of futures to offset a previously-established short position.

Covered Interest Arbitrage — Interest arbitrage transaction that is hedged against exchange rate fluctuation. For example, an American arbitraging to take advantage of higher interest rates in Germany would cover by selling Deutschemarks forward at the same time that he purchased them in the spot market. Usually done in short-term instruments. See Arbitrage, Interest Arbitrage.

Crop Year — The period of time from one harvest or storage cycle to the next; varies with each commodity.

Cross-Rate — In foreign exchange, the price of one currency in terms of another currency, in the market of a third country. For example, a London dollar cross-rate could be the price of one U.S. dollar in terms of Deutschemarks on the London market.

Customer's Man — A person employed by and soliciting business for a futures commission merchant. See Registered Representative.

Day Order — Orders that are placed for execution, if possible, during only one trading session. If the order cannot be executed that day, it is automatically cancelled.

Day Trading — Refers to establishing and liquidating the same position or positions within one day's trading.

Deferred Futures — Future contracts which expire during the more distant months. See Nearbys.

Deficit — Where "outgo" exceeds income, or expenses exceed receipts. In balance of payments, it implies that more of a country's currency went abroad than foreign currencies came into the country.

Delivery — The tender and receipt of an actual commodity, or warehouse receipt or other negotiable instrument covering such commodity, in settlement of a futures contract.

Delivery Commitment, Buyer's — The written notice given by the buyer of his intention to take delivery against a long futures position on delivery day.

Delivery Commitment, Seller's — The written notice given by the seller of his intention to make delivery against a short futures position on delivery day.

Delivery Month — A specified month within which delivery may be made under the terms of the futures contract.

Delivery Notice — The written notice given by the seller of his intention to make delivery against an open short futures position on a particular date.

Delivery Points — Those points designated by futures exchanges at which the physical commodity covered by a futures contract may be delivered in fulfillment of such contract.

Delivery Price — The price fixed by the Clearing House at which deliveries on futures are invoiced, and also the price at which the futures contract is settled when deliveries are made. See Settling Price.

Depreciate — Decrease in value. A currency depreciates when its "price," or exchange rate, in terms of other currencies, goes down.

Devaluation — A formal "official" decrease in the exchange rate, made with International Monetary Fund agreement, or unilaterally by a country. For example, when the British devalued the pound in 1967, the exchange rate, or price in terms of U.S. Dollars, went from $2.80/pound to $2.40/pound.

Differentials — See Allowances.

Discretionary Account — An account over which any individual or organization, other than the person in whose name the account is carried, exercises trading authority or control.

Discount — Less than. If a future delivery is selling at a discount to the spot delivery, then it's selling for a lower price than the spot price. See Premium.

Dominant Future — That future having the largest number of open contracts.

Dumping — Selling goods in a foreign country cheaper than they are sold at home. Under the rules of the General Agreement of Tariffs and Trades (GATT), dumping occurs when the wholesale price to the importer is lower than the wholesale price charged to the buyer in the country of origin.

Equity — The residual dollar value of a futures trading account, assuming its liquidation at the going market price.

Eurodollar — U.S. dollar deposits held *abroad*. Holders may include individuals, companies, banks, and central banks.

Evening Up — Buying or selling to offset an existing market position. See Liquidation.

Exchange Rate — The "price" of one currency stated in terms of another currency.

Ex-Pit Transaction — Trades executed, for certain technical purposes, in a location other than the regular exchange trading pit or ring.

First Notice Day — The first date, varying by commodities and exchanges, on which notices of intentions to deliver actual commodities against futures are authorized.

Floating — The establishment of exchange rates by free market forces. "Clean floats" involve no government intervention to manipulate the exchange rates. "Dirty floats" involve government manipulation of the price.

Floor Brooker — A member who executes orders for the account of one or more clearing members.

Floor Trader — A member who executes trades for his own account, or for an account controlled by him. Also referred to as a "local."

Foreign Exchange — Foreign currency. On the foreign exchange market, foreign currency is bought and sold for immediate or future delivery.

Forward — In the future.

Forward Market — Refers to informal (non-exchange) trading of contracts for future delivery. Contracts for forward delivery are "personalized," i.e., delivery time and amount are as determined by the customer.

Free Supply — The storage supply of a commodity outside of government-held stocks; the amount available for commercial sale.

Futures — A term used to designate the standardized contracts covering the sale of commodities for future delivery on a commodity exchange.

Futures Commission Merchant — A firm or person engaged in soliciting or accepting and handling orders for the purchase or sale of commodities for future delivery on, or subject to, the rules of a futures exchange and who, in connection with such solicitation or acceptance of orders, accepts any money or securities to margin any resulting trades or contracts. Must be licensed under the Commodity Exchange Act.

F.O.B. — Free-on-Board. A term describing the cost of placing commodities on board whatever shipment conveyance is being used.

Give Up — At the request of the customer, a brokerage house which has not performed the service is credited with the execution of an order.

Grading Certificate — A paper setting forth the quality of a commodity as determined by authorized inspectors or graders.

G.T.C. — Good-'til-Cancelled. An order to your broker to buy or sell at a fixed price. The order holds until executed or cancelled.

Group of 10 — The 10 leading industrial nations of the free world. Specifically, the United States, Canada, England, Belgium, France, Germany, Italy, The Netherlands, Sweden, and Japan.

Hardening — Describes a price which is gradually stabilizing.

Heavy — A description of a market in which prices are demonstrating either an inability to advance or a slight tendency to decline.

Hedging — A means of risk protection against extensive loss due to adverse price

331

fluctuations. In the futures market, a purchase or sale for future delivery as a temporary substitute for a merchandising transaction to be made later.

Interest Arbitrage — The operation wherein foreign debt instruments are purchased to profit from the higher interest rate in the foreign country over the home country. The operation is profitable only when the forward rate on the foreign currency is selling at a discount *less than* the premium on the interest rate. For example, if the interest rate in West Germany is 2% *higher than* in the U.S., interest arbitrage profits are possible if the forward rate for Deutschemarks is *higher than a 2% discount* over the spot rate. This is one fundamental factor affecting forward rates of exchange. See Interest Rate Parity.

Interest Rate Parity — The formal theory of interest rate parity holds that under normal conditions the forward premium or discount on a currency in terms of another is directly related to the interest rate differential between the two countries. An interest rate parity, the forward rate discount (or premium) on Swiss francs in terms of dollars would equal the premium (or discount) of interest rates in Switzerland over (or under) those in the U.S. *This theory holds only when there are unrestricted flows of international short-term capital.* In reality, numerous economic and legal obstacles restrict the movement, so that actual parity is rare. See Interest Arbitrage, Coverent Interest Arbitrage.

International Monetary Fund — An organization of 126 countries created to 1) promote international cooperation; 2) facilitate expansion and balanced growth of international trade; 3) promote exchange stability; 4) avoid competitive exchange depreciation; 5) assist in establishment of a multi-national system of payments and elimination of foreign exchange restrictions; and, 6) provide members with resources to correct short-term imbalances of payments. Created by Bretton Woods, New Hampshire, in July, 1944.

Intervention Limits — Outer limit of variation of the par value (as agreed upon by the IMF) of the spot price of a currency. At this point IMF members are obligated to keep the price within this limit. The intervention takes the form of open market sales or purchases of the currency. For example, if the Deutschemark is at the lower intervention limit, the German central bank will buy Deutschemarks, usually with U.S. dollars, to decrease the supply of Deutschemarks and thereby raise its "price" above the lower limit. If the upper limit were approached, the government would sell Deutschemarks. The current intervention limits used (though not yet officially ratified by the IMF) are 2¼% above and below the par value established.

Inverted Market — A futures market in which the nearer months are selling at premiums to the more distant months.

Invisible Supply — Usually refers to uncounted stocks in hands of wholesalers, manufacturers and ultimate consumers, and sometimes to producers' stocks which cannot be counted accurately.

Last Trading Day — The final day under an exchange's rules during which trading may take place in a particular futures delivery month. Futures contracts outstanding at the end of the last trading day must be settled by delivery.

Limit Order — An order given to a broker which has restrictions upon its execution, such as price and time.

Liquidation — Same as offset. Any transaction which offsets or closes out a long or short position. A market in which open interest is declining.

Long — One who has bought a futures contract to establish a market position and who has not yet closed out this position through an offsetting sale. Opposite of Short.

Long Hedge — The purchase of a futures contract to offset the forward sale of an equivalent quantity of a commodity not yet owned. Used as protection against an advance in the cash price. See Hedge.

Long The Basis — The purchase of a cash commodity and the sale of a future against unsold inventory to provide protection against a price decline in the cash market. Synonymous with Short Hedge.

Maintenance Margin (Maintenance Security Deposit) — A sum, usually smaller than, but part of, the original margin (security deposit) which must be maintained on deposit at all times. If a customer's equity in any futures position drops to or under the maintenance margin level, the broker must issue a call for the amount of money required to restore the customer's equity in the account to the original margin level.

Margin — On all commodity exchanges, except the International Monetary Market, a cash amount of funds which a customer must deposit with the broker for each contract as a sign of his good faith in fulfilling the contract terms. It is not considered as part payment of purchase. On the IMM, an amount of funds which must be deposited by a clearing member with the clearing house for each contract as a guarantee of fulfillment of the futures contract. See Security Deposit.

Margin Call — A demand for additional cash funds because of adverse price movement. See Maintenance Margin.

Market Order — An order for immediate execution given to your broker to buy or sell at the best obtainable price.

Maximum Daily Price Fluctuation — The maximum amount the contract price can change up or down during one trading session, as fixed by exchange rules.

Minimum Price Fluctuations — Smallest increment of price movement possible in trading a given contract. For example, the minimum price fluctuation on one pork belly contract is 2½/100¢ per pound, or $9.00 per contract. See Point.

M.I.T. — Market-if-Touched. A price order that automatically becomes a market order if the price is reached.

Monetary Policy — Governmental actions to control a country's domestic economy by adjusting the money supply. Used in conjunction with fiscal policy which injects funds into an economy via public works, grants, and federal contracts with the government as the buyer of goods and services.

Nearbys — The nearest delivery months of a commodity futures market.

Negotiable Warehouse Receipt — A legal document issued by a warehouse describing and guaranteeing the existence of a specific quantity (and sometimes a specific grade) of a commodity in the warehouse.

Nominal Price — Price quotation on futures for a period in which no actual trading took place.

Notice Day — A day on which notices of intent to deliver pertaining to a specified delivery month may be issued.

Offer — Indicates a willingness to sell a futures contract at a given price. It is the opposite of Bid.

Offset — See Evening Up, Liquidation.

Omnibus Account — An account carried by one futures commission merchant with another futures commission merchant in which the transactions of two or more persons are combined and carried in the name of the originating broker rather than designated separately. See Futures Commission Merchant.

333

Open Contracts — Contracts which have been bought or sold and are still outstanding, not having been delivered upon or offset. See Open Interest.

Open Interest — Number of open contracts. Refers to unliquidated purchases *or* sales, never to their combined total.

Open Order — An order to your broker that is good until it is cancelled or executed.

(The) Opening — The varying time period at the beginning of the trading session officially designated by the exchange during which all transactions are considered made "at the opening." The precise time varies with the amount of activity at the opening. See Close.

Opening Price — The price (or range) recorded during the period designated by the exchange as the official opening.

Option — Sometimes used as a synonym for "Contract Month," technically the term is incorrect in the sense that "Options" are agreements with a seller or buyer permitting the holder to buy or sell, if he chooses to do so, at a given price within a given period.

Original Margin — The margin needed to cover a specific new position.

Overbought — A market that has had sharp advance. Rank and file traders (who were bullish and long earlier) have turned bearish.

Oversold — A market that has had a sharp decline. Rank and file traders (who were bearish and short earlier) have turned bullish.

P & S — Purchase and Sale Statement. A statement provided by the broker to a customer showing the change in his net ledger balance after the offset of a previously established position.

Par — Refers to the standard delivery point or points, or to quality specifications of the commodity represented in the contract. Serves as a benchmark upon which to base discounts or premiums for varying quality. In foreign exchange, an exchange rate arbitrarily set by the country of issuance and ratified by the IMF.

Parity — Par rate.

Per Annum — Per year. Usually refers to interest rates, a basis of comparision of rates among various debt instruments of less than one year duration.

Point — The minimum unit in which changes in futures prices may be expressed; e.g., 1/10th of a cent per ounce for silver.

Position — One's interest in the market, either long or short, in the form of open contracts.

Position Limit — The maximum number of contracts, as prescibed by an exchange or the Commodity Exchange Authority, either net long or net short, in one commodity future or in all futures of one commodity combined, which may be held or controlled by one person or firm in its own name. Does not apply to bonafide hedgers.

Premium — Above par. Used to quote one price in reference to another. In foreign exchange — above spot. If the forward rate for Italian lira is at a premium to spot lira, it is selling *above* the spot price. See Discount.

Primary Market — Important distribution centers at which spot commodities are originally accumulated for shipment into commercial channels.

Prime Rate — The interest rate charged by banks to their biggest and most creditworthy customers. Other interest rates are scaled up from the prime rate. It is a good indication of general interest rate levels within a country.

Put — An option to sell a commodity or security at a predetermined price within a specified period of time.

Pyramiding — Using the profits on a previously-established position as margin for adding to that position.

Rally — An upward movement of prices following a decline.

Range — The high and low prices recorded during a specified time.

Reaction — A decline in prices following an advance — the opposite of rally.

Reciprocal — Any number divided *into* "1." A number multiplied by its reciprocal equals one. In foreign exchange, it is a handy way of expressing currency prices in terms of each other. For example, if one British pound = $2.6057, then $1 = 1/2.6057 = .3838 pounds.

Recovery — Usually describes a price advance following a decline.

Regulated Commodities — Those commodities over which the Commodity Exchange Authority exercises regulatory supervision for the purpose of seeing that trading is conducted in the public's interest.

Registered Representative — See Customer's Man.

Roundturn — Procedure by which the long or short position of an individual is offset by an opposite transaction or by accepting or making delivery of the actual commodity.

Reserves (Official) — Official foreign exchange reserves are kept to insure a government's ability to meet *current or near-term claims*. The primary reserve currency is the U.S. dollar, with the British pound being the secondary reserve currency. Gold is used in official reserves. As long as reserves grow faster than current claims, their adequacy increases. When claims grow faster, reserve adequacy decreases. Therefore, a particular volume of reserves has little significance because the "adequacy" concept is a relative one. Official reserves are a debit entry on a country's balance of payments; i.e., they are an asset.

Revaluation — A formal "official" increase in the exchange rate or price of currency.

Scalp — To trade for small gains. Involves establishing and liquidating a position quickly, within the same day or sometimes within the same hour.

Security Deposit — On the IMM, the amount of funds which must be deposited by a customer with his broker for each futures contract as a guarantee of fulfillment of the contract. It is not considered as part payment of purchase. See Margin.

Security Deposit Call — A demand for additional cash funds because of adverse price movement. See Maintenance Security Deposit.

Settling Price — The daily price at which the clearing house clears all trades and settles all accounts between clearing members for each contract month. Settlement prices are used to determine both margin calls and invoice prices for deliveries.

Short — One who has sold a futures contract to establish a market position and who has not yet closed out his position through an offsetting purchase or delivery. The opposite of being long. See Long.

Short Hedge — The sale of futures contracts to reduce the possible decline in value of an approximately equal amount of the actual commodity held.

Short Selling — Selling a contract with the idea of buying it back at a later date.

Seller's Option — Refers to the seller's right to select from among a range of alternatives regarding quality of the commodity, time, and place of delivery.

Short Squeeze — A situation in which a lack of supplies tends to force those who have sold to cover their positions by offset in the futures market rather than by delivery.

Short The Basis — The forward sale of cash commodity hedged by the purchase of a future against the cash position. Synonymous with Long Hedge.

335

Sold-Out Market — Market situation in which liquidation of weakly-held positions has been completed and offerings have become scarce.

Speculation — Any investment that aims at profit through price fluctuation. It is the assumption of an existing risk in expectation of a profit.

Speculator — One who attempts to anticipate price changes and through market activities make profits; he is not using the futures market in connection with the production, processing, marketing, or handling of a product.

Spot — Market of immediate delivery of the product and immediate payment. Also refers to the nearest delivery month on a futures contract.

Spread — 1. Difference in the prices of a currency between various future deliveries, or between the spot market and a future delivery. 2. To take a simultaneous long and short position, aimed at a profit via fluctuation of *differential* in two prices. For example, the purchase of May corn and the sale of September corn if it is felt the difference in price between the two would *widen* (if May were at a premium to September). If it is felt the price difference will narrow, you would sell May and buy September. Also called a Straddle.

Stop-Loss Order — An order which immediately becomes a market order when the "stop" level is reached. Its purpose is to limit losses. It may be either a buying order or a selling order. For example: "Sell two December British pounds at $2.6000 Stop" indicates that the buyer has bought two contracts at a price higher than $2.6000 and wants to limit the loss to that amount. An order to buy or sell at the market when a definite price is reached either above or below the prevailing price when the order is given.

Straddle — In futures trading, the same as the spread. Straddles (spreads) are between delivery months.

Surplus — Excess. In reference to balance of payments, income exceeds total payment to foreigners.

Swap — In foreign exchange, an exchange of bank balances. For example, when a bank sells Swiss francs for U.S. dollars, the actual funds are not shipped both ways across the Atlantic Ocean. Instead, the U.S. bank and a correspondent bank in Switzerland, via a swap agreement, exchange a franc balance in the Swiss bank for a dollar balance in the U.S. bank.

Switching — Liquidating an existing position and simultaneously reinstating that position in another contract month of the same commodity or currency.

Technical Rally — A price movement attributed to conditions developing from within the futures market itself. These conditions include changes in open interest, volume, and extent of recent price movement.

Tender — Delivery against futures.

Tick — See Point. Refers to minimum change in price.

Trade Balance — The net amount of *goods* exported and imported. Does not include import and export services, capital flows, or official settlements.

Treasury Bills — Government debt obligations. They are sold at something less than their value at maturity, the difference thereby being the yield. For example, a one-year U.S. Treasury Bill worth $10,000 at maturity may sell at $9,600. The $400 difference would be the yield, which is 4.17% (400/$9,600). They are considered a good barometer of interest rates.

Trend — The general direction of the market.

"To-Arrive Contracts" — A transaction providing for subsequent delivery within a stipulated time limit of a specific grade of a commodity. In reality, the "to-arrive" sales contract was the forerunner of the present day futures contract.

336

Visible Supply — Usually refers to supplies of a commodity in licensed warehouses. Often includes afloats and all other supplies "in sight" in producing areas.

Volume — The number of purchases *or* sales of a commodity futures contract made during a specified period of time.

Wire House — A firm operating a private wire to its own branch offices, or to other firms, commission houses; a brokerage house.

INDEX

A

alternate orders, 44-45
American Stock Exchange, 8, 324
arbitrage, 165-169
Arbitration Committee, 290
ascending triangle, 78-80
Audits and Investigation Department, 289

B

Baker, William G. III, 31
balance of payments, 162-163
bar charts, 67-69, 74
barley, 100
Barron's, 251
basis, 100-101, 107, 109, 111, 119-120, 128
broilers, 140
broker, 31-40, accounts, 37-40, firms, 34-36, hedge, 129-130, options, 218-219
Business Conduct Committee, 292

C

cash market, 108, 119, 124, 128
cattle, 96, 100, 105-107, 110, 119-123, 134, 136, 141, 257-258
chart formations, 77-81, bottom, 77, top, 77
Chicago Board of Trade, 187-189, 213, 273-274, 297, 310-312, 321
Chicago Board Options Exchange, 324

Chicago Mercantile Exchange, 10, 33, 54-55, 110, 138, 177, 239, 274-275, 297, 312
clearing house, 296-298
Clearing House Committee, 292
cocoa, 265
coffee, 264
Coffee, Sugar and Cocoa Exchange, 315, 322
combination orders, 44-46
commissions, 29, 101
Commitments of Traders reports, 250
Commodities Report, 251
Commodity Exchange (Comex), 315, 322
Commodity Exchange Act, 213
commodity futures exchanges, 287, 299, administration, 288-289, committees, 290-292, executing trades, 293-295, time-stamping, 295-296, trading floor, 292-293
commodity futures trading, 10-14, characteristics, 275-277, function, 10-14, historical development, 267-285, law, 277-285
Commodity Futures Trading Commission (CFTC), 4, 8, 33, 36-37, 85, 100-101, 214, 224, 250, 279-285, 295-296
commodity information, 252-266
Commodity Price Charts, 68
Commodity Research Bureau, 251
Commodity Yearbook, 251

339

I

J

K

L

M

N

O

P

partnership, limited, 39
Philadelphia Stock Exchange,
326
placing an order, 46
plywood, 140
point-and-figures charts, 67,
69-73
pork bellies, 108, 136, 259
potatoes, 100, 254
price, forecasting, 47-55, 57,
66, instructions, 42,
limits, 7
prime rate, 208

R

rallies, 76
random walk, 89-91
ratios, 60-61
reactions, 76
resistance, 76
risk, 3, 13, 94, 101-102, 137,
171-172, 186-187
Ross, Raymond, 19, 34

S

scale orders, 44
scalpers, 10
seasonality, 57-58, 87-88
selling short, 7-8
silver, 136
Smidt, Seymour, 90
Smith, Adam, 89
soybeans, 87, 100, 141, 253,
meal, 141, oil, 141
speculation, 10, 15-21
spot market, 160
spread, 101, 133-145, inter-
commodity, 45-46, 141-142,
inter-crop, 140, inter-
exchange, 140, inter-
market, 45-46, inter-

season, 139, intra-
commodity, 45-46, orders,
45, perishable, 138-139,
time, 135-137
Standard & Poor's 500,
239-242
Stanford University, 33
stock index futures, 239-247
stocks vs. commodity futures,
2-14
stop limit order, 44
stop orders, 28, 43-44
storage, 107-108, 137, 140
straddle, 134
sugar, 263
supply, 50-52
supply and demand, 12
Supreme Court, 102

T

taxes, 142-144, options, 231,
rules, 102
technical analysis, 26-27, 47,
67-81, 88-89
time-of-day orders, 41
Toronto Stock Exchange, 319
trader, average, 10-12,
position, 10
trading plan, 19-21, 23-30
Treasury bills, 73, 177-188,
204-205, 207-208, delivery,
178-179
Treasury bonds, 187-188, 204
Treasury notes, 187-188, 204
trends, 60, 74-77

U

United States Department of
Agriculture (USDA), 7, 26,
33, 50, 54-55
University of Illinois, 33-34
University of Wisconsin, 33
uptrend, 74-75

V

Value Line Average, 240-241
volume, 47, 83-91

W

Wall Street Journal, 251
wheat, 87, 100, 119, 252
Winnipeg Commodity
    Exchange, 320, 323
Working, Holbrook, 90, 97-98

Y

yield curve, 199-205